The Condition of Democracy

Recent years have seen contestations of democracy all around the globe. Democracy is challenged as a political as well as a normative term, and as a form of governance. Against the background of neoliberal transformation, populist mobilization, and xenophobic exclusion, but also of radical and emancipatory democratic projects, this collection offers a variety of critical and challenging perspectives on the condition of democracy in the 21st century.

The volumes provide theoretical and empirical enquiries into the meaning and practice of liberal democracy, the erosion of democratic institutions, and the consequences for citizenship and everyday lives. With a pronounced focus on national and transnational politics and processes, as well as postcolonial and settler colonial contexts, individual contributions scrutinize the role of democratic societies, ideals, and ideologies of liberal democracy within global power geometries. By employing the multiple meanings of *The Condition of Democracy*, the collection addresses the preconditions of democratic rule, the state this form of governance is in, and the changing ways in which citizens can (still) act as the sovereign in liberal democratic societies.

The books offer both challenging theoretical perspectives and rigorous empirical findings on how to conceive of democracy in our times, which will appeal to academics and students in social and political science, economics, and international relations amongst other fields. The focus on developments in the Middle East and North Africa will furthermore be of great usefulness to academics and the wider public interested in the repercussions of Western democracy promotion as well as in contemporary struggles for democratization 'from below'.

During the last 50 years, liberal democracies have been exposed to a fundamental reorganization of their politico-economic structure that transformed them through the impact of neoliberal economic doctrines focused on low taxation, free markets, and out-sourcing that have little regard in reality for democratic institutions or liberal values. The failures of the neoliberal 'remedy' for capitalism are now dramatically obvious through the banking crisis of 2008–2011, the increase in income inequality, the social and psychological damage caused by the austerity packages across Europe, and widespread dependence on experts whose influence over government policies typically goes without public scrutiny. While this has only accelerated the destruction of the social fabric in modern Western societies, the dramatic redistribution of wealth and an open 'politics for the rich' have also revealed the long-time well-covered alliance of the global oligarchy with the Far Right that has the effect of undermining democracy. The contributions to this volume discuss a wide variety of processes of transformation, the social consequences, dedemocratization, and illiberalization of once liberal democracies through the destructive impact of neoliberal strategies. These strongly politico-economic contributions are complemented with general sociological analyses of a number of cultural aspects often neglected in analyses of democracy.

Jürgen Mackert is Professor of Sociology and co-director of the 'Centre for Citizenship, Social Pluralism and Religious Diversity' at Potsdam University, Germany. His research interests include sociology of citizenship, political economy, closure theory, and collective violence. Recent publication: Social life *as* collective struggle: Closure theory and the problem of solidarity, SOZIALPOLITIK.CH (2021).

Hannah Wolf is a Researcher and Lecturer at the Chair for General Sociology at the University of Potsdam, and associate member at the DFG-collaborative research centre 'Re-Figuration of Spaces'. Her research interests include urban sociology, theories of space and place, and citizenship studies. Latest publication: *Am Ende der Globalisierung: Über die Refiguration von Räumen* (ed. with Martina Löw, Volkan Sayman, and Jona Schwerer), 2021, transcript.

Bryan S. Turner is Research Professor of Sociology at the Australian Catholic University (Sydney), Emeritus Professor at the Graduate Center CUNY, Honorary Max Planck Professor at Potsdam University, Germany, and Research Fellow at the Edward Cadbury Center, University of Birmingham, UK. He holds a Cambridge Litt.D. In 2020 with Rob Stones he published 'Successful Societies: Decision-making and the quality of attentiveness', *British Journal of Sociology*, 71(1), 183–202.

The Condition of Democracy

Volume 1: Neoliberal Politics and Sociological Perspectives

Edited by Jürgen Mackert, Hannah Wolf and Bryan S. Turner

Routledge
Taylor & Francis Group
LONDON AND NEW YORK

First published 2022
by Routledge
2 Park Square, Milton Park, Abingdon, Oxon OX14 4RN

and by Routledge
605 Third Avenue, New York, NY 10158

Routledge is an imprint of the Taylor & Francis Group, an informa business

British Library Cataloguing-in-Publication Data
A catalogue record for this book is available from the British Library

Library of Congress Cataloging-in-Publication Data
A catalog record has been requested for this book

ISBN: 978-0-367-74533-2 (hbk)
ISBN: 978-0-367-74535-6 (pbk)
ISBN: 978-1-003-15836-3 (ebk)
ISBN: 978-0-367-74540-0 (set)

Typeset in Times New Roman
by Deanta Global Publishing Services, Chennai, India

Contents

Illustrations

Figures

Tables

Contributors

Thomas Biebricher is an Associate Professor at the Department of Management, Politics and Philosophy at Copenhagen Business School. His recent publications include *The Political Theory of Neoliberalism* (Stanford University Press, 2019).

Rosario Forlenza, PhD, is a Fellow at the Remarque Institute, New York University. He is a historian of modern Europe, and he has worked at the University of Cambridge, Princeton University, Columbia University, and the University of Padua. His most recent book is *On the Edge of Democracy: Italy 1943–1948* (Oxford, 2019).

Andreas Kallert is a Postdoctoral Researcher in Political Science at Marburg University. His studies on the European Banking Union were supported by the Fritz-Thyssen-Foundation through a Postdoctoral Research Grant (04/2018–03/2020). His research interests are the political economy of finance, rural area studies, and state theory.

Nancy MacLean is the William H. Chafe Distinguished Professor of History and Public Policy at Duke University and the author of several award-winning books, most recently, *Democracy in Chains: The Deep History of the Radical Right's Stealth Plan for America*.

Christian Schmidt-Wellenburg, Dr. rer. pol., Assistant Professor for sociology at University of Potsdam. Research areas: transnationalization, European integration, political sociology of economic thought, field and discourse analysis, relational sociology. Current publications: *Charting Transnational Fields*, Routledge, 2020; 'Struggling over Crisis', *HSR* 43(3), 2018; 'Europeanization, Stateness, and Professions', *EJCPS* 4(4), 2017.

Margaret R. Somers is Professor Emerita of Sociology and History, University of Michigan, and specializes in the political economy of citizenship, moral worth, predistribution, and the work of Karl Polanyi. Her books include *Genealogies of Citizenship: Markets, Statelessness, and the Right to Have Rights* (2008) and, with Fred Block, *The Power of Market Fundamentalism: Karl Polanyi's Critique* (2014).

Bryan S. Turner is Research Professor of Sociology at the Australian Catholic University (Sydney), Emeritus Professor at the Graduate Center CUNY, Honorary Max Planck Professor at Potsdam University, Germany, and Research Fellow at the Edward Cadbury Center, University of Birmingham, UK. He holds a Cambridge Litt.D. In 2020 with Rob Stones he published 'Successful Societies: Decision-making and the quality of attentiveness', *British Journal of Sociology*, 71(1), 183–202.

Stephen Turner is currently Distinguished University Professor at the Department of Philosophy, University of South Florida, USA. His books include *Liberal Democracy 3.0: Civil Society in an Age of Experts* (2003) and essays collected in *The Politics of Expertise* (2013).

Preface

After the end of World War II, Sir Winston Churchill cynically stated that 'democracy is the worst form of Government except for all those other forms that have been tried from time to time'. Indeed, democracy and specifically liberal democracy has been promoted globally throughout the 20th century and seems to have become 'the world's new universal religion' as Corcoran said. However, this is not to say that this process of global democratization has been a success story. Seventy years after Churchill's statement, not only looking at the West and Global North but also at the Global South, the Middle East, and North Africa, one might wonder whether liberal democracy has actually become nothing but a 'lesser evil', or a floating signifier. Past decades have witnessed a fundamental transformation of the structural and cultural preconditions of liberal democracy in seemingly stable democratic societies: while political apathy is growing, populist and extremist mobilization and radicalization are on the rise; economic and environmental crises put societies and governments under pressure, demanding fast decisions and thus weakening public participation in decision-making processes; and neoliberal projects further undermine democratic procedures and legitimacy. Furthermore, the global promotion of the liberal democratic model has often entailed violent and destructive processes, while neglecting alternative and pluralist conceptions of democracy. Against this backdrop, it seems all too necessary to investigate the *Condition of Democracy*: what state is democracy in, both as a concept and as an empirically observable figuration? What are the preconditions of democratic rule? And what are the conditions that democracies establish for both citizens and non-citizens of diverse political communities?

The collection brings together critical perspectives on the condition of democracy in at least three senses of the term – the preconditions of democratic rule, the state this form of governance is in, and the changing ways in which citizens can (still) act as the sovereign in liberal democratic societies. Thus, it offers analyses and case studies of neoliberalism's hollowing out of democratic processes of decision-making, the fundamental transformations of the rule of 'the people', and the still effective ideological invocation of citizens to behave *as* democratic subjects.

Against the background of this conceptual idea, the three volumes of *The Condition of Democracy* provide theoretical analyses and case studies to promote a critical debate on liberal democracy by discussing the profound challenges it faces, the institutional transformation it is going through, and the blind spots in the various discourses concerning liberal democracy.

Neoliberal Politics and Sociological Perspectives discusses the fundamental transformations of once liberal democracies and how they have been transformed and hollowed out by neoliberal procedures and practices. It presents various aspects of this development such as the now transnational alliance of the wealthy oligarchies and the authoritarian and fascist right. With a focus on both empirical case studies and politico-economic theory, the contributions analyse processes of dedemocratization in the face of ongoing neoliberal re-regulations, address issues of expertise and hegemony in the realm of democratic decision-making processes, and discuss the long-term consequences of the global banking crises. Furthermore, the volume proposes the perspective of a cultural sociology in order to make sense of hitherto largely neglected aspects of democracy, by discussing its respective relationships with Catholicism, populism, and digital culture.

Contesting Citizenship sheds light on the changing figurations that structure and regulate relations and practices between states and citizens, as well as amongst individual citizens and non-citizens. The volume presents and discusses spheres and areas in which democracy's crucial relationships, within and beyond national borders and boundaries, are being contested and rearranged through heterogeneous practices, as well as their impact on core democratic principles of accountability, legitimacy, participation, and trust. Three vantage points, usually underrepresented in the discussion of democracy in political and social sciences, are offered to make sense of both current political and social processes as well as of changing conceptions of democracy altogether: migration, violence, and the refiguration of institutions. The contributions bring together empirical analyses and conceptual considerations, assessing how democratic societies regulate access to citizenship rights, the ways in which institutional reforms pave ways towards authoritarian regime transformations, and the crucial position that violence has with regard to maintaining or undermining a democratic social order.

Postcolonial and Settler-Colonial Contexts concentrates on the broken promises of liberal democracies in non-Western contexts and points to the dark side of these regimes as postcolonial and settler-colonial geopolitical actors. Here, talk of 'democracy' is followed by military action, the support of military, despotic, and even fascist regimes in the name of democratic freedom. The contributions discuss the Israeli settler-colonial regime and its illegal occupation of Palestine that Western liberal democracies wholeheartedly support, and the failures of liberal democracy to develop policies that would contribute to enhancing equality and reducing injustices in post-Apartheid South Africa, and offer hope for new forms of democracy in the social movements in Algeria and Rojava.

The publication of these three volumes would not have been possible without the support of the Deutsche Forschungsgemeinschaft (DFG), the Alexander-von-Humboldt Stiftung, and the Max-Planck-Gesellschaft. Finally, we would also like to thank Josepha Hoferichter and Eda Tatlici for their assistance during the production of these volumes.

Introduction

Waves of democracy

Bryan S. Turner

John Dunn opened his influential *Western Political Theory in the Face of the Future* with heavy irony in the claim 'We are all democrats today', but with the important qualification that 'Democratic reality is certainly pretty thin on the ground' (Dunn, 1979, pp. 1–2). In short, there was a striking disjuncture between theory and reality. Nevertheless, the United States was moving into a more settled period in which the prospects for democratic progress were promising. With Richard Nixon's resignation after Watergate on a charge of perjury in 1974 and the end of the Vietnam War in 1975, the United States and most western democracies began to enjoy a period of relative peace and prosperity. In particular, there was evidence of the spread of democratic institutions and progressive values.

America was emerging into a more stable and progressive period of its modern history. In 1972, *Roe v. Wade* recognized the right to abortion under specific conditions. In 1976, the desegregation of school bussing was legislated, albeit with widespread opposition and divided opinion. Nevertheless, the decennial celebrations on 4 July 1976 caused President Ford to conclude that he had brought healing to the nation. Ronald Reagan's 1984 election campaign promoted a sense of security and well-being with the political advertisement, 'It's morning again in America' that summarized the promise that American society would be 'Prouder, Better, Stronger'. With the landing on the moon in 1969 as the ultimate triumph of American technological prowess, this period defined American supremacy. Bill Clinton became the US President in 1993 and, with the support of the US Trade Representative, economic advantage became the core objective of foreign policy (Dryden, 1995).

As an indication of the optimistic mood in the final decades of the century, Samuel Huntington wrote about the positive prospects for the world in his *Democracy's Third Wave: Democratization in the Late Twentieth Century* (1991), in which he explored the causes of democratic change across the globe. Huntington also noted the changing role of the Roman Catholic Church after Vatican II (1962–1965) which had moved from entanglement with military regimes in Latin America to becoming an opponent of authoritarianism. In this volume, Forlenza and Turner examine the complex relationship between the Catholic Church and democracy, noting the role of the Church in the Christian Democratic parties in modern Europe. While the Church developed a democratic and progressive posture in its external relations, it retained its internal hierarchical structures that are based on priestly authority. However, perhaps paradoxically the Pope has often adopted attitudes that are more progressive than many of the bishops and cardinals, such as his attitude towards civil unions. In his Encyclical *Fratelli Tutti* of 3 October 2020, he repeated his criticisms of limitless consumerism and the throwaway world of capitalism.

The third wave was not confined to Europe as democratic progress was being recorded in Asia and Africa. Two critical events were significant in this political transformation: the Carnation Revolution in 1974 that overthrew the Caetano regime in Portugal and the fall of the Berlin Wall and the subsequent break-up of the Soviet Union into a collection of independent states, thereby bringing the Cold War (1947–1991) to a dramatic end. There was of course ample criticism of Huntington's argument (Schmitter, 1993). It was noted that reversals to authoritarianism were as frequent as breakthroughs into democracy. Larry Diamond writing a decade later adopted a more cautionary approach arguing that

> it is more likely that in the next five years democratic regressions (as in Zambia) or breakdowns (as in Niger and the Gambia) will largely offset new breakthroughs to electoral democracy and that some few transitions to democracy will be aborted (as in Nigeria in 1993) or otherwise largely drained of democratic content as happened through political violence, repression, and fraud in Cambodia and many of the former Soviet states.
>
> (Diamond, 1999, p. 60)

Despite the criticisms of the Huntington thesis and American triumphalism among academics, the mood of political optimism was widespread. The sociology of globalization, along with cosmopolitanism and multiculturalism, can be considered the academic response to what was seen to be a more open and stable world. In retrospect, globalization theory, perhaps best signalled by the early work of Roland Robertson in his collection of essays, *Globalization: Social Theory and Global Culture* (1992), envisioned an emerging cosmopolitan world based on international co-operation. In this new world, it was argued that sociology needed new paradigms. For Ulrich Beck (2000), methodological nationalism had to give way to methodological cosmopolitanism. In the work of John Urry (2000), sociologists had to think in terms of mobility, flexibility, and fluidity. In the same year, Zygmunt Bauman (2000) published his *Liquid Modernity*, claiming that, in the new order, modernity would be 'light and liquid'.

Authoritarian communism was in retreat and the United States, as the leader of the free world, was enjoying the benefits of its global dominance. Although there were plenty of critics at the end of the century, there was an awareness of a bright new world of international co-operation despite its manifold risks (Hutton & Giddens, 2000). These optimistic perspectives on the global society can be contrasted with analyses in the 1950s and 1960s that were critical of the failures of democracy and the powerful elites that dominated western societies. C. Wright Mills published his classic *The Power Elite* (1956) that described an elite that exercised power and legitimacy over society as a whole. The 1950s was also a decade in which McCarthyism divided American society around the Red Scare and the rise of the Far Right (Bell, 1964).

My reference here to C. Wright Mills provides me with the pretext, before we enter into a discussion of the various chapters that constitute Volume 1, to consider the differences between democracy as a central topic of political science and the sociology of the condition of democracy which is the theme of our publication. I start with a caveat that one cannot draw a sharp distinction between political science and political sociology. For example, it would be difficult to study the role of political oligarchies and bureaucracies without reference to the work of Robert Michels and Max Weber, both of whom are regarded as sociologists. Indeed the subtitle of Michels' famous *Political Parties* was *A Sociological Study of the Oligarchical Tendencies of Modern Democracy* (Michels, [1911] (1999). Having said that, the chapters in these volumes are written primarily by sociologists, and their research exhibits various features that defines its sociological character. The role of sociology is to pay attention to the social processes and forces that lie behind and define much of the visible structures of political power. These social factors include the role of experts in defining policies and policy objectives, the role of ideologies that characterize the distribution of resources as a natural order and not a contrived order, the role of religion especially Roman Catholicism in shaping European political parties, the new role of digital culture outside official sources of information in shaping social attitudes, and the role of emotions in underpinning social *Weltanschauung*.

Catastrophe and the condition of democracy

I have argued that the United States and the West more generally were enjoying a period of prosperity and peace in the remaining decades of the twentieth century. My argument is not that they were entirely trouble-free decades. There were early populist fears often centred on the notion of a 'deep state' that controls the agenda of democratic politics. To understand the rise of right-wing militia groups in the United States and theories about the deep state, we have to return to the 1990s. The origins of the politics of extremism start with the Ruby Ridge siege in Idaho in 1992, when the FBI was involved in the killing of members of the Weaver family in a firefight that lasted several days. The Ruby Ridge siege was seen to be the response of an over-reaching government against its own citizens. After Ruby Ridge, there was the Waco Siege of April 1993 when the FBI attempted to remove a community of Branch Davidians on charges of drug and child abuse. In the 51-day siege, many Davidians were killed, including women and children. In response to those incidents, Timothy McVeigh and Terry Nicholas bombed the Alfred P. Murrah Building in Oklahoma City on April 19 1995, killing 168 people. These events have had a long-term impact on the rise of right-wing militia groups and have become historic dates in the Far Right calendar. These events were not seen to be catastrophic for democracy at the time, but they have had long-term consequences for Far Right beliefs about the deep state.

Four catastrophes, or at least radical and largely unforeseen transformations, have shaken the optimistic world of peace and plenty of the late twentieth century. At least three are essentially American catastrophes, but they shook the world and specifically destabilized the liberal democracies and transformed the condition of democracy. In referring to these changes as catastrophes, we should be reminded that the original meaning of the word referred to the denouement of a sequence of events in Greek drama. By the seventeenth century, catastrophe had come to mean an overturning of existing social and political arrangements, especially an overturning of government. The first catastrophe was the attack on the Twin Towers on 11 September 2001. This event, taking place at the core of global capitalism, transformed America's relationship with the outside world and led to the invasion of Iraq, the war in Afghanistan, and the destabilization of the Middle East. One immediate consequence of 9/11 was the transformation of President Bush's foreign policy. Bush, previously an amicable Methodist from Texas, embraced a 'theology of empire' whereby he pledged America to fight the evil forces behind the attack (Wallis, 2004). The result has been a series of 'never-ending wars'. The global refugee crisis, that has been acute in the Middle East and North Africa, also contributed to right-wing populist responses to the sudden influx of refugees. The ongoing political crisis in the European Union is yet another feature of the consequences of American foreign policy and the wars in the Middle East. The decision to engage in war with Iraq was taken in 2003 according to the *Manning Memo* between President Bush and Prime Minister Tony Blair before there was any conclusive evidence that Saddam Hussein posed any real threat to the West. Blair's decision to support Bush was a 'blunder' (Porter, 2018) that destroyed his political legacy.

In conducting 'The Global War on Terror', the United States used or endorsed a range of measures that undermined the spirit if not the actuality of human rights. These included so-called 'enhanced interrogation techniques' such as 'waterboarding' and the development of 'black sites' around the world to hold terror suspects under 'indefinite detention'. Perhaps the most notorious development was the Guantanamo Bay Detention Camp, where, at one stage, 779 prisoners were held without any legal safeguards. Equally problematical was the use of 'extraordinary rendition' whereby suspects were subject to extra-judicial transfers by the CIA and held for interrogation. By such measures, which were defined by the United Nations as crimes against humanity, the United States departed from the human rights culture of which it had been the creator and custodian. The western democracies developed strategies such as 'plausible legality' to secure legitimacy for erstwhile proscribed or dubious practices (Sanders, 2017). These developments after 9/11 brought into focus the fragile character of legality and human rights in democratic societies.

President Bush's strategic goals included the expansion of democracy around the world and the enhancement of national security. These two goals raise of course the question as to how far democratic freedoms and national security can easily be combined. This tension came to a head with the passing of the Patriot Act in 2001. The 9/11 crisis had in fact shifted the balance away from individual rights to national security, and the Patriot Act gave legal recognition to this transition. In the wake of 9/11 and the Patriot Act, many governments passed anti-terrorism legislation, which also had the effect of limiting the rights of citizens (Whitaker, 2007). Whether this wave of legislation made these societies any safer is debatable. What is clear is that many governments used the legislation to silence critics and quell legal protest. In short, security took precedence over democracy.

The second catastrophe, or the overturning of structures, was the financial crisis of 2008–2011, which underlined the general dangers resulting from the financialization of capitalism (Marazzi, 2011). The fall of the Lehman Brothers investment bank, which filed for bankruptcy in 2008, exposed many of the problems arising from Chicago economics, the subprime mortgage strategy, an over-heated housing market, and the false expectations of the 'trickle-down effect' whereby the expenditures of the rich would produce employment and income for the rest of society. The fall of the Lehman Brothers and Bear Stearns demonstrated that the crisis in finance capital was systemic and not accidental. While the effect was highly damaging for Lehman's 25,000 employees, the long-term global consequences were equally disastrous.

Economic uncertainty, the emergence of the 'precariat', growing income inequality, the erosion of pensions, and soaring house prices were consequences of neoliberalism and the specific financial crisis of 2008–2011. Social historians will reasonably wish to push the origins of these economic and social problems back to the economic policies of Ronald Reagan and Margaret Thatcher. 'Thatcherism' was the general term to describe her policies of privatization, low taxes, cutting public spending, and reducing inflation. Thatcherism was not driven by the debates in Germany about economics and politics that are discussed in Thomas Biebricher's chapter in this volume. Ordoliberalism, as Biebricher explains, emerged from the Freiburg school of law and economics. It shares with liberalism a commitment to the free market, but argues that state intervention is required to protect the competitive character of capitalism. Thatcher might be described as a neo-liberal in her economic policies, but she was not a liberal in the tradition of J.S. Mill. There were clear elements of authoritarianism in her version of conservatism. Her strategy had one clear objective, which was to weaken the power of the trade unions, especially the National Union of Miners that in 1971 demanded a 43 per cent pay rise and oversaw the miners' strike of 1974 and that was taken from Shakespeare's Richard III to describe the industrial disputes that crippled the economy. Her economic policies were originally popular against the background of Edward Heath's government that had been battered by industrial strikes, the three-day working week, electricity shortages, and rising oil prices, allowing Thatcher to replace him as the leader of the Conservative Party in 1975. Thatcher was successful in curbing trade union power and their industrial tactics, such as the wildcat strike. Her second objective was the political ambition to create a strong state. This objective was possibly obscured by her opposition to the legacy of Keynesianism and an overextended state. Her strong state ambitions became more obvious in her foreign policy. It was the Falklands War with Argentina in 1982 that restored support for her government. The lesson is that a democratic leader with declining fortunes can gain support with a short, sharp, and successful war.

Reaganomics had a similar beginning and history. Reagan inherited an economic environment from Presidents Ford and Carter that was characterized by slow economic growth and high unemployment. His strategy was in many ways parallel to Thatcherism and was based on supply-side economics and the trickle-down effect: reduce government expenditure, reduce taxes on both individuals and corporations, cut regulation, and slow down the money supply. His tax theories were based on the so-called Laffer Curve in which, over time, tax cuts would have a neutral effect as the tax base expanded with growing employment (Wilentz, 2008). In simple terms, the economic and political agenda of Reagan and Thatcher was to overturn Keynesian economic theories, that had been so central to building up the welfare state, the National Health Service, and commitments to full employment and pension rights.

While the influence of political leaders such as Reagan and Thatcher is well known and widely researched, there are other figures in the transformation of capitalist economies and their political ideologies who are less well known or less fully discussed. Nancy MacLean addresses this gap in her chapter on the 'Enchaining democracy: The now-transnational project of the US corporate libertarian right' and in her book *Democracy in Chains* (2017). Her original focus was on the Koch brothers (Charles and David), who employed their wealth to drive American society in a direction that was consistent with their libertarian values. However, the ideas behind the Koch project came from an economist James McGill Buchanan whose aim was to severely limit the capacity of democratic institutions to impede the unrestrained growth of capitalism. Buchanan and his associate G. Warren Nutter essentially applied Chicago economics to political behaviour, arguing that political actors should be seen as individuals rationally seeking their own self-interest rather than the common good. The driving idea was to prevent governments from extracting taxes from citizens who did not support government objectives such as improving the standard of living of the marginalized poor. For Buchanan, taxation was theft. The contemporary strategy of the majority of western democratic governments has been to reduce personal taxation on the assumption that there would be trickle-down effect. The consumption of the rich would stimulate the economy, providing employment for the majority. The negative consequences of crumbling public buildings, decaying transport systems, under-funded hospitals, and failing welfare systems were of little concern provided individual freedoms were unlimited by legislation and uncompromised by government ineptitude. What alarms MacLean is the global reach of Koch ideas and interests through their funding of the Atlas Network and affiliates, and their ability to shape political agendas from Brexit to attacks on the science of global warming.

It is evident that the economic and social consequences of Reaganomics and Thatcherism have been long-term. There is little agreement however among economic historians as to the success or failure of their economic policies. While they were successful in the short run, the long-term effects were less encouraging. It has been argued that Reaganomics shifted expenditure from the domestic sector to defence demands. The social effects were largely negative. Income inequality has been a persistent problem. For example, the crises of financial capitalism came in tandem with evidence of widespread corruption and mismanagement of the banking sector. In Australia, the Royal Commission into Misconduct in the Banking, Superannuation and Financial Services Industry, that reported in 2019, found widespread evidence of mismanagement, disrespect for clients, and cheating, such as selling insurance to people who were dead. The global economic crisis had many casualties, including the social groups who suffered from the policies that created austerity packages. The burden of austerity packages was especially heavy for Spain, Greece, and Portugal. These arrangements also exposed the fragile relations between the various states of the European Union, especially between the weaker economies and the core economies of Britain, Germany, and France.

Many of these financial and political problems that initially flowed from the financial crisis of 2008–2011 are explored in this volume by Andreas Kallert from the perspective of cultural political economy (CPE). This perspective helps researchers to explore the causal narratives behind economic policies. Returning to Stephen Turner's chapter, these narratives draw heavily on experts whose policy recommendations are thus grounded in discursive strategies that in turn are justified by available scientific evidence. Kallert's chapter covers the history of the financial crisis which posed a threat not just to the European banking system but also to the integration and survival of the European Union as a whole. The immense burden of the financial crisis passed from shareholders and creditors to taxpayers, but the impact across countries was uneven. From the perspective of CPE, it is evident that creditors and banks were able to avoid being bailed-in. With a bail-out strategy it was possible to achieve a socialization of private losses, and therefore the redistribution of taxpayers' money into private hands was essentially a political struggle that cannot be understood within the perspective of pure economics. Another way to understand this development is to recognize that the increasing power of finance capital lends support to money capital under the pretext of securing financial stability.

Margaret Somers in her chapter reminds us of the cruel logic of free markets where 'freedom' typically means freedom from state interference to protect citizens from the precarious circumstances of employment and security. Thus, a market-driven society constantly pits inequality against egalitarian citizenship. The morality of capitalism thus rests on the notion of 'just deserts' in which striving and hard work are rewarded by wealth, but this morality overlooks the way in which rewards are conditioned by what Somers calls 'predistributive' political engineering. Free market morality is based on the notion that I should not be taxed to support citizens who through laziness and turpitude have fallen by the wayside. This moral logic, among other problems, ignores the ways in which inherited wealth is passed from generation to generation. As she explains, social and economic inequalities are seen in capitalism's political economy as natural divisions rather than sustained by the power of elites. The idea of 'just deserts' is perhaps illustrated by the fact that Donald Trump, who inherited considerable wealth from his father and, according to a report by Russ Buetterner and Susanne Craig on *The President's Taxes* on 29 September 2020 in the *New York Times*, enjoyed a tax rebate of $72.9 million, paid some $750 in tax in 2016 and 2017. The president claims that the Internal Revenue Service treats him badly. It is perhaps unsurprising that in Trump's world Obamacare disrupts the moral logic of a free society. We might usefully describe Trumpian economics by reference to the King James translation of the Gospel according to St Matthew (13:12): 'For whosoever hath, to him shall be given, and he shall have more abundance; but whosever hath not, from him shall be taken away even that he hath'.

Returning to the history of the United States, over a period of some 30 years after World War II America emerged as a middle-class society, but between 1979 and 2007, these gains in terms of middle-class prosperity were slowly reversed as the real income of the top 1 per cent quadrupled. Thus, 'by 2007, America was about as unequal as it had been on the eve of the Great Depression – and sure enough just after hitting this milestone, we plunged into the worst slump since the Depression' (Krugman & Wells, 2012, pp. 7–8). In this crisis, the response was to repeat the mistakes that had perpetuated the Great Depression and, in the contemporary political context, the polarization of Republicans and Democrats in Congress has hindered any consensus over measures that would create employment and reduce inequality. The polarization of American politics intensified during the Obama Presidency and continued with Trump's Presidency, making meaningful co-operation over policy impossible, including how to manage the Covid-19 crisis (McCarthy, Poole & Rosenthal, 2006).

The third catastrophe has been political, namely a general crisis of the democratic states of the West, which can be seen in part as an effect of 9/11 and the financial crisis of 2008–2011. This general political and social crisis is the principal topic of *The Condition of Democracy*. The effects of austerity and the inequalities within the European Union have been destabilizing, but they were compounded by the refugee crisis, which galvanized the Far Right in its hostility to immigration, and by what members of the Far Right see as the loss of sovereignty, political independence, and cultural and ethnic coherence of the nation. These multiple difficulties have been important in the rise of right-wing populism, and the further destabilization of democratic institutions. It is signalled by increasing authoritarianism in Austria, Poland, and Hungary, and growing racism across Europe. These crises, alongside status, class, and regional inequalities, played a role in the British vote to leave the European Union or Brexit, with increasing post-Brexit political instability in the United Kingdom (Outhwaite, 2017).

Any discussion of the condition of democracy will include some consideration of populism. Over the last decade, populism has become a dominating theme of political science and has been fuelled by the financial crisis, the implementation across Europe of austerity policies, rising income inequality, and the erosion of citizenship by neo-liberal individualism, and by Thatcherism and Reaganomics. Alongside these objective transformations of the living conditions of citizens, there is the perception by the populace of the indifference and corruption of political elites. The crisis surrounding Brexit and the aftermath in many respects bring many of these changes into a single political issue – the political crisis of liberal democracy. Given the populist appeal of President Trump, there is ample criticism of populist leaders and populist rhetoric from serious journalists and from such sources as the Public Broadcasting Service in the United States. Stephen Turner in his chapter on 'The ideology of anti-populism and the administrative state' in this volume raises important objections to the standard interpretations of populist movements and their ideologies. The relationship of populism to democracy is often described as resembling the drunken unwanted guest at a dinner party. Turner argues that populism rejects the superiority of the elites and their governments that dismiss the claims of populists by reference to the claims of experts. Populist movements emerge when governments fail to deliver on expected goods or impose policies that increase the hardship and suffering of citizens who are at the bottom of the social hierarchy as was the case with the austerity measures after the financial collapse. Experts are not accountable to the people and are often an invisible branch of administration. For Turner, Woodrow Wilson provides a basic illustration of distrust of the people and the need to protect the administration from scrutiny. Wilson sought to limit elections and protect administrators from popular control. Bureaucrats within the administrative state have no pressing requirement to be attentive to the needs of the populace (Stones & Turner, 2020). The role and nature of experts are also taken up by Christian Schmidt-Wellenburg in his chapter in this volume. Experts have played a critical role in the movement for EU integration, but the composition of the experts has changed over a time span of 50 years in which academics were slowly replaced by recruits from business, civil lobby groups, and the Commission itself. The result was the politicization of expert knowledge. This process has not contributed to the further democratization of EU policies and practices, which has in turn fuelled opposition from both left and right populist movements.

Many of the issues and arguments around populism raise significant theoretical problems (Fitzi, Mackert & Turner, 2019). The notion of 'populism' – 'the people' in opposition to the state which is no longer trusted – lacks specificity and is hardly a new concept or development, given the rise of populism in Russia in the 1870s as the commune versus the state or populism in the Mid-West in the 1870s, which involved rural political opposition to 'big business' and eastern elites. Contemporary populism is driven by a similar distrust of the state and the elites that control it, but right-wing populism has acquired additional ammunition from widespread opposition to immigration, especially from Middle East societies with predominantly Muslim populations. A new theme of populism is opposition to what is seen to be uncontrolled flows of migrants into the West, whose high fertility rates spell the erosion of the dominance of the 'native' population.

One basic theoretical difficulty with contemporary interest in populism is the assumption that populism is only driven by right-wing extremists. This general classification ignores the complexity of modern politics in which extremism characterizes both the left and the right. Indeed, modern populism is indicative of the fact that the left–right distinction is no longer clear-cut in modern politics. In Spain, *Podemos* – regarded as a left-wing development in response to economic inequality and political failures – draws its intellectual inspiration from the conservative jurist Carl Schmitt (Booth & Baert, 2014). The election victory of Donald Trump in 2016 demonstrated the growing division in the Democratic Party between eastern sea-board highly educated voters in metropolitan centres and the working class, poorly educated white voters of small communities. Many 'Trump Democrats' supported Trump without changing allegiance to the GOP (Muravchik & Shields, 2020).

Populist movements, including Brexit and Trump's electoral base, are often depicted and condemned by academics and a large section of the press as 'the left behind' or 'the deplorables' who are too badly educated to understand the causes of their problems. However, these assumptions (typically only implicit in academic publications) often overlook the real hardship suffered by working people in a modern economy with poor pay, eroding pensions, instability in the labour market, and declining health care. The precarious nature of their employment and indeed their lives has been captured by the notion of a precariat. A further assumption behind the idea of 'the deplorables' is that their ideas and their worldview lack any intellectual coherence and have little credibility. Populist movements also appear to promote incivility in the public domain – Trump's vulgar language about women's bodies, attacks on members of parliamentary assemblies, the acceptance of crude and violent language in political debates, and outright dismissal of alternative viewpoints. Incivility is a defining feature of aggressive masculinity. Incivility has become acceptable within the elite and is no longer seen to define the working class. The pre-election debate between President Trump and Joe Biden on 29 September 2020 was perhaps the modern nadir of public civility.

While we typically think of incivility as simply referring to bad behaviour, it is important to remember a deeper and more important meaning of civility that was captured by Edward Shils in a variety of publications, many of which eventually appeared in *The Virtue of Civility* (Shils, 1997). For Shils, civility was not about good manners, or only about them. As a foundation of citizenship and democracy, it embraces the norms of self-respect and due consideration for others. Regarding the modern day, there is a widespread sense of the incivility of modern societies as evidenced by threats to the lives of members of parliament, the intimidation of public figures, the abuse of women in public places, and the growth of hate speech on social media. Civility also includes the norms of free speech in which open dialogue is maintained by respect for conflicting viewpoints.

Truth isn't truth

Modern political campaigns appear to draw their spokespersons and leaders from TV shows and popular films rather than from the traditional sources of political information and recruitment. Ronald Reagan had a film career before becoming President. Donald Trump was the host of the popular *The Apprentice* series before he became President of the United States. Trump now consults Kim Kardashian West on prison reform, while Hope Hicks, a former model, served as White House director of strategic communications in 2016. This development may be simply part of the new celebrity culture (Rojek, 2001). While this may be the ultimate outcome of popular culture, it raises acute questions about the reliability and accuracy of the information that is consumed by the electorate. Political slogans – 'Let's Get Brexit Done' or 'Jobs, Jobs, Jobs' – are a poor substitute for political debate. However, slogans are not the exclusive property of Fox News or Republican conventions. Jesse Jackson's 1984 campaign for the Democratic nomination with his 'Run, Jesse, run' slogan promoted Jackson with revivalist rallies that exaggerated his support from the black community (Payne, 1984).

Perhaps what is more damaging is the idea of 'alternative facts' from Kellyanne Conway, counsellor to the President, in her defence of Sean Spicer's claim that the crowds at Trump's inauguration were far larger than the turn-out for Barack Obama's inauguration. Perhaps more challenging was Rudy Giuliani's observation that 'Truth isn't truth' in response to allegations that Russia had interfered in American politics. Similar examples can be taken from recent British history during the referendum on membership of the EU when claims about improved funding for the National Health Service were false. 'Let's get Brexit done', which was addressed to a tired and confused electorate, has still not been settled over four years after the June 2016 referendum, and a hard exit was almost inevitable. President Obama's philosophy was summarized by 'Yes we can'. These speeches and similar slogans are addressed to a post-literate electorate that wants its political aspirations wrapped up in easy comforting phrases. Of course the transformation of political messages can be dated to President Reagan who specialized in one-liners – 'It's morning again in America' or 'Here's my strategy for the Cold War: We win, they lose'. It is clear that we live in a political world of slogans that work on the same level and with similar contents as advertisements for cornflakes or coffee. The simplicity of the message may give emotional comfort but little else to an electorate regarding issues – such as leaving the EU or the advantages of solar heating – that are fundamentally complex and on which there may be no clear-cut answers. However, the slogans rarely or never incorporate or address real policy options.

In any future historical or sociological analysis of the twenty-first century, it may turn out to be that fake news, conspiracy theories, misleading slogans, and redefinitions of the meaning of truth played a major role in defining the negative condition of democracy. In making such a claim, I anticipate that one response would be to find ample historical examples of misinformation in political slogans. One example might be British Prime Minister Harold Macmillan's 'You've never had it so good' speech at Bedford in 1957. It is worth keeping in mind, however, that Macmillan's optimistic slogan was to counter the views of his ministers who favoured cutting welfare and letting unemployment rise to control inflationary pressures in the economy (Heppell, 2014, p. 23). Later in his African speech in 1960 on the 'Winds of Change' he argued, to the South African Parliament, that black consciousness was a fact and that we all had to accept that fact. Macmillan was also realistic in recognizing that political life is often shaped primarily by accidents and the unexpected. In his retirement, when asked what were the main problems he faced during his Prime Ministership, he replied, 'Events, dear boy, events'.

The struggle for power has always included struggles to control the means of communication. While Roman elites in the ancient world had 'bread and circuses' to entertain and control the masses, Tibor Dessewffy in this volume draws our attention to the role of the new media, popular culture, and collective emotions in the quest for hegemony. For Dessewffy, the 'emotional design' of online media has become a prerequisite for political success in the digital age. He takes as one example the slogan 'Get Brexit Done', and I would add the emotional appeal of support for the National Health Service, which has in the British imagination a virtually sacred status. The Trump election success of 2016 and the vote to leave the European Union caught 'the experts' by surprise. Indeed, David Cameron was so confident of success in supporting the Remain campaign that he took the decision to hold a referendum without consulting his own cabinet. Dessewffy reminds us that Trump's victory came to depend heavily on an 'aggressive troll army' that spread Trump's message. New channels of communication – 4chan, 8chan, Reddit – are rapidly replacing the traditional channels of political communication. These new forums have become channels for the disgruntled voice of those sections of society that believe their voice and their issues have not only been ignored by the traditional media, but they have been scorned as the ideas of 'the deplorables'. Their anger, especially against feminism, has been channelled through such movements as incels or involuntary celibates.

The Trump Presidency has established new criteria to blur any distinctions between truth and make-believe. The examples are numerous, such as building the Mexican wall and getting the Mexican government to pay for it, the treatment of Covid-19 infections with disinfectant, the alleged foreign policy successes with North Korea and the Middle East, and claims regarding the potential for widespread voter fraud with mail voting. His foreign policy objectives and the promise to 'Make America Great Again' (MAGA) have only served to divide the United States and alienate what have been America's staunch allies for the last 75 years. MAGA has been described by the Democrats as 'Make America White Again'. Other critics call it a 'white political theology' that aims 'to build on the racialist Anglo-Saxon thesis, one whose defining narrative is that of a "magistrate of God" under siege by the generally perceived ills of mixity, migration, and multiculturalism' (Mukherjee, 2018, p. 2).

The *coup de grâce* of American democracy came in September 2020 when President Trump encouraged his base to commit a criminal act by voting twice, once by mail and once in person at a ballot booth. This recommendation was combined with a general attempt to make voting more difficult. These processes are a direct attack on democracy. Let me return to Huntington's minimalist definition of democracy as involving the selection of decision-makers through 'fair, honest, and periodic elections in which candidates freely compete for votes and in which virtually all the adult population is eligible to vote' (Huntington, 1991, p. 7). The condition of democracy itself is threatened by attempts to limit the eligibility of the voters and to make the actual act of voting as difficult as possible.

While voting to elect governments is an important aspect of a functioning democracy, we need more substantive notions to measure democratic success and failure. One important criterion must be the capacity of a democracy to enhance the well-being of its citizens, namely, their happiness, by which I mean much more than satisfaction. To give this idea a more substantive measure, I refer to Amartya Sen's reference to mortality as an indication of economic success or failure (Sen, 1998). Life expectancy is a reliable measure of economic development and offers an important insight into patterns of equality in a given society. Sen also draws attention to patterns of gender inequality, for example, by reference to the 'missing women' in the Chinese population in the 1960s. Sen's argument was stated in a basic claim that no democracy (or at least a society with a free press) has experienced a famine (Sen, 1994). Famine is almost never caused by food shortages (D'Souza, 1994).

This research into the social causes of mortality offers us a demographic insight into the condition of democracy. Research by Anne Case and Angus Dutton (2017) identified increases in mortality and morbidity among white non-Hispanic Americans in midlife since the turn of the century. Alongside increases in all-cause mortality, there were additional increases in drug overdoses, suicides, and alcohol-related liver mortality. The patterns of morbidity and mortality are complicated, and Case and Dutton eschew any set of simple economic explanations to account for variance between different social groups. However, they suggest that there is an important long-term explanation, namely, the slow decline of employment opportunities and income of the working class from the 1970s, which was the beginning and the end of the 'blue-collar aristocracy'. Alongside these economic changes, there were equally important transformations in marriage, community, and religion, and growing social isolation that may explain the sense of hopelessness in these people's lives. These changes in turn explain growing suicide rates in this section of the population. They conclude that behind the familiar stories about globalization and automation,

> changes in social customs that have allowed dysfunctional changes in patterns of marriage and childrearing, the decline of unions … and the pathologies that accompany that decline may provide a deeper insight into the malaise of the white working class.
>
> (Case & Dutton, 2017, pp. 438–439)

It is precisely this sector of the declining working class that forms a significant component, but not the only component, of President Trump's 'base'. In conclusion, an account of the condition of democracy requires a careful analysis of the changing economic circumstances of the citizens but also an inquiry into their sense of well-being and the meaningfulness of their lives.

Conclusion: A coda for Covid-19

The Covid-19 pandemic of 2020 is the fourth catastrophe of my modern history of socio-political disasters. The early manifestations of the health crisis arrived long after the Potsdam conference on *The Condition of Democracy* of 2019 where these chapters were originally presented. Nevertheless, the pandemic has exposed the underlying weakness of the western democracies and the fragility of the global system that were well in place long before the arrival of the disease. The pattern of infections and deaths has exposed the pattern of social inequality in the democracies, with the poor, the migrants, and the elderly being the primary victims. The pandemic has also shown the difficulty for democracies in locking down populations, enforcing social distancing, and closing their borders. The crisis has also fuelled the agenda of the Far Right in confirming their suspicions about the role of 'the deep state'. It is, however, difficult to include a comprehensive discussion of this catastrophe in this conclusion because we do not yet know if and when the pandemic can be brought under effective control, and hence we cannot be certain what its effects will be in the long term. What is clear is that the global order will not remain the same. With restrictions on movements within and between societies, the crisis may usher in new social and political formations, but will they be democratic?

Acknowledgements

The research for this chapter was made possible by an Australian Research Council grant. Project title: 'Far Right in Australia: Intellectuals, Masculinity and Citizenship'. Australian Research Council Discovery Grant DP200102013. Prof Bryan S. Turner, Prof Pam Nilan, Ass Prof Joshua Roose, Dr Mario Peucker. Note: since the initial data collection phase of this funded project was postponed owing to the Covid-19 pandemic, the project support for this book is primarily intellectual, drawing on the expertise of the distinguished research team.

References

Bauman, Z. (2000). *Liquid modernity*. Cambridge: Polity Press.

Beck, U. (2000). The cosmopolitan perspective: Sociology of the second age of modernity. *British Journal of Sociology*, *51*(1), 79–106.

Bell, D. (Ed.). (1964). *The new American right*. Garden City: Anchor Books.

Booth, J., & Baert, P. (2014). *The dark side of Podemos? Carl Schmitt and contemporary progressive populism*. London: Routledge.

Case, A., & Dutton, A. (2017). Mortality and morbidity in the 21st century. *Brookings Panel on Economic Activity*. Retrieved from https://www.brookings.edu/wp-content/uploads/2017/08/casetextsp17bpea.pdf.

Diamond, L. (1999). *Developing democracy toward consolidation*. Baltimore: Johns Hopkins University Press.

Dryden, S. (1995). *Trade warriors: USTR and the American crusade for free trade*. New York: Oxford University Press.

D'Souza, F. (1994). Democracy as a cure for famine. *Journal of Peace Research, 31*(4), 369–373.

Dunn, J. (1979). *Western political theory in the face of the future*. Cambridge: Cambridge University Press.

Fitzi, G., Mackert, J., & Turner, B.S. (Eds.). (2019). *Populism and the crisis of democracy. Vol. 1. Concepts and theory*. London: Routledge.

Heppell, T. (2014). *The Tories: From Winston Churchill to David Cameron*. London: Bloomsbury.

Huntington, S.P. (1991). *Democracy's third wave: Democratization in the late twentieth century*. Norman: University of Oklahoma Press.

Hutton, W., &Giddens, A. (Eds.). (2000). *Global capitalism*. New York: New Press.

Krugman, P., & Wells, R. (2012). The widening gyre: Inequality, polarization, and the crisis. In J. Byrne (Ed.), *The occupy handbook* (pp. 7–17). New York: Back Bay Books.

Marazzi, C. (2011). *The violence of financial capitalism*. Los Angeles: Semiotext(e).

McCarthy, N., Poole, K.T., & Rosenthal, H. (2006). *Polarized America: The dance of ideology and unequal rights*. Cambridge: MIT Press.

Michels, R. [1911] (1999). *Political parties. A sociological study of the oligarchical tendencies of modern democracy*. New Brunswick: Transaction Publishing.

Mills, C.W. (1956). *The power elite*. Oxford: Oxford University Press.

Mukherjee, S.R. (2018). Make America great again as white political theology. *Revue LISA*, *XVI*(2), 1–16.

Muravchik, S., & Shields, J. (2020). *Trump's democrats*. Washington: Brookings Institution Press.

Outhwaite, W. (Ed.). (2017). *Brexit: Sociological responses*. London: Anthem Press.

Payne, L. (1984). Black reporters, white press—and the Jackson campaign. *Columbia Journalism Review* (July/August), 32–37.

Porter, P. (2018). *Blunder: Britain's war in Iraq*. New York: Oxford University Press.

Robertson, R. (1992). *Globalization: Social theory and global culture*. London: SAGE.

Rojek, C. (2001). *Celebrity*. London: Reaktion.

Sanders, R. (2017). Human rights abuses at the limits of law: Legal instabilities and vulnerabilities in the 'global war on terror'. *Review of International Studies*, *44*(1), 2–23.

Schmitter, P.C. (1993). Democracy's third wave. *The Review of Politics*, *55*(2), 348–351.

Sen, A. (1994). Liberty and poverty: Political rights and economics. *New Republic*, *210*(10), 31–37.

Sen, A. (1998). Mortality as an indicator of economic success or failure. *The Economic Journal*, *108*(446), 1–25.

Shils, E. (1997). *The virtue of civility*. Indianapolis: Liberty Fund.

Stones, R., & Turner, B.S. (2020). Successful societies: Decision-making and the quality of attentiveness. *British Journal of Sociology*, *71*(1), 183–202.

Urry, J. (2000). Mobile sociology. *British Journal of Sociology*, *51*(1), 185–203.

Wallis, J. (2004). George W. Bush's theology of empire. *Mississippi Review*, *32*(3), 60–72.

Whitaker, B.E. (2007). Exporting the patriot act? Democracy and the 'war on terror' in the third world. *Third World Quarterly*, *28*(5), 1017–1032.

Wilentz, S. (2008). *The age of Reagan: A history 1974–2008*. New York: HarperCollins.

Part 1

Neoliberalism and the meltdown of democratic life

1 Enchaining democracy

The now-transnational project of the US corporate libertarian right

Nancy MacLean

Introduction

Over the past decade, it has become ever more obvious that American politics are in profound crisis, both in Washington and a majority of the states. A government that once claimed to be of, by, and for the people has been captured by corporations whose agendas are driving unmatched inequality and planetary crisis. With the presidency of Donald J. Trump, even elementary norms of civic decency were imperilled.[1]

Anyone who follows American politics knows this. What you may be struggling to figure out is how things reached this pass and what that means for the wider world, given the dominance of the United States in the global political economy and its rule-making bodies – and, as I will explain in concluding, the international ambitions of the country's Radical Right. The watershed in US public life has been fed by many streams, of course. They include the kind of movement conservatism that made Barry Goldwater the Republican candidate for President in 1964, just after his vote against the Civil Rights Act of 1964. Another – and related stream – is the Religious Right. And there is the white Supremacist Right that has resurfaced with a vengeance of late. All of these are important, and have yielded votes to effect radical policy change.

But I want to address another piece of the puzzle: a missing piece in the literature and media coverage that explains much that otherwise remains mysterious. My subject is the ideas that are guiding the billionaire-funded libertarian right made notorious by Charles Koch, one of the world's richest men. He and his brother David, now deceased, have assembled over 600 likeminded wealthy donors into the largest private political network the world has ever seen, one that outstrips in size and sophistication the Republican Party which it has turned into a delivery vehicle for the donors' unpopular agenda. Other researchers have captured well the scale and audacity of the Koch network's bid for power.

What they have not identified are the ideas this network has weaponized to climb from utter marginality to breathtaking power. I believe knowing about these ideas – and how the Koch's networks operations have used them to gain a sway this arch-right billionaire project otherwise could not – is important not just in its own right, to see more clearly what is happening and why and how, but also because having that knowledge may equip concerned citizens to stop this speeding train before it is too late. A public health nurse who read my book on the subject used this analogy: 'I see now, she said, that we need to get the diagnosis right before we can determine the best treatment plan'.

Why does getting the diagnosis right matter so much? Because there is an unmarked hazard in our current situation in how the noisiest threats are getting the most attention – among them the now chronic race-baiting and mafia-like intimidation coming from the White House. But as the sitting President at this writing, whom I've come to think of as the Distractor in Chief, draws nearly all media attention, an even more extreme plan is moving along apace out of the spotlight – in the 30 states now totally dominated by the Koch cause through a party it has bent to its purposes, in federal departments and agencies, and in the courts. This plan is being pursued, not by a surprise president with a limited attention span, but by a highly strategic network that is archly determined and breathtakingly well-funded. And this cause's architects aim to rewrite the rules of our society, permanently. To do so, they have shown that they are willing to use those other, popular sections of the right – the Religious Right and the Racist Right, to say nothing of the Trump presidency itself – to get what they want, in the knowledge that they otherwise could not achieve it.

I will state my case concisely: behind all the seeming chaos and dysfunction in US public life, there is a strategy in play, a cold-eyed, calculated strategy. And that strategy is far along. One of its field generals said this in late 2015: 'We're close to winning … they [the critics] don't have the real path'. That was Mark Holden, then head of Koch Industries' government and public affairs operation, gloating to an invitation-only audience of billionaire and multimillionaire donors. It was an academic economist, I learned in the archives, whose work supplied the strategic path to which Holden referred. This scholar taught Charles Koch that for capitalism to thrive, democracy must be enchained: not overthrown in a coup, but rather quietly rigged so that it can no longer provide what citizens have looked to it to provide – from workers' rights and retirement security to protection from discrimination and environmental degradation.

My research thus provides an unknown backstory to this pivotal moment, as it uncovers and explains the 'real path' to which Mark Holden referred. It exposes how the lives of this thinker and CEO converged, beginning in the early 1970s, through a shared commitment to transform the model of government that western capitalist nations built up over the twentieth century. The thinker was a Tennessee-born economist, James McGill Buchanan, the first US Southerner to be awarded the Nobel Prize in Economic Sciences. The CEO is, of course, the Kansas-based Charles Koch, who spent most of his adult life building Koch Industries into a fossil fuel-based behemoth while also seeking a way to make his country – and the world, in fact – conform to an arch vision of economic liberty, a kind of free-reign capitalism beyond the reach of voters and their governments. The history my conveys is, first, of the crucible in which Buchanan came up with the idea of enchaining democracy to insulate economic liberty: as the civil rights movement made headway in his adopted state of Virginia and in the nation in the late 1950s and 1960s. Then the focus turns to how Koch began funding an apparatus to make that idea a reality, in a messianic quest that has produced the volatile situation now compounded by the COVID pandemic (MacLean, 2017a).

As the final section of this chapter will convey, while my book's story was mainly US-based, the Koch project is transnational. Indeed, readers may be surprised to learn that the Mont Pèlerin Society – so formative in promoting neoliberalism around the world – is now chock-full of Koch-funded academics and operatives (Readfearn, 2014). And the Atlas Network, first launched by England's Antony Fisher in 1981, is now more vast and influential than Fisher could ever have imagined, thanks in no small part to funding from the United States and the Koch network in particular (Atlas Network, 2020a, b; Teles & Kenney, 2007).

Forget Chicago: The crucible of our current crisis is to be found in the Virginia School

Here, rather than summarize the book, I want to share the story of how I stumbled upon the trail that led me to these findings. Knowing the circuitous route that led to the stark conclusions I have just stated will give readers an even sharper sense of the stakes, I believe. Because it turns out that what we are seeing in today's world is not the first time the libertarian right has shown itself willing to exploit racism and demagoguery to advance a cause I have come to think about as property supremacy – a property supremacy that is now endangering the entire planet.

The story is one of serendipitous discovery. I had never heard of either Charles Koch or James Buchanan when I embarked on the research that led to *Democracy in Chains* (MacLean, 2017a). I am a historian of social movements and their impact on public life, with a particular interest in the US South. In 2006, on a chance visit to an archive, I came across the tragic tale of Prince Edward County, Virginia, whose white officials answered the US Supreme Court's call to desegregate their public schools without further delay by, as the county leaders put it, 'going out of the public school business entirely'. They shuttered every public school in the community, leaving black children with no formal education whatsoever as their white counterparts headed off to a private segregation academy knowing that they would have state-subsidized tuition grants: vouchers. And the county officials kept the public schools shut for five years, until the courts compelled them to reinstate a school system.

Shocked, I started to research this history and learned that tax-funded school vouchers were crucial to this kind of 'massive resistance' to *Brown v. Board of Education*. I also discovered that the Chicago libertarian economist Milton Friedman had issued his first manifesto calling for such vouchers to undermine the 'government monopoly' of education in 1955, the year after the *Brown* decision, in the full advanced knowledge of how it would aid segregationists. So Friedman became part of my story. But in following a footnote, I learned of a 1959 report, as this Prince Edward County threat was in the air to close the schools that fall when a court ultimatum would take effect, by two *other* economists, both trained at the

University of Chicago, who had recently set up a new centre at the University of Virginia in Charlottesville, one of them being James Buchanan.

Their report attempted to refute a movement of moderate whites – led by mothers and liberal clergy – who were trying to save Virginia's public education system from the segregationists. How did the economists fight? By making a case that these moderates had the math wrong: that if the state sold off its facilities to private operators it could break up the 'government monopoly' in schooling and provide better education at less cost with 'liberty' (liberty from the federal courts being the crucial subtext). The economists' report, in effect, called for privatizing the South's schools, before that verb even existed. And they did so in the full knowledge that the schools thus funded would be white segregation academies because those were the only private schools in question. Black parents and their organizations opposed the vouchers to a person, seeing them as the policy tool to perpetuate segregation they were. Indeed, the economists issued their report with timing that abetted a segregationist effort to alter the Virginia constitution to eliminate its guarantee of a 'public' education.

It stunned me, as a professor myself, to see two university faculty members making a case for what their state's most arch segregationists were seeking. (Two cosmopolitan faculty, I might add: Buchanan read in five languages and had just returned from a fellowship in Italy; his colleague and co-author, G. Warren Nutter, a student of the USSR's economy, would go on to work for the Central Intelligence Agency and the Nixon administration Defense Department.) It also intrigued me that they advocated the diehard racists' policy not in racial terms, but in economic terms, self-consciously leveraging the authority of their discipline to back up the state's powerful right-wing elite and Buchanan's stature as the new chair of the Economics Department in 'Mr. Jefferson's University', as Virginians referred to it, paying homage to its designer, Thomas Jefferson. Buchanan and Nutter knew they were exploiting the rage of white supremacists to move their libertarian economic agenda, one they referred to as 'the free society' even as they showed no sympathy whatsoever for the civil rights activists whose mantra was 'Freedom Now'. Their cover letter to legislators with their report said that they were speaking out, 'letting the chips fall where they may'. The professors were fully aware, in other words, of the harm these actions would inflict. As an educator myself, I wondered how anyone could do such a thing – not in irrational frenzy, but in cold-eyed calculation, to move an otherwise unpopular neoliberal agenda?

With curiosity piqued, I began seeking more information about Buchanan. I learned that he had gone on to win the Nobel Prize in Economic Sciences in 1986. He was awarded it for having pioneered a new way of thinking called public choice economics, which also became influential in political science and law – and, I learned, among activists and elected officials on the Right. What Buchanan did that was new was, in his phrase, the economic analysis of politics. But it was a distinctive economic analysis: he applied Chicago-style and Austrian-style libertarian economic assumptions to political actors to argue that they should only be understood as individuals rationally seeking their own personal self-interest – not the common good as they claimed.

That theoretical premise led Buchanan to a new explanation of deficits, because he made sense of why the governments would overspend in times of prosperity, not just depression or recession as Keynesian economics would predict. As a thinker who specialized in public finance and who identified with the political Right in the South and nationally, Buchanan made it his mission to find ways to reduce taxes and shrink the expanding public sector, then in its heyday of expansion. In 1963, he and his colleague and co-author Gordon Tullock founded what became the Public Choice Society (a society to which Charles Koch now contributes, by the way, and whose journal has been edited by many Koch-funded faculty since its founding). With public choice economics, Buchanan turned new attention to what he liked to call 'the rules of the game of politics': to the taxing and spending incentives of the political process, and to how altering the rules of the process might yield different outcomes.

Public choice ideas have since interested some people not on the political Right, I hasten to add. Among them is Cass Sunstein, a Harvard Law School professor who worked on regulatory matters in the Obama administration, and co-author of a book called *Nudge*, which shows how altering certain incentives could, say, improve public health (Sunstein & Thaler, 2008). But I also learned that Buchanan's own subset of the larger school, known as the Virginia School of Political Economy, was always distinctive – and tendentious. Buchanan himself said, looking back, that his goal was 'to tear down' the very idea of 'the public interest'. Why, I thought, would anyone want to do that?

Reading more, I learned that to a libertarian like Buchanan, there *is* no common good. Any such notion of shared purpose will lead government to coerce those who do not agree with the majority. Democracy, Buchanan and his colleagues came to argue, violates the individual liberty of the minority. The minority he was concerned with was that of wealthy taxpayers who do not share the majority's view of the public interest. And government, Buchanan and his colleagues argued, all but steals their property, if it taxes them for purposes they do not share. Indeed, even in his scholarly work he made this point very agitationally. In what he viewed as his master work, *The Limits of Liberty* (Buchannan, 1975a), written during the 1970s crime panic, Buchanan compared government 'coercion' of the unwilling taxpayer to 'the thug who steals his wallet in Central Park'.

We should not be our brothers' keeper, Buchanan insisted – or at least, we should not be able to use government to transfer tax revenues from one citizen to another. He made that case aggressively in a 1975 article called 'The Samaritan's Dilemma' (Buchanan, 1975b), which argued that the ethics of Jesus produced perverse results in the modern world. Buchanan summarized this piece of what he termed 'prescriptive diagnosis' thus: 'We may simply be too compassionate for our own well-being or for that of an orderly and productive free society'. He then applied a game theory thought experiment – never, of course, empirical research, which he spurned – to make the case. His 'hypothesis' was 'that modern man has become incapable of making the choices that are required to prevent his exploitation by predators of his own species, whether the predation be conscious or unconscious'. *Predators of his own species?* It was a perverse appropriation of the parable of the Good Samaritan, in which a kind resident of Samaria comes to the aid of a Jewish traveller who has been stripped, robbed, beaten, and left to die – a victim, in other words, in the story Jesus used to show his followers that one should love every person as himself, even when the person was a member of a despised out-group, as Samaritans and Jews were.

But in the view of the libertarian economist, Jesus was a sop for weak minds. What society needed (and Charles Koch would ultimately supply) was the 'strategic courage' to restore the market to proper ordering. By this logic, what seemed to be the ethical thing to do – help someone in need – was not the right thing to do, because the assistance would encourage the neighbour to 'exploit' the giver rather than to solve his own problems. Buchanan used as an analogy the spanking of children by parents: it taught 'the fear of punishment that will inhibit future misbehavior'. 'The potential parasite' needed harsh discipline to prevent future efforts 'to live parasitically off and/or deliberately exploit' society's 'producers'. More than any other piece, this article captured the stark morality of libertarianism. As the economist noted in conclusion, 'welfare reform' was 'only one of many applications, and by no means the most important' (Buchanan, 1975b, pp. 71, 74–76, 84). It was true. He had bigger targets in mind.

Over the ensuing years, Buchanan came to talk about all this in very stark and foreboding terms that are now widespread on the Right, owing to decades of inculcation by Buchanan's team and the think tanks with which they worked. A case in point: when Mitt Romney, campaigning for the presidency in 2012 at a $50,000 a plate dinner for donors, spoke disdainfully of what he called 'the 47 per cent' of Americans who he said would never vote for him because they were too 'dependent' on government as net tax recipients, millions of Americans were shocked. Many pundits thought it cost him the election. But Romney was not offering a new idea, in fact. By then, the Heritage Foundation was maintaining an 'annual index of dependency' derived from public choice economics. It was Buchanan who gave scholarly imprimatur to such thinking. And he did not hold back. He spoke of net tax recipients as 'parasites on the productive'; he warned of 'predators and prey'. His very vocabulary made fellow citizens appear as menaces, not even truly human. It is a vocabulary that is disinhibiting, one that licenses hostility. And it, too, is rife on the Right today.

As I read more, I learned that for those who think this way, social justice is an oxymoron. As Buchanan's colleague Walter E. Williams, the John M. Olin Distinguished Professor of Economics at George Mason University and a frequent guest host for the right-wing radio pioneer Rush Limbaugh, put it on the Conservative Political Action Conference circuit: 'Let me offer you my definition of social justice: I keep what I earn and you keep what you earn' (Civitas, 2014).

From theory building to trial of radical rules change with Chile's 'Constitution of Liberty'

But Buchanan did not stop with developing theory that he hoped would undermine the legitimacy of the modern welfare and regulatory state. Believing fiercely in the rightness of his cause, he moved in the 1970s from scholarship to organizing to apply that theory, urging right-wing donors to help build a 'counterintelligentsia'. How? By creating what he called 'a gravy train' to bring men into the libertarian fold and train them for intellectual battle with Keynesians and social justice advocates. As he organized, he also shifted from diagnosis to prescription; he began developing the field he called *constitutional economics*.

In the belief that all existing constitutions were 'failures' as far as protecting the wealthy minority from the grabbing majority was concerned, Buchanan set out to design a new legal regime. Its aim would be to protect capitalists from government – to enshrine the rights of the wealthy minority to a degree no society anywhere had ever done, making them all but impervious to intrusion by democracy.

Buchanan took pride in being an 'academic entrepreneur', and this venture showed his acute sense of timing. For he turned to constitutional design in the mid-1970s just as the military junta of General Augusto Pinochet in Chile was facing intense international pressure to return to representative government – yet wanted to lock in the radical transformation of the political economy it had forced upon the country, including the privatization of social security and education.

In 1980, the dictatorship's corporate allies invited Buchanan to Santiago to try out his ideas for how to devise a constitution that would protect capitalism from government; the result – the so-called 'Constitution of Liberty' ratified in a rigged plebiscite – is still achieving that purpose. In 2013, Michelle Bachelet, a president elected by two-thirds of the Chilean people to carry out far-reaching reforms after huge and vastly popular demonstrations by Chilean students protesting the high cost of privatized university education, soon complained that the constitution's 'authoritarian trammels' were keeping her from delivering to that supermajority because it put 'locks and bolts' on what government can do. Indeed, in 2019, 20 people lost their lives in the massive struggle for a new constitution that might again be responsive to the will of the vast majority (McSherry, 2020).

Sadly, the Chilean experience is not a detour of purely historical interest, but rather, a case of past as prologue. That kind of constitution – a constitution not of checks and balances, but of locks and bolts – is now coming to the United States, owing to pressure from the Koch network, which is determined to achieve the kind of binding changes Buchanan urged, without informing the public of their true goals. Thanks to assiduous organizing by the apparatus these arch-right donors fund – above all the American Legislative Exchange Council (ALEC) and a Republican Party that the donors have all but taken over and turned into a delivery vehicle with the threat of primary challenges – this cause now has in place 28 of the 34 states' authorizations needed to call the first constitutional convention since 1787. It is an incredibly radical and reckless gambit, and it is perhaps a few years away, at the rate things are going. The citizens group Common Cause calls this convention push 'the most serious threat to our democracy flying almost completely under the radar' (Riestenberg, 2018; MacLean, 2017b).

A slow-motion revolution launched at the state level

You might be wondering how I was able to put together the way that Buchanan's ideas were guiding 'the real path' the Koch network is following to shackle democracy through a quiet constitutional revolution. The answer is, again in good part, coincidence. I happened to move to North Carolina in 2010, just as a radicalized Republican Party, dominated by Koch-backed Tea Party figures, won majorities in both houses of the state legislature. And suddenly, the prescriptions I was reading in Buchanan's work that still seemed so abstract became concrete as the General Assembly's lead donor, Art Pope, a long-time Koch ally, boasted of the 'Big Bang' his grantees were delivering to make this once-moderate state 'a laboratory' for the cause, using measures derived from public choice thought (Mayer, 2011, 2016; Hertel-Fernandez, 2019).

To appreciate the nature of this big bang, a public policy variant of the 'shock and awe' strategy of warfare, it helps to know that Buchanan had long urged his teammates on the Right to stop focusing on *who* rules, and study *the* rules. He explained to like thinkers and those who funded them – including Charles Koch – that if you did not like the outcome of public policy over a long period of time (as libertarians despised the policy fruits of twentieth-century democracy) and wanted to achieve, instead, the kind of radical U-turn that libertarians did, you must focus laser-like on systematically changing the rules of governance.

What unfolded in North Carolina was a stunning barrage of radical rules changes on this model, one after another – among them, the most extreme and sophisticated gerrymandering in US political history to misrepresent the will of the electorate; new measures to undermine workers' ability to organize in unions, particularly public sector unions, with teachers unions now the most powerful and progressive in America; attacks on public education at all levels and radical cuts in funding for it; refusal to accept the Medicaid expansion of the Affordable Care Act despite a crying need for health care subsidies in this low-wage state; and rolling back measures to protect the environment and reduce global warming. Also, the new majority broke with customary governing practices like public hearings before passing legislation and transparency about the process; instead, they worked with breakneck speed and often secrecy. And then, to cap it off, they passed what has come to be known as the monster voter suppression bill, which in some 15 different ways tried to keep those least likely to support the corporate libertarian agenda – including African Americans, Latinos, and young people – away from the polls. 'Getting dramatic economic change at the federal level is very difficult', Tim Phillips, President of the Koch organizing enterprise Americans for Prosperity, later explained. So 'a few years ago, the idea we had was to create model states. North Carolina was a great opportunity to do that – more so than any other state in the region' (Mayer, 2016; NC Policy Watch, 2015).

The new Republican majority, I could see from my research, was applying James Buchanan's ideas to achieve what they otherwise could not, certainly not if they had campaigned openly for the policies they were rushing through. Indeed, at the very same time, Scott Walker, the Koch-allied Governor of Wisconsin, was running a similar operation, taking away collective bargaining rights from public sector workers to destroy the labour movement there, under the false pretext of a 'budget repair bill' (Kaufman, 2018).

Because of my research, I could also see how the critics of all this – progressive activists and other good people who had helped make their once-poor state a beacon to the South and now were shocked at the U-turn their beloved state was taking – were missing the deep operational strategy that unified all these far-flung measures. They could not see that the men pushing this agenda were not misinformed about the likely consequences of the agenda they were pushing: they fully understood that it would inflict harm on many of their fellow citizens. But they believed their endgame was worth that price. They were, in cold calculation, yet again 'letting the chips fall where they may'.

What critics of all this also did not see was that this agenda was backed by an ethical system that gave the new-style Republican elected officials confidence and let them feel heroic enough to weather all the criticism and opposition. I understand why they could not, not even the prophetic leader of the Moral Mondays movement, the Reverend Dr William J. Barber II, who has since been awarded a MacArthur 'Genius Grant'. Why not? Because this ethical system runs counter to the best in all the world's great religious traditions (Barber, 2016; Nichol, 2020).

But it is an ethical system, one that has its own harsh coherence, which must be understood to deal with the crisis that Buchanan's ideas and Koch's money have created. To wit: the libertarian morality deems it better to have people die from lack of health care than receive it from government, from taxes paid by others. This, really, is what they mean, ultimately, by personal responsibility: you *should* be on your own, for all your needs. And if you fail to anticipate and save for those future needs, you deserve your fate. Not only that, your suffering will have instructive value for others in the new world the libertarians are ushering into being: watching what happens to you, as government no longer helps you, will teach others that they must save. What they seek, in short, is a world in which we are kept from using government to help ourselves and one another: by ironclad new rules.

The Koch network's weaponization of bases in higher education

I learned all this and more in 2013, when James Buchanan died, at the age of 93, and finally that September I was able to gain access to his unprocessed archive at George Mason University (GMU), his last institutional home. In his records going back to the 1940s, I found my developing understanding of all this confirmed – in a way that left me gobsmacked more than once. Just one example: in his private office on the second floor, I found a pile of documents stacked on a chair, which exposed how Charles Koch and some of his most trusted operatives, GMU economics faculty, the law school dean, the president and provost, and a politically appointed Board of Visitors presided over by Ed Meese III, Ronald Reagan's long-time ally, had collaborated to establish a base camp for this political project at a public university, just across the Potomac from Washington, DC.

This was in 1997, when Koch gave his first $10 million gift to GMU to support a big new Center for Political Economy (he has since become the university's top donor, having given well over $100 million to support his units there). Koch made it clear in the speech that accompanied his money that he wanted bold steps. Buchanan's theory and implementation strategies were the right 'technology', to use the favourite phrase of this MIT-trained engineer. But the professor's team had not employed the tools forcefully enough to 'create winning strategies'. The operatives Koch put in place on the campus would. One of them was Buchanan's former colleague, the aptly named Richard Fink, who by that point had become Koch's chief political strategist. Fink made clear that establishing beachheads in higher education was crucial because, as he has told donors: 'It's an integrated strategy that uses universities, think tanks and political spending for the implementation of policy change' (UnKoch My Campus; Koch Docs).[2]

With a respectable base camp secured at GMU, a short ride from the nation's capital, Koch would turn to assembling what he said he sought when he gave that first multi-million-dollar 1997 gift, with the proclamation that 'I want to build the kind of force that propelled Columbus to his discoveries'.

To make the remainder of the story short, America and the world have felt that force since. And just as it did not, in fact, start with President Obama's election, so it will not stop with the end of the Trump administration, however that happens.

Promoting corporate libertarian transformation on every continent

In closing, though, let me pull the lens back out from this flagship campus outpost to the overall Koch project of social and political transformation. It is so radically new in human history in its scope, audacity, and strategic sophistication that the social sciences lack even a concept for it. The Koch donor network funds an infrastructure of literally hundreds of organizations. It includes dozens of ostensibly separate national bodies such as the Cato Institute, the Heritage Foundation, the American Legislative Exchange Council, the Heartland Institute, and the Federalist Society. It also includes over 150 state-level organizations whose work is aligned through the State Policy Network. It further contains organizing enterprises such as Americans for Prosperity, Concerned Veterans for America, the LIBRE Initiative (aimed at Latinos), and Generation Opportunity. And it boasts centres at colleges and universities – with George Mason University as the flagship enterprise, but faculty at over 300 colleges now getting funding. Thus, we are talking about hundreds of organizations working to radically alter government and society in a quest to bring unfettered free-reign capitalism into being – without being honest with the people. Not surprisingly, with all this capacity, the Koch network has been able to bend the Republican Party to its agenda nationally, in the courts, and in the majority of states, with a discipline Joseph Stalin could have admired (Mayer, 2016; Hertel-Fernandez, Skocpol & Sclar, 2018).

But there's more: this was never just a US project. With capitalism a global system, governed by global rule-making bodies, why would such shrewd strategists confine their efforts to a single country? Just as Marxists knew a workers' revolution would have to be international to succeed, so have these revolutionary capitalists reached the same conclusion. Their vehicle is something called the *Atlas Network*, which at this writing claims over 400 affiliates in 95 countries, their operations partly funded by Koch and allied capitalists, with heavy support from fossil fuel-based fortunes. In fact, Atlas can now claim to be the largest think tank network in the world (Desmog, 2020; Fischer & Plehwe, 2017; Djelic & Mousavi, 2020; Salles-Djelic, 2017).

Yet, the organization is all but unknown to most scholars and trackers of neoliberalism. Atlas presents itself to the global public as a non-profit body 'strengthening the worldwide freedom movement'. Its mission, according to its website, is to '[increase] global prosperity by strengthening a network of independent partner organizations that promote individual freedom and are committed to identifying and removing barriers to human flourishing'. Atlas says that it 'cultivates a network of partners that share this vision' (Atlas Network, 2020b). It all sounds so harmless.

As in the case of the Koch network's operations in the US, the rhetoric of freedom packages a cause which does more than simply compete in the marketplace of ideas to win converts. Even from the very limited investigations undertaken to date, numerous Atlas affiliates have been found to sway public opinion with disinformation, operate in secrecy, violate tax laws on charitable endeavours, and more (MacLean, 2020). Most concerning here is the key role a number of its affiliates have played in the rise of right-wing populism, the topic with which I will end.

Scholars and journalists interested in corporate-driven neoliberalism and climate denial have only begun to study the Atlas Network and its far-flung affiliates. So far the work has focused on Australia, Latin America, the United States, and Western Europe (particularly England, Germany, France, and Sweden). Much more research needs to be done on Atlas affiliates' operations in these places, as well as in Africa, East and Southeast Asia, Eastern Europe, and the Middle East (Salles-Djelic, 2017; Fischer & Plehwe, 2017; Djelic & Mousavi, 2020).

The global organizing appears to track the intensification of the US project in the late 1990s and thereafter. Between 1995 and 2015, the number of Atlas affiliates quadrupled, and longer standing member organizations also grew in size (Djelic & Mousavi, 2020). Why such a global push? The timing suggests one critical prompt. While the Atlas Network had been created a decade and a half earlier, its work notably escalated at this particular moment in the late 1990s. That was just as global recognition of climate change spread and parties across the spectrum began coordinating policies to address it, with the Kyoto Protocol adopted in 1997 being the prime example (Kelly, 2019; Djelic & Mousavi, 2020).

To pass on the knowledge and techniques honed by the cause, instructional exchanges between national affiliates are common. The most common seem to involve those outside the United States being visited by representatives of key American Koch-funded hub organizations – such as the Cato Institute, the Heartland Institute, and the Heritage Foundation – or spending time in the United States to learn first-hand how the US organizations operate. The Australian groups, a study of them notes, are 'in constant contact and working in tandem' with US allies (Kelly, 2019).

First-hand exposure is no doubt ideal for tutoring in the kind of stealth tactics practiced by many US affiliates. Thus, the Atlas affiliates studied to date all rely on undisclosed donors. Australia's Institute for Public Affairs (IPA), for example, rebuffs inquiries about its donors, despite transparency being the national norm. Still, journalists managed to discover that its lead donor is the coal mining magnate Gina Rinehart, one of the country's richest individuals. Her contributions alone account for between a third and half of the revenue of the IPA (Readfearn, 2018). So, too, England's Institute for Economic Affairs has been indicted for violating the country's Charities Law, which requires that alleged non-profits refrain from meddling in politics (Pegg, Lawrence & Evans, 2019).

Still more toxic to democracy, some affiliates have been found to use strategic disinformation to stop policy action that the dark-money donors view as harmful to their interests. As a Canadian scholar of climate denial notes, many of the self-described think tanks 'have become heavy-duty weapons in the battle for public opinion and political support'. The disinformation has included, above all, the avid promotion of climate science denial by multiple Atlas affiliates (Hoggan, 2009).

The original Atlas affiliate, the Institute for Economic Affairs (IEA) in England, is a case in point: it was recently exposed for having 'undermin[ed] climate science' for decades. Similarly, the Heartland Institute offered to pay any scientist who would help 'generate international media attention' for and attend an 'International Conference on Climate Change' designed to downplay the danger. Elected officials would enjoy all-expenses paid 'scholarships' to the conference thus publicized (Hoggan, 2009; Pegg & Evans, 2019; MacLean, 2020).

More broadly, many of the democracy-undercutting developments scholars have been studying under the rubric of 'the new constitutionalism' have their origin among thinkers of the Mont Pèlerin Society, whose ideas Atlas seeks to implement. Its leading intellectuals, the European historian Quinn Slobodian has shown, 'did not see democracy and capitalism as synonymous'. Nor were they seeking an international laissez-faire system. On the contrary, their distinguishing intuition was that 'the market does not and cannot take care of itself'. That is why they sought to re-make institutions 'to inoculate capitalism against the threat of democracy' – on a global scale, by 'redesigning states, laws, and other institutions to protect the market'. A premier example is trade treaties with terms that curtail national sovereignty to regulate corporations and preclude democratic claims from national citizenries (Gill & Cutler, 2014; Slobodian, 2018). Future research is needed to track just how the operatives of the Atlas Network and their allies in political parties have implemented ideas first conceived by MPS members.

With hard-core libertarian ideas being so unpopular, journalists have found that Atlas affiliates in several countries enlisted divisive demagogy to move their policy agenda. US Tea Party mobilizations against the Obama administration showed the utility of such demagogy – a point further proved by the election of Donald Trump. Indeed, Australian Atlas affiliates soon held an event entitled

'Trump in Oz! Could "the Donald" Happen Here?' (Atlas Network, 2017b). In Latin America, the journalist Lee Fang reports that the long-time Atlas director Chafuen 'lit up when U.S. President Donald Trump came up, offering praise for the president's appointees', such as Atlas allies Mike Pence and Betsy DeVos (Fang, 2017). Much more research needs to be done in dozens of nations to understand how Atlas affiliates operate, but I will conclude here with some preliminary investigations by others to convey what makes this research so urgent.

Historian Janek Wasserman in his 2019 study of the Austrian economic tradition, long promoted by Charles Koch and many of his grantees throughout the world, points to the existence of a 'libertarian-to-alt-right pipeline'. In the United States, it manifests in the slippage of numerous libertarians from arcane economic theory to neo-Confederacy, white supremacy, and even Holocaust revisionism. In Europe, some Atlas members have peeled off to neo-fascism. Not all, to be sure, or even most. And those who go this way have encountered attempted rebuttal by some of their fellow believers. But significantly placed individuals and groups continue to join the alt-right in a manner that may hint at what is to come as the war of ideas and policy gets tougher while the number of climate refugees from the global South to Europe continues to grow. Indeed, the leading Koch-backed Austrian economist in the United States, GMU's Peter Boettke, a past MPS president, admits that the 'paleolibertarian' racists have won the battle for the mantle of Austrian economics. He says of the too-sullied standard: 'We have to let it go' (Wasserman, 2019).

With even the intellectuals unable to hold the line, not surprisingly, their allied operatives and the donors often turn to right-wing populist candidates and officials to get what they otherwise could not.

Brexit is a good example. Pushing it from the outset, in fact, was the founding organization of the Atlas umbrella, the venerable IEA. Originally funded by Antony Fisher, IEA has since come to be supported by UK-based multinational corporations, including the fossil fuel giant British Petroleum – and by Charles Koch and some of his allied donors. 'Wealthy US donors gave millions to right-wing UK groups', in the apt summary of one *Guardian* headline, reporting on 11 Americans who together gave $3.7 million between 2014 and 2019 – in the run-up to Brexit, that is. Five of the groups in the vanguard of the push for it were Atlas partners, which met regularly with organizers from other non-Atlas groups 'to agree on a common line'. The IEA could soon boast that 14 of those in Boris Johnson's cabinet were its own alumni 'liberty-lovers.' That achievement, in turn, was abetted by top US Koch-funded think tanks, including the Heritage Foundation and the American Enterprise Institute, having done their utmost to help those who would achieve and implement Brexit (Gordon, 2018).

As one member of Parliament and chair of a committee inquiry into the role played by disinformation summarized: 'We've got to recognize the bigger picture here. This is being coordinated across national borders by very wealthy people in a way we haven't seen before' (Mayer, 2018).

As with Brexit, so with Bolsonaro. Atlas affiliates seem to have played a leading role in Brazil's sharp right turn, by helping to empower Jair Bolsonaro, an open racist and virulent homophobe – and ally of local and multinational capital. Back in 1999, Bolsonaro shared his dream of a civil war that would let him 'do the job that the military regime didn't do: killing 30,000' people deemed obstacles to the right's agenda (Simões, 2018). Brazilian Atlas affiliates brought him closer to that dream by helping 'to fuel a cultural war against the Workers Party and its representatives', in the words of researcher Karin Fischer (2018). Reporting from the front, Hernán Ramírez pointed to the prominent role of Atlas think tanks in spreading the doctrine that primed the pump for radical change and of Students for Liberty, a transnational Atlas affiliate, whose in-country members organized the massive street demonstrations that prepared the way for the parliamentary coup (Ramírez, 2018).

Indeed, the long-time Atlas director Alejandro Chafuen boasted of the role the Free Brazil Movement (sometimes called Brazil's Tea Party) played in the street demonstrations and later impeachment under false pretences of Workers' Party leader Dilma Rousseff, in what Brazil specialists have called a parliamentary coup. Leadership in the fight came from alumni of Atlas. The federal judge who prosecuted Rousseff and drove her from office, since charged with improper conduct, was a featured speaker at the 2018 Atlas-sponsored Forum da Liberdade, which claimed over 6000 participants, including 6 presidential candidates. For the Brazilian transformation, Atlas relied on well-trained activists, many of them tutored by US affiliates, nearly 30 in-country libertarian think tanks (up from 3 a decade ago), far-right voices waging 'a constant war' in the media, particularly on social media, and faculty allies at donor-funded campus centres to provide 'defense' with 'the credibility of academic institutions'. All of these operations had 'quiet support from local industrial conglomerates', notes Lee Fang in the most detailed English-language coverage to date (Fang, 2017; Atlas Network News, 2018; Phillips, 2018; Rocha, 2019). As the well-regarded outlet Brazil Wire summed up: '[The] election was not a free or fair process' (Mier, 2018).

Nowhere is the application of the whatever-it-takes-to-win ethos of Atlas more chilling than in Central Europe, the original spawning ground of Naziism. Some Atlas participants are building cosy relationships with neo-Nazi parties in Germany and Austria. This is all the more interesting and starkly instrumental on both sides, since the original fascists were enthusiasts of state planning and welfare provision, anathema to founding libertarians like Friedrich Hayek. But in the quest to stop government action on climate change, many of their successors seem to be of the mind that any enemy of social democratic environmentalism is a friend. 'The transnational emergence of the 'New Right', observes a historian of Central Europe, 'demonstrates an alarming degree of interaction between rightists and "Austrian" supporters of free markets and economic liberty' (Wasserman, 2019). Where one side brings numbers and street energy, the other brings wealthy donors, highly placed political and intellectual allies, and a coherent policy agenda.

In Austria itself, two organizations that got most of their seed money from the Koch Foundation and the Atlas Network, the Friedrich Hayek Institute and the Austrian Economics Center, saw some of their leading members join the

Freedom Party of Austria (FPÖ). A right-wing populist party par excellence, it is anti-immigrant, ethnonationalist, and hostile to the European Union. In other words, 'a seed bed of incipient neo-Naziism'. Yet the Director of the Friedrich Hayek Institute, Barbara Kolm, has served the (FPÖ) as an economic advisor, denouncing the EU and trumpeting the US Tea Party, 'all in the name of Hayek and Austrianism'. But, then, she succeeded in bringing the FPÖ to embrace the economic agenda of the arch-capitalist donor network: 'deregulation, privatization, decreased corporate and income taxes, [and] decreased social services' (Wasserman, 2019; Booth, 2010).

Germany, too, has seen disturbing collaboration. Here again, the US Tea Party, hailed as a beacon, encouraged some libertarians to summon old demons for new purposes. The Alternative für Deutschland (AfD) developed as a significant player in German politics in 2013, criticizing the EU, arguing for anti-statist economics, and evoking comparisons in its reactionary populism not only to the Tea Party but also to France's National Front and Austria's FPÖ. With Germany's acceptance of two million refugees in 2014–2016, the AfD became more shrill in its 'ethnonationalist, xenophobic, and anti-Muslim message'. When a rare female member of the Hayek Society, Karen Horn, criticized how this body was becoming a 'hotbed of the AfD', her speaking out 'ignited a firestorm'. Two dozen members attacked her and demanded she resign, as in fact she – and 60 others – soon did. Those who remained doubled down on their new affinity; the Hayek Society now includes 'several prominent AfD figures', including its 2017 candidate for Chancellor of Germany. Still, the Society membership in the Atlas Network continues unabated, just like that of Kolm's Hayek Institute (Wasserman, 2019; Slobodian, 2018).

To be sure, there is some dissent within Atlas on the part of those uncomfortable with the direction in which their cause is moving. But their answer is always more rigid application of the same toxic medicine that feeds the right-wing populist movements, including austerity and anti-democratic 'constitutional reform' (Atlas Network, 2017a). With fossil fuel ideologues like Charles Koch determined to win at any cost, the rest of us would be wise to learn as soon as we can what, exactly, Atlas is doing. If history is any guide, this cause is too dogmatic and determined for self-redemption. But to be defeated, it must be understood.

Notes

1 This article originated as a keynote address in the form of a book talk on Nancy MacLean, *Democracy in Chains: The Deep History of the Radical Right's Stealth Plan for America* (New York: Viking/Penguin, 2017). So as to keep the documentation for this chapter manageable, the reader should be aware that any evidence or interpretation in the text that is not documented through other sources in this chapter can be found there using the index or a simple word search.

2 See http://www.unkochmycampus.org/charles-koch-foundation-george-mason-mercatus-donor-influence-exposed/ and https://kochdocs.org.

References

Atlas Network. (2017a). The right-wing authoritarian threat to Europe. Foundation for Economic Education (FEE). (9 August 2017). Retrieved from https://fee.org/articles/the-right-wing-authoritarian-threat-to-europe/.

Atlas Network. (2017b). CIS: Trump in Oz!: could 'the Donald' happen here? Retrieved from https://www.atlasnetwork.org/event/cis-trump-in-oz-could-the-donald-happen-here.

Atlas Network. (2018). Fórum Da Liberdade 2018 is the 'Voice of Change' in Brazil. *Atlas Network News*. (20 April 2018). Retrieved from https://www.atlasnetwork.org/news/article/forum-da-liberdade-2018-is-the-voice-of-change-in-brazil.

Atlas Network. (2020a). *Global directory*. Retrieved from www.atlasnetwork.org/partners/global-directory.

Atlas Network. (2020b). *Our story*. Retrieved from https://www.atlasnetwork.org/about/our-story.

Barber, W.J. (2016). *The third reconstruction: how a moral movement is overcoming the politics of division and fear*. Boston: Beacon Press.

Booth, R. (2010). A very British tea party: US anti-tax activists advise UK counterparts. *The Guardian*. (9 September 2010). Retrieved from https://www.theguardian.com/world/2010/sep/09/tea-party-britain-us-tax.

Buchannan, J.M. (1975a). *The limits of liberty. Between anarchy and leviathan*. Chicago: The University of Chicago Press.

Buchannan, J.M. (1975b). The samaritan's dilemma. In E. Phelps (Ed.), *Altruism, morality and economic theory* (pp. 71–85). New York: Russell Sage.

Civitas. (2014). Walter Williams, Gov. McCrory at CLC. *Civitas Capitol Connection*. (7 April 2014). Retrieved from https://issuu.com/civitasreview/docs/ccc_february_2014_-_for_web.

Desmog (2020). *Atlas network*. Retrieved from https://www.desmogblog.com/atlas-economic-research-foundation.

Djelic, M.-L., & Mousavi, R. (2020). How the neoliberal think tank went global: the Atlas network, 1981 to the present. In D. Plehwe, Q. Slobodian & P. Mirowski (Eds.), *Nine lives of neoliberalism* (pp. 257–282). London: Verso.

Fang, L. (2017). Sphere of influence: how American libertarians are remaking Latin American politics. *The Intercept*. (9 August 2017). Retrieved from https://theintercept.com/2017/08/09/atlas-network-alejandro-chafuen-libertarian-think-tank-latin-america-brazil/.

Fischer, K. (2018). The Atlas network: littering the world with free-market think tanks. *Global Dialogue. Magazine of the International Sociological Association*, *8*(2), 10–11. Retrieved from https://globaldialogue.isa-sociology.org/the-atlas-network-littering-the-world-with-free-market-think-tanks/.

Fischer, K., & Plehwe, D. (2017). Neoliberal think tank networks in Latin America and Europe: strategic replication and cross-national organizing. In G. Murray & A. Salas-Porras (Eds.), *Think tanks and global politics—key spaces in the structure of power* (pp. 159–186). New York: Palgrave MacMillan.

Gill, S., & Cutler, C. (Eds.). (2014). *New constitutionalism and world order*. New York: Cambridge University Press.

Gordon, C. (2018). *Brexiters: research questions and aims*. Unpublished report (2 November 2018) in author's possession.

Hertel-Fernandez, A. (2019). *State capture: how conservative activists, big businesses, and wealthy donors reshaped the American states—and the nation*. New York: Oxford University Press.

Hertel-Fernandez, A., Skocpol, T., & Sclar, J. (2018). When political mega-donors join forces: how the Koch network and the democracy alliance influence organized U.S. politics on the right and left. *Studies in American Political Development*, *32*(2), 127–165.

Hoggan, J. (2009). *Climate cover-up: the crusade to deny global warming*. Vancouver: Greystone Books.

Kaufman, D. (2018). *The fall of Wisconsin: the conservative conquest of a progressive bastion and the future of American politics*. New York: W. W. Norton & Company.

Kelly, D. (2019). *Political troglodytes and economic lunations: the hard right in Australia*. Carlton: La Trobe University Press.

MacLean, N. (2017a). *Democracy in chains: the deep history of the radical right's stealth plan for America*. New York: Viking Press.

MacLean, N. (2017b). The GOP tax bill could kill two birds with one stone. *The Hill*. Retrieved from https://thehill.com/opinion/finance/366488-the-gop-tax-bill-could-kill-two-birds-with-one-stone.

MacLean, N. (2020). 'Since we are greatly outnumbered': why and how the Koch network uses disinformation to thwart democracy. In L. Bennett & S. Livingston (Eds.), *A modern history of the disinformation age: communication, technology, and democracy in transition* (pp. 120–149). New York: Cambridge University Press.

Mayer, J. (2011). State for sale. A conservative multimillionaire has taken control in North Carolina, one of 2012's top battlegrounds. *The New Yorker*. (3 October 2011). Retrieved from https://www.newyorker.com/magazine/2011/10/10/state-for-sale.

Mayer, J. (2016). *Dark money: the hidden history of the billionaires behind the rise of the radical right*. New York: Doubleday.

Mayer, J. (2018). New evidence emerges of Steve Bannon and Cambridge Analytica's role in Brexit. *The New Yorker*. (17 November 2018). Retrieved from https://www.newyorker.com/news/news-desk/new-evidence-emerges-of-steve-bannon-and-cambridge-analyticas-role-in-brexit.

McSherry, J.P. (2020). Chile's struggle to democratize the state. *NACLA*. (24 February 2020). Retrieved from https://nacla.org/news/2020/02/24/chile-struggle-democratize-state-plebescite.

Mier, B. (2018). Why Bolsonaro won: beyond the cliches. *Brazil Wire*. (31 October 2018). Retrieved from https://www.brasilwire.com/why-bolsonaro-won-beyond-the-cliches/.

NC Policy Watch. (2015). *Altered state: how five years of conservative rule have redefined North Carolina*. Retrieved from https://www.ncpolicywatch.com/wp-content/uploads/2015/12/NC-Policy-Watch-Altered-State-How-5-years-of-conservative-rule-have-redefined north carolina-december-2015.pdf.

Nichol, G.R. (2020). *Indecent assembly: the North Carolina legislature's blueprint for the war on democracy and equality*. Winston-Salem: Blair Publishing.

Pegg, D., & Evans, R. (2019). Revealed: top UK Thinktank spent decades undermining climate science. *The Guardian*. (10 October 2019). Retrieved from https://www.theguardian.com/environment/2019/oct/10/thinktank-climate-science-institute-economic-affairs.

Pegg, D., Lawrence, F., & Evans, R. (2019). Rightwing thinktank breached charity law by campaigning for hard Brexit. *The Guardian*. (5 February 2019). Retrieved from https://www.theguardian.com/politics/2019/feb/05/rightwing-thinktank-breached-charity-law-by-campaigning-for-hard-brexit.

Phillips, T. (2018). Bolsonaro business backers accused of illegal WhatsApp fake news campaign. *The Guardian*. (18 October 2018). Retrieved from https://www.theguardian.com/world/2018/oct/18/brazil-jair-bolsonaro-whatsapp-fake-news-campaign.

Ramírez, H. (2018). The Brazilian neoliberal think tank network. *Global Dialogue*. Retrieved from http://globaldialogue.isa-sociology.org/the-brazilian-neoliberal-think-tank-network/.

Readfearn, G. (2014). Exclusive: Mont Pelerin Society revealed as home to leading pushers of climate science denial. Retrieved from www.desmogblog.com/2014/01/15/exclusive-mont-pelerin-society-revealed-home-leading-pushers-climate-science-denial.

Readfearn, G. (2018). Gina Rinehart company revealed as $4.5m. donor to climate sceptic think tank. *The Guardian*. (20 July 2018). Retrieved from https://www.theguardian.com/business/2018/jul/21/gina-rinehart-company-revealed-as-45m-donor-to-climate-sceptic-thinktank.

Riestenberg, J. (2018). U.S. constitution threatened as article V convention movement nears success. *Common Cause Background Memo*. (21 March 2018). Retrieved from https://www.commoncause.org/resource/u-s-constitution-threatened-as-article-v-convention-movement-nears-success/.

Rocha, B.L. (2019). Letter from Bolsonaro's Brazil: 'Sarah Palin and Rush Limbaugh would feel at home here!' *Indypendent.Org*. (25 January 2019). Retrieved from https://indypendent.org/2019/01/letter-from-bolsonaros-brazil-sarah-palin-and-rush-limbaugh-would-feel-at-home-here/.

Salles-Djelic, M.-L. (2017). Building an architecture for political influence: Atlas and the transnational institutionalization of the neoliberal think tank. In C. Garsten & A. Sörborn (Eds.), *Power, policy and profit: corporate engagement in politics and governance* (pp. 159–186). Cheltenham: Edward Elgar Publishing.

Simões, M. (2018). Brazil's polarizing President, Jair Bolsonaro, in his own words. *New York Times*. (28 October 2018). Retrieved from https://www.nytimes.com/2018/10/28/world/americas/brazil-president-jair-bolsonaro-quotes.html.

Slobodian, Q. (2018). Neoliberalism's Populist Bastards. Public Seminar. (15 February 2018). Retrieved from https://publicseminar.org/2018/02/neoliberalisms-populist-bastards/.

Sunstein, C., & Thaler, R. (2008). *Nudge: improving decisions about health, wealth, and happiness*. New Haven: Yale University Press.

Teles, S., & Kenney, A. (2007). Spreading the word: the diffusion of American conservatism in Europe and beyond. In J. Kopstein & S. Steinmo (Eds.), *Growing apart? America and Europe in the twenty-first century* (pp. 136–169). New York: Cambridge University Press.

Wasserman, J. (2019). *The marginal revolutionaries: how Austrian economists fought the war of ideas*. New Haven: Yale University Press.

2 Ordoliberalism, authoritarianism, and democracy

Thomas Biebricher

Introduction

While ordoliberalism in its original configuration has all but ceased to exist as a specific paradigm within the discipline of economics, this does not mean that it is merely a 'dead man walking' (Hien & Joerges, 2018). Both its contemporary heirs who cast themselves as practitioners of *Ordnungsökonomik* as well as its (self-proclaimed) adherents in politics ensure the continued influence of at least some aspects of ordoliberal thought – as do the various economic crises of the last decade: when the Financial Crisis hit, ordoliberalism was quickly extolled as the one version of neoliberalism that had always refused to descend into the rabbit hole of 'self-regulating markets' now supposedly proven to be a fatal illusion. Furthermore, when the Eurozone crisis almost burst asunder the European Monetary Union, commentators began to wonder about the extent to which the German-orchestrated austerity strategy to deal with the crisis was fuelled more or less directly by ordoliberal ideas of monetary stability and individual liability. This chapter will focus on a particular aspect within the ambiguous framework of ordoliberal thought, namely the nexus between democracy and authoritarianism, and proceed in two steps. The starting point is an examination of primary ordoliberal sources from its formative years in the 1930s and 1940s, focusing on two protagonists, Walter Eucken and Alexander Rüstow. What emerges here is a critique of pluralist democracy and a corresponding positive appraisal of what one might call a 'de-pluralized' democracy with more or less pronounced authoritarian intimations. In a second step, I will turn to the post-war history of ordoliberalism and scrutinize the various narratives that describe it – up to its contemporary incarnation as *Ordnungsökonomik* – as chastened of earlier fantasies of 'strong states' and unflinchingly committed to the ideals of liberal democracy. However, while there are undoubtedly considerable transformations taking place within ordoliberalism, what I will try to show is that its scepticism with regard to popular sovereignty and mass democracy is hardly revoked but only reconfigured.[1]

To preface these steps, I will conclude this introduction with a brief conceptualization of neoliberalism as I conceive of it, and briefly address the relation between ordoliberalism and neoliberalism.

Neoliberalism was officially born in 1938, when the term was first used as a shared label by the participants of the so-called *Colloque Walter Lippmann* (Reinhoudt & Audier, 2018). The original neoliberals were formulating their political and intellectual project as a response to the undeniable crisis that held liberalism in its grip ever since the end of World War I, which also spelt the undoing of the classical liberal era lasting throughout the '100 years peace' from 1814–1914, as Karl Polanyi referred to it. Against the backdrop of the Great Depression, the New Deal, the slow but steady ascent of Keynesianism, and the meteoric rise of deeply antiliberal political forces from Soviet Communism to European fascism and German National Socialism, liberalism was clearly on the defence. In order to regain a footing in this political and intellectual contestation, the neoliberals sought to reassert liberal ideas, but to do so would also require a modernization of the liberal framework, including a thorough review of its tenets with regard to their continued timeliness or obsolescence. What emerged from the discussions at the *Colloque* was the belief widely shared among the participants – excluding only Ludwig von Mises – that laissez-faire and 'Manchesterism', as they referred to it, was an aberration that had done more harm than good to the liberal cause and thus ought to be abandoned. Thus, neoliberalism positioned itself not only against what was typically referred to as 'collectivism', be it of the communist or the fascist kind, but also the politics of laissez-faire and self-regulating markets, which was almost vilified for its flaws and took on the more or less deserved role of a scapegoat for liberal failure – when in fact nineteenth-century 'laissez-faire' was a fairly broad tent that contained various positions, some of which even approximated a genuinely neoliberal point of view. What is specific about this neoliberal perspective then? Neoliberals sought to revitalize and revise liberal ideas, but they did so in such wide-ranging variations that it seems impossible to distil a positive essence of neoliberalism. Rather, what emerges from the twofold distancing from collectivism and laissez-faire is a shared *problematic* (Biebricher, 2019): neoliberals assert the superiority of markets against collectivism but they are no longer content to leave them to themselves (if anyone in the history of economic thought ever was). Thus, the problematic that unites neoliberals concerns the conditions of possibility of functioning markets, i.e. markets on which the price mechanism reigns as unperturbed as possible. If this is correct, then a number of issues can be inferred from this. First of all, contrary to common parlance neoliberalism is properly understood not as market fundamentalism and the unwavering belief in the self-regulatory capabilities of markets. True, during the last 30 years there have been some prominent proponents of such notions, such as Chicago economist and 2013 Nobel laureate Eugene Fame with his now somewhat infamous 'Efficient Market Hypothesis'. But in the light of what has been said here, he ought to be considered at least an extreme outlier in the field of neoliberalism, if not a representative of a different paradigm altogether. Far from suggesting that 'the market' solves all problems, neoliberal thought turns the market into the prime problem to be addressed in the sense of securing the complex preconditions of its functioning. This is what differentiates neoliberalism from classical liberalism and laissez-faire. While the naivety of both of the latter with regard to the precarious existence of functioning markets is clearly embellished by the neoliberals in an effort to give their own position a clearer profile and distance themselves from what were widely considered discredited frameworks at the time, it is true that the neoliberal outspokenness with regard to the constant monitoring of markets and other state tasks beyond the minimal state prominently envisioned by Wilhelm von Humboldt in the late 1790s is hard to find in nineteenth-century discourses on liberal political economy – at least this side of the para-social democratic liberalism of a T.H. Green or the late John Stuart Mill, which the neoliberals also viewed as an aberration from true liberalism.

Second, if the key to neoliberal thought is the reflection upon the interactive effects between the economic and the non-economic spheres of society, it follows that neoliberalism is not the kind of economism that assumes markets exist in a vacuum, as its critics often suggest, but that it is properly understood as political economy. This implies that neoliberalism is as much concerned with strictly economic matters as it is with matters of politics and society – at least as far as they pertain to the preconditions of functioning markets. Accordingly, the issues addressed in this chapter are not some annex to neoliberal thought but rather front and centre to it: as will become clear, democracy emerges as one of the crucial specific problems within the overall neoliberal problematic, prompting various recommendations as to how to deal with it, including the authoritarian option.

Finally, identifying the neoliberal problematic as the bond that holds neoliberals together leaves room for a considerable range of positions. The neoliberal problematic animates not only the work of the usual neoliberal suspects such as Friedrich August von Hayek and Milton Friedman but also that of the German ordoliberals from Walter Eucken and Wilhelm Röpke to Franz Böhm and Alexander Rüstow. And it is equally characteristic of the architect of the so-called Virginia School, James Buchanan. Ordoliberalism is thus best understood as a sub-current within neoliberalism, whose relative unity lies in a broadly shared pattern of response to the challenge that is posed by the neoliberal problematic (Biebricher, 2017). Elucidating this pattern in its basic parameters is the task of the following section.

Ordoliberalism and democracy

Both protagonists we focus on in the following, Walter Eucken and Alexander Rüstow, had a considerable distance to travel in order to finally arrive in the harbour of ordoliberalism. Rüstow had been a longstanding supporter of religious socialism before he broke with it decisively towards the end of the 1920s – not the least due to his increasingly close companionship with Eucken, whom he had already come to know during World War I. But Eucken himself was not a born (ordo-)liberal either. Influenced by his philosopher father Rudolf Eucken he was socialized into an amalgam of various strands of conservatism that would combine the belief in tradition, religion, and nation with a Nietzschean apotheosis of agency and action, moving the entire framework close to what would come to be referred to as Young Conservatism. As has been chronicled in much detail (Dathe,

2009), Eucken incrementally disengaged from the at times militantly conservative positions arising out of this intellectual milieu and became an increasingly ardent supporter of liberalism – at least as far as economics are concerned: while conservatives (and many other political factions) were clamouring for protectionism, Eucken lauded the benefits of free trade and distanced himself from the nationalist undertones of this and many other political demands and projects. In the late 1920s, Eucken and Rüstow were both engaged in the everyday 'battle' over public opinion, writing op-eds and participating in public debates, but especially Eucken simultaneously embarked upon the project of outlining a *science* of economics that would seek to combine the idiosyncratically German heritage of the so-called Historical School championed by Gustav Schmoller with a more abstract or theoretical way of economic reasoning. This science, the basic parameters of which Eucken laid out in *Wozu Nationalökonomie* (1938) and, particularly, in the seminal *Foundations of Economics* (1950), was to engage in a morphological analysis of economic orders, assuming that these strictly economic orders were *interdependent* with other societal orders. *Nationalökonomie* as it was called at the time was thus, in the final instance, a scientific practice aimed at grasping the totality of society or at least the totality of a given political economy. This has major implications for the issues at stake in our context, because a sound economic policy would have to be based upon an understanding of the specific interactive effects that prevail in this interdependence of orders and Eucken as well as most of his fellow ordoliberals were decidedly uneasy about leaving this most intricate task in the wayward hands of democracy. At the heart of the economic policy along Euckian lines lay the notion of a competitive order as the proper framework of markets, based on several constitutive principles, and to be monitored and fine-tuned according to another set of regulative principles, which are presented and discussed in Eucken's *Grundsätze der Wirtschaftspolitik* (Eucken, [1952] 2017a). In a somewhat simplified manner one can summarize the task of the state as being the guardian of the competitive order (in addition to science and the church), so why should this guardianship not be entrusted to democratically elected politicians?

Two main lines of reasoning can be found and distinguished in the ordoliberal thought of Eucken and Rüstow but also Böhm and Röpke. First of all, there is a concern that is hardly exclusive to the ordoliberals at the time, namely the rise of mass society. In their critique of the masses, the ordoliberals inscribed themselves in a tradition that can be traced back at least to Tocqueville and Mill, who had problematized conformism and a levelling mediocrity as prominent characteristics of contemporary and especially democratic societies. Towards the end of the nineteenth century this *topos* of a more or less explicit tyranny of the majority was enriched with social-psychological but also 'race-theoretical' facets by writers such as Gustave Le Bon. In the 1920s this tradition reached an immense level of academic and public attention through José Ortega Y Gasset's (1949) contribution, which bore the telling title *Revolt of the Masses*. Gasset's book was well-known among ordoliberals and other early neoliberals – Ortega Y Gasset was invited to the *Colloque Walter Lippmann* but did not attend – and summed up all the liberal-conservative fears at the time: here was a populace (although Ortega Y Gasset thought mass man could in principle also belong to the upper classes) that was as anaemic and mediocre as Nietzsche's 'Last Man' but still presumptuous and disrespectful of all authority in society. Furthermore, although mass man was typically indolent and passive, the masses were potentially unruly and could easily be whipped into action by demagogues: masses can be moulded and manipulated because, as Le Bon (and also Sigmund Freud) had confirmed, the power of reason was reduced once individuals coagulated into masses and an inherent tendency towards the irrational took hold of the latter. Masses are thus easy prey for those who present deceivingly easy solutions to complex problems, e.g. socialists who advocated a planned economy but also fascists who presented the homogeneous national community as a panacea for all problems. But even when mobilized by incendiary and effusive demagoguery, the masses were still volatile and wayward, prone to violence and destruction. As Eucken notes, the masses only have the 'power to destroy'; they are like 'microbes', and once the 'edifice of culture has become ramshackle, the masses bring about its collapse' (Eucken, [1952] 1960, p. 16).[2]

Depending on the author in question, massification – to borrow a term prevalent in the more sociologically oriented works by Röpke and Rüstow – was either a universal (Le Bon) or a specifically modern phenomenon that originated in the urbanization and proletarianization processes unleashed by capitalism, which tended to be the ordoliberal point of view. Still, irrespective of these differences, what united Le Bon, Ortega Y Gasset, and the ordoliberals was the conviction that massification had only turned into a real problem in the wake of democratization. Now the masses had actual political power beyond the streets within their reach. 'The entry of the popular classes into political life' (Le Bon, 2001, p. 35) makes all the difference, and Eucken concurs when he bemoans 'the democratization of the world and the consequent unleashing of the demonic powers of peoples' (Eucken, [1932] 2017b, p. 69). Mass democracy thus hands over responsibility of the collective livelihood of a society to mass man, whom Ortega Y Gasset described as a 'spoiled child' or 'rebellious savage' (Ortega Y Gasset, 1949, p. 105), and the cunning political entrepreneurs who were using ideology and demagoguery to instrumentalise him.

If the irrationality of the masses is the one main concern the ordoliberals harbour with regard to (mass) democracy, the very strategic rationality of those who make use of the masses to gain leverage for their demands, i.e. interest groups and political parties, or particularistic actors in general, is the other. Across the entire spectrum of ordoliberal thought we can see a vehemently articulated critique not only of mass democracy but also of pluralist democracy. The basic pattern that concerns the ordoliberals is easily summarized: (economic) interest groups – and it is no stretch to assume that trade unions figured prominently in this category for the ordoliberals – were trying to gain influence on state policy and strove for exemptions from the 'lash of competition' (Eucken, [1932] 2017b, p. 52) engendered by the competitive order or other forms of special treatment. Democratic politicians and entire parties were ultimately forced to do the bidding of these special interests, and thus the general welfare and the state itself were threatened with dissolution. As Rüstow put it in vivid imagery, 'a state which begins to feed the beasts of organized business interests will finally be devoured by them' (Rüstow, 2017a, p. 159). 'What we are facing here, is, to use another term from Carl Schmitt, "pluralism", and a pluralism of the worst kind. What takes place here accords with the motto: "The state as prey"' (Rüstow, 2017b, p. 147).

And again, this influence peddling and the subsequent merging of state, economy, and society into what Eucken terms the 'economic state' were laid at the feet of democracy: 'But the chief factor was that the simultaneous process of democratization lent the parties, the masses and interest groups that they organized, much greater influence over the management of the state, and so upon economic policy' (Eucken, [1932] 2017b, p. 59). Along similar lines, Rüstow elaborates:

> The democratic, parliamentary structure of some of the economically leading states caused the economic corruption to spread to the internal policy of the state, to the political parties, and to parliamentarism itself. The political parties were slowly transformed into parliamentary agencies of economic pressure-groups and were financed by them.
>
> (Rüstow, 2017a, p. 159)

Given this 'pathological form of government' (Rüstow, 2017a), i.e. pluralism, a democratic economic policy is bound to be triturated between competing interests pulling state action into potentially opposing directions. In sum, the combination of mass democracy and pluralism renders the appropriate politics of the competitive order, as the ordoliberals conceived of it, all but impossible – which brings us to the alternatives considered by Eucken and Rüstow.

There are two texts that stand out as the *loci classici* of the case for an at least semi-authoritarian transformation of the political status quo by Eucken and Rüstow, respectively, which we have already quoted from in the above. Both stem from the end days of the Weimar Republic in 1932, and further below we will return to this fact to assess the context-bound nature of the ordoliberal demands. Eucken's *Structural Transformations of the State and the Crisis of Capitalism* ([1932] 2017b) covers a wide terrain of issues all the way to questions of world politics. However, the narrative that interests us begins with the transformation of the 'liberal' state into the already mentioned 'economic' state, induced by democratization. As noted above, the economic state is characterized by a problematic conflation of state, society, and economy, ultimately leaving the state at the mercy of societal interests and incapacitating it with regard to its actual function, which is the safeguarding of the common good by acting as the guardian of the competitive order. Consequently, Eucken places his hopes in a disentanglement of the state from the fatal embrace by societal/economic interest groups, so it can return to its actual task instead of catering to the varying lobbying groups – or at least this must be inferred *ex negativo* from the respective passages:

> Nevertheless, much more serious is the way in which close integration with the economy *has undermined independent decision-making on the part of the state*, something upon which its very *existence* depends ... The state of fifty years ago was cautious in using its powers but made its own decisions; today, by contrast, it makes substantial and wide use of its powers, but lacks the real independent power to make its own decisions.
>
> (Eucken, [1932] 2017b, pp. 59, 60)

In other words, the ideal state would be one that was placed in a position for its own independent and unified will formation to take place undistorted by societal influences pulling in various and often opposite directions. Only if the state can regain this status as something French constitutional theory once introduced as a *pouvoir neutre*, the crisis of capitalism Eucken refers to, which is really a crisis of the political framework of capitalism, can be overcome. This implies not necessarily the abolition of democracy but the shielding of the state from undue societal influence, especially in matters of economic policy. In this field, state action should not necessarily be informed by democratic opinion and will formation processes but rather the authority of science. As Eucken writes in the same text:

> First of all, a rigorous training in economic theory is needed to be able to understand the order in the economic processes that exist in a free capitalist economy, but which is destroyed in the transformation of the state into an economic state. The lay person has no such training, but most ideologists of the planned economy also think they can do without it.
>
> (Eucken, [1932] 2017b, p. 70)

The conviction that only science can pierce the arcane nature of capitalist economics and thus has a veritable duty to provide political decision-makers with expertise is even more pronounced in the so-called *Ordo-Manifesto* jointly written by Eucken, Franz Böhm, and Hans Großmann-Doerth and published in 1936 (see Böhm, Eucken & Großmann-Doerth, 2017). Here the 'dethronement' of law and economics is lamented, followed by a call for the reinstatement of their academic representatives to their proper position because

> they are also the only ones who ... are capable of forming an objective judgment, independent of their own immediate economic interests, about economic measures appropriate in particular circumstances ... [Consequently], we wish to bring scientific reasoning, as displayed in jurisprudence and political economy, into effect for the purpose of constructing and reorganizing the economic system.
>
> (Böhm, Eucken & Großmann-Doerth, 2017, pp. 27, 35)

The formula that emerges here is a state shielded from undue democratic influence on all matters related to the economy and instead guided by the scientific expertise of lawyers and economists.

Rüstow largely concurs with Eucken, although the state's agenda is a slightly different one: while Eucken's assumes that a strong state is required that can make independent decisions even if they go against some particularistic interests and that commands sufficient enforcing power to implement even controversial decisions that are contested by powerful societal and economic actors, Rüstow envisions a state that goes even further and engages in what he at times calls liberal interventionism.

> As opposed to the interventionism practiced in the past, which served the interests of some, or even a large number, of interested parties, the kind of intervention that I demand – namely, one that catalyses those changes that such parties feel to be obstacles or threatening – the interested parties are, for selfish reasons, not interested in at all.
>
> (Rüstow, 2017b, p. 147)

What state could engage in such a politics that is likely to provoke criticism from any number of actors?

> For that reason, to carry out what I propose requires a strong state that stands above individual groups and above interested parties – a requirement, incidentally, that also needs to be fulfilled if we simply want to guarantee a free market and fair competition with the same rules applied to all … The new liberalism, which I and my friends promote, demands a strong state … And with this confession of faith in a strong state that promotes liberal economic policies, and … in liberal economic policies that promote a strong state, with this confession I should like to end.
>
> (Rüstow, 2017b, pp. 148–149)

This is the end of a talk Rüstow gave at a meeting of the *Verein für Socialpolitik* in 1932, the title of which is considered to be the ordoliberal agenda in a nutshell by some: *Free Economy, Strong State* (see Bonefeld, 2017).

Let us sum up what we can infer from these quotes about the way the defects of democracy ought to be overcome, according to ordoliberal reasoning. Irrespective of what exactly they consider to be the proper function of the state, Eucken and Rüstow clearly agree that its agenda requires statehood which is sufficiently insulated from societal influences, makes autonomous decisions based on scientific insight, and stringently implements these decisions making use of all means at its disposal. It is not a stretch to say that this is a technocratic and also a fairly elitist programme, but is it warranted to refer to this as an authoritarian vision of politics? To be sure, any number of observers of widely differing political persuasions would agree that influence-peddling by lobbyists and organizations is a massive problem for any liberal representative democracy, so this ordoliberal concern in itself can hardly be sufficient grounds for the charge of authoritarianism. However, there are two reasons that seem to justify this assessment.

First, while many proponents of liberal democracy will agree that lobbying efforts are a cause for concern, they will hardly make the case that the pursuit of particularistic interests per se is illegitimate. Still, this is the *impression* that the ordoliberal accounts give because there is no visible effort to distinguish acceptable from excessive lobbying, e.g. by introducing rules regarding donations, transparency of consultations, etc., – which, incidentally, is surprising for a school of thought often thought of as overly fixated on rules by its critics.[3] Furthermore, one has to assume that the ordoliberal concern is not limited to backroom dealings and what public choice theorists today call 'regulatory capture', but also extends to official democratic channels of will formation, expressed through elections and political parties in parliament who are at times portrayed as hardly more than dupes of (economic) interest. These two more or less implicit assumptions turn the anti-pluralism of ordoliberalism into a full-blown critique of liberal democracy.

The second and related reason is the ordoliberal view of the state, which is organicist in nature, as it presupposes that there is something like an independent will of the state itself that should manifest itself again, as Eucken notes in the passages quoted above. More generally, though, it is a view that puts a premium on the unity of the state and thus inevitably is sceptical of any forces that would jeopardize this unity. There is a systematic reason for this heavy emphasis on an 'undivided' state apparatus that borders on the monolithic, which I will consider further below, but for now let us simply note that such a truly unified state is bound to come into conflict with separation of powers requirements and – once again – basic tenets of liberal democracy, which is built on the notion that there is a proper balance between unity and separation within states as well as a balance of particularistic interests and considerations of the common good. The thrust of the ordoliberal argument is to tilt this balance toward a one-sided appreciation of the state as a unified guardian of the common good – and in the terminological repertoire we have at our disposal to describe regimes, in my view this comes close to an authoritarian one.

Authoritarianism examined: Strong states and changing circumstances

The accuracy but also the pertinence of the nexus between the critique of democracy and the espousal of authoritarian politics I have attributed to ordoliberal thought in the preceding chapter are challenged in a number of different respects. As far as I can see there are two sets of arguments that are mobilized against the notion that ordoliberalism may exhibit authoritarian leanings.

The first is the one that most directly challenges the interpretive accuracy of the account I have given here: according to this view the ordoliberals attributed a completely different meaning to the notion of the strong state that is not authoritarian and while they may not be model democrats their misgivings are explainable by the specific conceptualization of democracy that underlies their assessment.

The second argument does not so much question the accuracy of my account but rather its continued pertinence. According to this view, the ordoliberals may have been para-authoritarians in the interwar era but the encounter with National Socialism and, subsequently, the experience of the young Federal Republic of Germany cleansed them of these questionable leanings and left them as ardent supporters of the basic framework of liberal democracy. There is also a variation of this argument, which concedes that there may have been a lingering authoritarianism in ordoliberalism during the post-war decades but the paradigmatic transformation of ordoliberalism into *Ordnungsökonomik* orchestrated by the third/fourth generation of the Freiburg School and its concomitant assimilation to constitutional economics finally put the framework on solid liberal democratic ground.

In this section I will first provide a slightly more elaborate exposition of the first line of reasoning in particular, before I offer a response to both arguments, defending the account I have put forward.

The *strong state* is obviously a signifier that is open to considerable interpretation. Consequently, the reading I have put forward in the preceding sections is subject to challenges. Most commonly, it is the following argument that can be found in Vanberg's (2014) discussion of the relation between democracy and (ordo-)liberalism and has since been repeated by a number of commentators who aim to rectify an alleged misreading of the ordoliberals as authoritarians (Young, 2017; Hien & Joerges, 2018). In this interpretation the strong state is based on the correct consequences drawn from the weakness of the 'economic state' that Eucken ([1932] 2017b) describes in his article 'Structural Transformation of the State and the Crisis of Capitalism': a state that assumes responsibility for an expansive social and economic policy agenda is bound to become the 'plaything' (Röpke) of the respective societal interests. In contrast to this weak state of pluralism that is constantly on the verge of dissolution, the truly strong state is simply strong because it radically limits the reach of its own actions, e.g. through self-binding rules or by simply denying that a state has any means to effectively combat unemployment or poverty.

Eucken – as well as virtually all other major neoliberals – indeed makes the argument,

> that this process of expansion, a process that in the post-Bismarckian period was initiated and developed by the economy, did not result in the strengthening of the state, but rather by contrast in its weakening; bringing with it, indeed, even the danger of state dissolution … today, every serious economic depression rocks the state itself, demonstrating the shackling of the state to the economy.
>
> (Eucken, [1932] 2017b, p. 59)

Far from the provocative authoritarian connotations that term might have for contemporary readers, Vanberg concludes, the strong state is a prudent state of self-limitation that almost paradoxically gains strength by forfeiting some of its potential powers (Vanberg, 2014, p. 15).

Thus, there is undeniable evidence that this theorem is part of the ordo- and neoliberal ideational cosmos and is commonly employed by its major representatives. Rüstow echoes the thrust of the argument when he refers to the 'withdrawal of the state into its own identity, this self-limitation as the foundation of self-affirmation' (Rüstow, 2017b, p. 148). Accordingly, I have no reason to challenge the idea that this is indeed one aspect of the notion of a strong state. Still, I have considerable doubts whether this really exhausts the intended meaning of the demand for it. Two reasons can be put forward to warrant this claim: first, the argument by Vanberg and others begs the question how this disentanglement through self-limitation should work if not through at least a suspension of democratic influence, assuming the ordoliberals are correct in their positing that 'the masses' will always use their democratically granted power to vehemently demand that the state take responsibility for any number of issues and cater to their needs. If the ordoliberal argument is to claim that the state has to be weakened in a certain sense in order to regain strength, it *presupposes* a strong state disentangled from democratic influence in the first place to implement this weakening in the sense of self-limitation – if the ordoliberals are correct in their assumptions on the predatory nature of mass democracy and influence-mongering interest groups. Given that the ordoliberals (as well as Hayek) were keenly aware of Carl Schmitt's analysis of pluralist/liberal democracy, it stands to reason that they were aware of this argument, which can also be found in one of his talks at the time:

> Only a strong state can depoliticize, only a strong state can effectively decree that certain activities … remain its privilege and as such ought to be administered by it, that other activities belong to the … sphere of self-management, and that all the rest be given to the domain of a free economy.
>
> (Schmitt, 1998, pp. 226–227)

The second reason pertains to the agenda the strong state is confronted with, which is – somewhat simplistically stated – to be the guardian of the competitive order and to govern the interdependence of orders the ordoliberals posit as a given. What is notable in the respective descriptions of this task is the emphasis on the coherence of the overall policy and the need to minimize heterogeneity. Consider in this regard Franz Böhm, arguably the closest collaborator of Eucken and an eminent ordoliberal scholar of law in his own right. In 1937 he writes that much of contemporary politics

> are incompatible with the substantive challenges posed by the task of organizing the functioning national economic totality in line with the correct procedural norms of a single operative idea, such that the reality of this highly-differentiated and no longer knowable national economic personality is mastered in the entirety of all of its manifestations. The only orders equal to this task are those generated by conscious and intelligent political will, and by an authoritative leadership decision founded in expert knowledge; there is no room here for silent growth … from the bottom up. Such social towers of Babel … result only in a hopeless babble of tongues should

> the ordering ideal … not be grounded in the phrase: everything obeys my command!
>
> (Böhm, 2017, p. 117)

In contrast to Hayekian let alone straightforward libertarian notions of spontaneous orders the ordoliberal Böhm leaves no doubt that order is a matter of will, authority, and decision, and that it hinges on a 'single operative idea' that leaves no room for plural notions of economic policy and the respective diversity. This is confirmed by Eucken, although he seemingly espouses diversity at first:

> A policy for the economic constitution has to be shaped for each different kind of market form, and so policy will be diverse. But despite this evident diversity that we encounter in reality, everything will be focused upon *one* aim. Although we start out from below registering a concrete *diversity*, we do eventually arrive at a unitary principle of order that is vital for the functioning of the economic process in this order.
>
> (Eucken, [1942] 2017c, pp. 93–94)

The unitary character of the economic policy and the ensuing systematic coherence indispensable in the governing of the precarious interdependence of orders is what makes for sound economic policy; and, conversely, it is the inability to deliver such coherence against the backdrop of pluralism which is one of the gravest defects of democracy. As Eucken writes in a letter to Rüstow from 21 February 1930: 'Implementing free trade requires a sense of systematic economic policy, but this sense of systematics – in all domains of politics – is lacking in democracy per se' (quoted in Dathe, 2009, p. 13; author's translation, underlining in the original). Accordingly, a strong state in the sense of a monolithic state that has expunged all contesting (economic and social) policy agendas and their proponents – of which empirical liberal democratic states are invariably rich – is the conclusive aim of the classical ordoliberals as they see no alternative way to realize a coherent, systematic, i.e. unitary economic policy. The demanding nature of such a task is reflected in the constant reminder that only economic experts have the knowledge to see through the complicated mechanisms to be governed, which are opaque to the mass of the people. Accordingly, it is sufficient for the principles of sound economic policy conveyed by experts to be understood only by the 'leading strata of a society that bears responsibility' (Eucken, 1960, p. 308) – although Eucken is even sceptical of their understanding: 'Only a few of the ruling class understand the problems and even they are not very clear as to what control of economic activity really means' (Eucken, [1948] 1989, p. 37).

As mentioned above, the corresponding strategy to exculpate Eucken in particular from the charge of being an anti-democratic semi-authoritarian with elitist leanings is to 'contextualize' his scepticism regarding democracy. Two arguments are prevalent in the respective discussions. First, there is the claim by Dathe that Eucken's critique of democracy rests on a rather narrow understanding of democracy, which is said to have been widespread in his age. Democracy, writes

Eucken in another letter to Rüstow, 'is bound to lead to an ever closer connection between the people and the state, or – if you will – ideally, towards the unity of both' (quoted in Dathe, 2009, p. 16). Thus, again, there is some textual evidence here but it seems questionable whether this really suffices as grounds for Dathe's claims that are picked up by Nientiedt and Köhler: Eucken, in this interpretation, is merely opposed to democracy because he only knows it in the version that Carl Schmitt derives from a particular reading of Rousseau, i.e. identitarian democracy. Against this identitarian democracy, Dathe, Nientiedt, and Köhler contend, Eucken maintained the crucial significance of individual freedom – which is also cited as one more reason why Eucken would have been opposed to an authoritarian strong state.

But not all of these arguments are fully convincing. Is it really plausible to claim that 'like so many of his contemporaries, Eucken only knows the identity concept of democracy but in contrast to many he is most clearly aware of its dangers' (Dathe, 2009, p. 17)? After all, Eucken was obviously surrounded by what he considered a non-identitarian democracy, namely what Rüstow referred to as a pluralist democracy – and which both criticized for this very pluralism. Therefore, it is puzzling for Nientiedt and Köhler to repeat this argument by Dathe, since they make mention of this critique pluralism (Nientiedt & Köhler, 2016, p. 1749), but they do not reflect upon the fact that they end up attributing a seemingly tension-laden position to Eucken. At least, it appears to be a difficult line to walk, being opposed not only to identitarian democracy but also its very opposite, simultaneously. Furthermore, the subtext to this argumentation, namely that Eucken is fundamentally at odds with Schmitt's views, is also somewhat questionable. Eucken may be opposed to identitarian democracy, but his narrative about the fusion of state, economy, and society is broadly congruent with Schmitt's critical account in *The Concept of the Political* (Schmitt, [1932] 1976). This is not to suggest in an intellectual shortcut that Eucken is simply a Schmittian, nor that his reputation ought to be considered tarnished just because he happens to concur with Schmitt on this. My point is simply that it seems at least a little far-fetched to argue that Eucken is critical of the economic state because of the looming danger of identitarian democracy when the prime proponent of this latter notion is just as critical of the economic state.

Finally, there is the basic point that Nientiedt and Köhler highlight and that also can be traced back to Dathe. Eucken's scepticism with regard to democracy is not due to authoritarian leanings or elitism, rather it is his 'concern for individual freedom' (Nientiedt & Köhler, 2016, p. 1744). The background narrative to this claim comes from Dathe who offers an elaborate account of Eucken's conversion from more or less radical conservatism to liberalism between the early 1920s and the mid-1930s. The basic claim that Eucken was a defender of individual freedom and autonomy seems plausible, and the same goes for his corresponding concern that democracy may transform itself into some kind of tyranny of the majority – a time-honoured worry among liberals. Still, it is not clear how this would serve as an immunization against authoritarian leanings. After all, the wager that the ordoliberals and a fair number of neoliberals, prominently including Hayek, enter into, is that authoritarianism may in fact prove to be a more suitable framework for individual liberty than democracy. Interestingly, Nientiedt and Köhler make reference to a letter from Eucken to Hayek, dating from 12 March 1946, which is to support their argument. Still, it is not entirely clear whether it actually serves this purpose or the opposite. In the letter, Eucken discusses Hayek's *Road to Serfdom* and indeed writes that 'there also exists, as you yourself show, democracy without freedom' (quoted in Goldschmidt & Hesse, 2012, p. 18). The truly interesting part, however, is contained in the preceding sentences where Eucken writes: 'You outline everything that needs to be said on this subject on p. 99', referring to the German edition of *The Road to Serfdom* (quoted in Goldschmidt & Hesse, 2012, p. 18). The passage he refers to reads as follows in the original English version:

> Democracy is essentially a means, a utilitarian device for safeguarding internal peace and individual freedom. As such it is by no means infallible or certain. Nor must we forget that there has often been much more cultural and spiritual freedom under an autocratic rule than under some democracies – *and it is at least conceivable that under the government of a very homogeneous and doctrinaire majority democratic government might be as oppressive as the worst dictatorship.*
>
> (von Hayek, 2007, p. 110 – emphasis added)

This is the controversial claim that Hayek will repeat many years later in the *Constitution of Liberty* (von Hayek, 1960) and, even more controversially, with reference to the Pinochet regime and its coup against the democratically elected Allende government in Chile in the 1970s – and Eucken is in explicit agreement with it. Thus, we see that the ordo-/neoliberal hope or at least assumption is indeed that there can be something like an authoritarian liberalism that might be preferable to what Hayek would call 'unlimited democracy'. Whether this is a defendable normative position or even a plausible empirical scenario is a discussion that lies beyond the scope of this chapter. In the present context we can rest with the conclusion that Eucken's long march towards liberalism, to paraphrase Dathe (2009), does not provide sufficient grounds to exonerate him categorically from the charge of authoritarian leanings and, almost needless to say, provides no argument to defend him against the charge of being at least highly sceptical with regard to mass democracy.

And there is no really convincing reason to assume that this changes due to the experience of National Socialism, which bring us to the second line of argument defending ordoliberalism and Eucken in particular: in a response to an article by Bonefeld (2012), in which he lays out the case for the ordoliberals to be supporters of a strong state squarely along the lines of the interpretive sketch I have given here, Berghahn and Young contend that the post-war contours of ordoliberalism had undergone a remarkable transformation because

> the Freiburgers were definitely among those who changed their mind about the 1930s, and it is hence doubtful that there is a straight line between their beliefs in a strong state across the divide of 1945 as Bonefeld makes out.
>
> (Berghahn & Young, 2013, p. 770)

Other commentators who argue similarly also make reference to Dathe's narrative about Eucken's conversion to liberalism to support their claims (see Hacke, 2018). But to stay with Berghahn and Young, what is surprising about their article is the dearth of textual evidence that they present. One would assume that they present references to ordoliberal texts, letters, or lectures from the post-war era, but it is only suggested that the current partisans of a *social market economy* as such could not be supporters of a strong state. But while Rüstow in particular was happy to embrace this label, it is also known that from an ordoliberal perspective, the social market economy in its actually existing form in Germany was not a panacea but remained wanting according to strictly ordoliberal standards (Ptak, 2009). More importantly, if we focus on the example of Eucken, it is quite difficult to make the case that there was a profound change of his basic point of view. After all, the quote above referring to the masses as destructive microbes is taken from the posthumously published *Grundsätze der Wirtschaftspolitik* from 1952, as are the following quotes: 'Many people now undergo a process of massification [...but the mass] loves myth and hates rationality'. Furthermore,

> everywhere there is an undermining of state authority by particularist forces, that represent particularist interests … but in contrast to the Middle Ages a state with a unitary and consequent will formation as well as a clearly demarcated agenda is indispensable today.
>
> (Eucken, [1952] 1960, pp. 131, 329)

Thus, it appears as if both the critique of mass and pluralist democracy as well as the respective conclusions regarding the need for a 'unitary' state remain largely unchanged until the very end of Eucken's life. This interpretive conclusion is supported or at least not challenged by other post-war writings by Eucken (see Eucken, [1948] 1989). And why would the basic Euckean stance change? This would imply that the argument for a coherent and unitary politics of the competitive order and its unfeasibility under pluralist democratic conditions has been revised, but there is no sign of this in Eucken's writings as far as I can see. Post-war ordoliberalism may have toned down its critique of democracy but while I do not mean to imply that there is no dynamic whatsoever in its tenets, there is also no notable distancing from its positions prior to 1945.

To a certain degree this is confirmed by those who contributed to triggering the major transformations that did take place over the course of the 1980s and 1990s and led to the rebranding of ordoliberalism as *Ordnungsökonomik*, which brings us to the variation of the argument mentioned above, which I will only deal with in a very cursory fashion.[4] In an article from 1988 that would come to have major repercussions, Gebhard Kirchgässner pointed to the lingering notion of the 'benevolent dictator' that continued to pervade ordoliberal thought, i.e. the assumption that elected representatives would heed the advice of economists and lawyers in implementing a rational and sound politics of the competitive order. Aside from other concerns, Kirchgässner hailing from a New Political Economy perspective doubted the realism of such an assumption but also called into question the legitimation of such technocratic politics (Kirchgässner, 1988). Thus, we see that even among those broadly aligned with the neoliberal cause, the lingering authoritarianism and the tension-laded relation to democracy in ordoliberalism was a concern. Partly in response to these charges but also due to other reasons, Vanberg and others sought to align ordoliberalism with constitutional economics à la James Buchanan (Vanberg, 1988), resulting in a paradigm of *Ordnungsökonomik* that overlaps considerably with Buchanan's framework. With this move, the spectre of technocratic authoritarianism in contemporary *Ordnungsökonomik* may be banned but at the price of importing the democratic scepticism specific to public choice and constitutional economics, i.e. the perpetual anxiety over 'rent-seeking', into its framework. Even if one does not share Nancy MacLean's concerns over a large-scale attack on democracy orchestrated by Buchanan's Virginia School in alliance with the Koch brothers and the ATLAS network (see MacLean's contribution to this volume), there is thus no reason to assume that the somewhat fraught relation to democracy has disappeared entirely from contemporary ordoliberalism.

Conclusion

Let me conclude with a caveat regarding the scope and implications of the argument developed here. While I have been referring to ordoliberalism throughout this chapter, the actual argument mostly focused on Eucken and, to a lesser degree, Rüstow. They are certainly not outliers in the field of ordoliberal thought but neither are they sufficiently representative of the latter to make a convincing *pars pro toto* argument. In other words, the picture of ordoliberalism in its relationship with democracy and authoritarianism becomes more complex as we include more of the tradition's representatives into the inquiry. Of particular interest in this regard would be Wilhelm Röpke, a crucial figure in the ordo- and neoliberal networks up to the early 1960s. His positions on mass society and democracy are similar to Rüstow's and Eucken's, but while his concerns also pertain to the danger of a pluralistic dissolution of the state, his solution to the problem is highly ambiguous: there are indeed passages in his work that suggest a certain affinity to authoritarian notions but the overall thrust of his state theoretical thinking points in the direction of the decentralization of state power and societal power structures in general. This position comes with its own normative/empirical problems, but it is certainly not a *straightforward* recipe for a strong, authoritarian state – although the contemporary constellation in Europe proves that authoritarian elements may also be incorporated into multi-level systems of governance. In other words, this study is not exhaustive of its topic and these limitations need to be borne in mind. Still, anyone who claims that the charge of a critical view of democracy in its mass and pluralist dimension with a corresponding inclination towards authoritarian solutions is inaccurate, polemical, and/or simply no longer pertinent to the ordoliberal tradition will have to dispel the points made in this chapter.

Notes

1 It is worth noting that the issue of authoritarian leanings within ordoliberalism has gained renewed salience in the aftermath of the Eurozone crisis and the respective reforms. A growing number of commentators problematize the politics of crisis management orchestrated predominantly by Germany as both ordoliberal and authoritarian in nature. Still, since I have written elsewhere extensively on this topic and a proper discussion would exceed the scope of this chapter, I will focus only on the debates over the characteristics of ordoliberal theory and its potentially authoritarian aspects. For the European dimension of the debate see Biebricher, 2013; 2018; 2019; Bonefeld, 2012; Matthijs, 2016; and Wilkinson 2019 who tend to affirm an authoritarian ordoliberalism on the European level, and Feld et al., 2015; Hien & Joerges, 2018; and Young, 2017 who deny it more or less categorically. For an excellent recent study of the issue see Bruno 2019; for a well-compiled edited volume that gives an informative overview of the various aspects of the debate see Dold & Krieger, 2020.

2 All translations from German are mine.

3 This is ultimately confirmed by the case of Röpke, who also criticizes that 'the monistic state of democratic doctrine has developed into the pluralistic state of democratic practice'. While he continues to introduce a differentiation between a 'sound' and an 'unhealthy' pluralism, the first simply amounts to minority rights against the undue use of the majority principle and the second entails what I have characterized as pluralist democracy (Röpke, 1960, pp. 142, 144).

4 For a more extensive treatment see Biebricher & Ptak, 2020.

References

Berghahn, V., & Young, B. (2013). Reflections on Werner Bonefeld's 'Freedom and the strong state: on German ordoliberalism' and the continuing importance of the ideas of ordoliberalism to understand Germany's (contested) role in resolving the eurozone crisis. *New Political Economy*, *18*(5), 768–778.

Biebricher, T. (2013). Europe and the political philosophy of neoliberalism. *Contemporary Political Theory*, *12*(4), 338–375.

Biebricher, T. (2017). Ordoliberalism as a variety of neoliberalism. In J. Hien & C. Joerges (Eds.), *Ordoliberalism, law and the rule of economics* (pp. 103–114). Oxford & Portland: Hart Publishing.

Biebricher, T. (2018). Zur Ordoliberalisierung Europas. *Leviathan*, *46*(2), 170–188.

Biebricher, T. (2019). *The political theory of neoliberalism*. Stanford: Stanford University Press.

Biebricher, T., & Ptak, R. (2020). *Soziale Marktwirtschaft und Ordoliberalismus zur Einführung*. Hamburg: Junius.

Böhm, F. [1937] (2017). Economic ordering as a problem of economic policy and a problem of the economic constitution. In T. Biebricher & F. Vogelmann (Eds.), *The birth of austerity: German ordoliberalism and contemporary neoliberalism* (pp. 115–120). London: Rowman & Littlefield International.

Böhm, F., Eucken, W., & Großmann-Doerth, H. [1936] (2017). The ordo manifesto of 1936. In T. Biebricher & F. Vogelmann (Eds.), *The birth of austerity: German ordoliberalism and contemporary neoliberalism* (pp. 27–39). London: Rowman & Littlefield International.

Bonefeld, W. (2012). Freedom and the strong state: on German ordoliberalism. *New Political Economy*, *17*(5), 633–656.

Bonefeld, W. (2017). *The strong state and the free economy*. London: Rowman & Littlefield International.

Bruno, F. (2019). *Ordoliberalism and the reform of the European economic governance during the euro crisis*. Unpublished dissertation manuscript at the Università degli Studi di Milano.

Dathe, U. (2009). *Walter Euckens Weg zum Liberalismus (1918–1934)*. Freiburg Discussion papers on Constitutional Economics 09/10.

Dold, M., & Krieger, T. (Eds.). (2020). *Ordoliberalism and European economic policy: between realpolitik and economic utopia*. New York: Routledge.

Eucken, W. (1938). *Nationalökonomie wozu?* Godesberg: Verlag H. Küpper.

Eucken, W. (1950). *Foundation of economics*. London: William Hodge and Company Ltd.

Eucken, W. [1952] (1960). *Grundsätze der Wirtschaftspolitik*. Tübingen: Mohr Siebeck.

Eucken, W. [1948] (1989). What kind of economic and social system? In A. Peacock & H. Willgerodt (Eds.), *Germany's social market economy: origins and evolution* (pp. 27–45). London: Macmillan.

Eucken, W. [1952] (2017a). What is the competitive order?. In T. Biebricher & F. Vogelmann (Eds.), *The birth of austerity: German ordoliberalism and contemporary neoliberalism* (pp. 99–107). London: Rowman & Littlefield International.

Eucken, W. [1932] (2017b). Structural transformations of the state and the crisis of capitalism. In T. Biebricher & F. Vogelmann (Eds.), *The birth of austerity: German ordoliberalism and contemporary neoliberalism* (pp. 51–72). London: Rowman & Littlefield International.

Eucken, W. [1942] (2017c). Competition as the basic principle of the economic constitution. In T. Biebricher & F. Vogelmann (Eds.), *The birth of austerity: German ordoliberalism and contemporary neoliberalism* (pp. 81–98). London: Rowman & Littlefield International.

Feld, L., Köhler, E., & Nientiedt, D. (2015). *Ordoliberalism, pragmatism and the Eurozone crisis: how the German tradition shaped economic policy in Europe*. CESIFO Working Paper 5368.

Goldschmidt, N., & Hesse J.-O. (2012). *Eucken, Hayek and the road to serfdom*. Freiburg Discussion Papers on Constitutional Economics 12/4. Freiburg: Walter Eucken Institut.

Hacke, J. (2018). *Existenzkrise der Demokratie. Zur politischen Theorie des Liberalismus in der Zwischenkriegszeit*. Berlin: Suhrkamp.

Hien J., & Joerges C. (2018). Dead man walking? Current European interest in the ordoliberal tradition. *European Law Journal*, *24*(2–3), 142–162.

Kirchgässner, G. (1988). Wirtschaftspolitik und Politiksystem: Zur Kritik der traditionellen Ordnungstheorie aus Sicht der Neuen Politischen Ökonomie. In D. Cassel, B. Ramb, & J. Thiema (Eds.), *Ordnungspolitik* (pp. 53–75). München: Vahlen.

Le Bon, G. (2001). *Crowds: a study of the popular mind*. Kitchener: Batoche Books.

Matthijs, M. (2016). Powerful rules governing the Euro: the perverse logic of German ideas. *Journal of European Public Policy*, *23*(3), 375–391.

Nientiedt, D., & Köhler, E. (2016). Liberalism and democracy—a comparative reading of Eucken and Hayek. *Cambridge Journal of Economics*, *40*(6), 1743–1760.

Ortega Y Gasset, J. (1949). *Revolt of the masses*. New York: W. W. Norton & Company Inc.

Ptak, R. (2009). Neoliberalism in Germany: revisiting the ordoliberal foundations of the social market economy. In P. Mirowski & D. Plehwe (Eds.), *The road from Mont Pelèrin* (pp. 98–138). Cambridge: Harvard University Press.

Reinhoudt, J., & Audier, S. (2018). *The Walter Lippmann colloquium: the birth of neo-liberalism*. New York: Palgrave.

Röpke, W. (1960). *A humane economy: the social framework of the free market*. Chicago: Henry Regnery.

Rüstow, A. [1942] (2017a). General sociological causes of the economic disintegration and possibilities of reconstruction. In T. Biebricher & F. Vogelmann (Eds.), *The birth of austerity: German ordoliberalism and contemporary neoliberalism* (pp. 151–162). London: Rowman & Littlefield International.

Rüstow, A. [1932] (2017b). State policy and the necessary conditions for economic liberalism. In T. Biebricher & F. Vogelmann (Eds.), *The birth of austerity: German ordoliberalism and contemporary neoliberalism* (pp. 143–150). London: Rowman & Littlefield International.

Schmitt, C. [1932] (1876). *The concept of the political*. Chicago: University of Chicago Press.

Schmitt, C. (1998). Appendix: Carl Schmitt, strong state and sound economy: an address to business leaders. In R. Cristi (Ed.), *Carl Schmitt and authoritarian liberalism: strong state, free economy* (pp. 212–232). Cardiff: University of Wales University Press.

Vanberg, V. (1988). 'Ordnungstheorie' as 'constitutional economics': the German conception of a 'social market economy'. *ORDO*, *39*, 17–31.

Vanberg, V. (2014). *Liberalismus und Demokratie: Zu einer vernachlässigten Seite der liberalen Tradition*. HWWI Policy Paper 85.

Von Hayek, F. (1960). *The constitution of liberty*. Chicago: University of Chicago Press.

Von Hayek, F. (2007). *The road to serfdom (The collected works of F.A. Hayek. Vol.2)*. Chicago: University of Chicago Press.

Wilkinson, M. (2019). Authoritarian liberalism in Europe: a common critique of neoliberalism and ordoliberalism. *Critical Sociology*, *45*(7–8), 1023–1034.

Young, B. (2017). Is Germany's and Europe's crisis politics ordoliberal and/or neoliberal? In T. Biebricher & F. Vogelmann (Eds.), *The birth of austerity: German ordoliberalism and contemporary neoliberalism* (pp. 221–237). London: Rowman & Littlefield International.

3 Toward a predistributive democracy

Diagnosing oligarchy, dedemocratization, and the deceits of market justice

Margaret R. Somers

Introduction

In the face of today's egregiously spiking inequality,[1] politically empowered plutocracy, and increasing moves toward autocracy,[2] many have called for a new 'moral economy' and have turned to Karl Polanyi's *The Great Transformation* (GT) (Polanyi, [1944] 2001) for inspiration.[3] Yet one of the great contributions of Polanyi's work is that it disabuses us of the sentimental delusion that when it comes to the economy, morality has a progressive heart. Too often misread as a story of confrontation between morality (good) versus markets (bad), Polanyi's GT makes clear that all matters economic traffic in morality, that classical (and modern) political economy is drenched in moral sentiments, and that those who fail to reckon with its moral justifications will fail to understand the power of capitalism.[4] Today's most grotesque forms of inequality, economic domination, and dedemocratization are not symptoms of the absence of morality; rather, they are signature expressions of the dominant neoliberal moral economy.

A moral economy is a normative apparatus that justifies specific economic arrangements on the grounds that they produce morally superior – fair and just – outcomes. The moral economy of capitalism is that of *market justice* – the normative claim that distributional outcomes produced by legally voluntary market transactions operating in a morally neutral price system are by definition morally just.[5] While he doesn't use the precise term, the concept of market justice is a neglected linchpin of Polanyi's analysis of market society's moral infrastructure that lays the predicate for capitalism's formidable *inequality regime* – a regime that in the name of market neutrality and efficiency relentlessly suppresses popular efforts to democratize the economy, all the while occluding the actual exercise of power and coercion that underlies unequal market distributions. As such, market justice provides a diagnostic window into the submerged foundations that prop up the market system, induce the suffering of so many, and which impel the forces of dedemocratization, oligarchy, and authoritarianism.

Using the conceptual tools derived from a Polanyian perspective,[6] the diagnosis is straightforward: like all moral economies, market justice rests on and advocates for a specific political economy – an analysis of both the empirical and the necessary relationship between economy and government, market, and state. The political economy of capitalism is that of *market naturalism* – the claim that the economy operates according to natural internal laws and regularities, symmetrical to the laws of nature, which tend toward maximum efficiency when left autonomous from government and politics. Market naturalism bestows moral privilege on market outcomes on the grounds of its alleged neutrality, voluntarism, and freedom from power and human bias. In fact, it rests on a market economy that is anything but natural and nonpolitical, but one constituted by a phalanx of *predistributive mechanisms of political and legal engineering*.

Claims that the market economy is free from government power are thus utterly fictitious. *Freedom from the power of democracy*, however, has been a structural constant of capitalism from its inception. There is a consequential flaw in this paradox of competing powers. Thomas Piketty (2014, 2020) reminds us that in democracies, where the professed equality of legal citizenship rights contrasts dramatically with vast economic inequalities, the contradiction is compensated for by the discourse of meritocracy – the claim that such extreme disparities are warranted by the differences in people's productive value and contributions. Here is the flaw: while capitalist democracies depend on meritocracy for their legitimation, both meritocracy and market justice are among the chief drivers of the very plutocracy and creeping autocracy that inexorably undermine the democracies they are supposed to buttress. That is the potency and the peril of capitalism's moral economy.

Clearly, for those distressed about the condition of democracy and the fate of citizenship today, the call for morality by itself is no panacea for our ills. Instead, the challenge is to *name* the specific kind of economy we seek as an egalitarian and democratic alternative to the moral economy of capitalism. This chapter advocates for a *predistributive democratic citizenship* as an alternative political and moral economy and a mandate for structural and ideational change, which diagnoses inequality not simply as a problem of income distribution but as one of the maldistribution of power and the acceleration of dedemocratization. The goal is to organize a system of *countervailing predistributive powers*, to substitute equality and democratic rights for market justice's inequality regime; to call for a decommodification of the workforce and democratization of the workplace; and ultimately to aim for what Polanyi aspired to in the name of his version of democratic socialism: '[To] transcend the self-regulating market by consciously subordinating it to a democratic society' (Polanyi, [1944] 2001, p. 242; see also Ferreras, 2020).

The invention of market justice

The story of market justice is rooted in classical political economy, which was from the outset handmaiden to a perceived political and social grievance: late 18th- and 19th-century property owners and economic liberals protested that Poor Law taxes were extracted from them coercively by the government in the name of morally invidious ideas of compassion.[7] The stepchild of political liberalism, economic liberalism skilfully deployed the former's rhetoric of liberty to demand freedom from the tyranny of government. But whereas political liberalism opposed the Crown in the name of rights, economic liberalism named the rights of the poor as instruments of coercion.[8]

For justification, political economy invented market naturalism, an idealized thought experiment that stipulates that the laws governing nature also govern the site of property.[9] The economy is not 'like' the natural world; the world of private property and the natural world are one and the same and regulated by the same laws and exigencies.[10] Market naturalism fabricated a bifurcated world in existential conflict between a biological-like organism that tends innately toward law-like equilibrium in so far as it is free of government and moral interference, and a hierarchically dominated coercive state that exercises power at will and arbitrarily imposes moral imperatives.

Market naturalism set the terms for modern economics' Rubicon-like divide between a voluntary contractual *nonpolitical* site of market processes and a coerced *political* site of governance. By appropriating the self-regulatory laws of nature, political economy declared economic society capable of self-management, as only a market anchored to the self-equilibrating laws of nature could usurp the government in its own administration. This was not, however, a divide separate but equal: market naturalism also dethroned the ruling authority of government and established the *primacy of the economic*. Whereas under mercantilism the economy served as a handmaiden to the priorities of state power ('trade follows the flag'), with market naturalism, the economy became the arbiter of policy. The imperative to shield the market from politically imposed distortions to the self-regulative process now trumped all competing goals. Legislation that neutralized potential threats to market autonomy were justified, but those aimed at reducing economic insecurity through social provisioning were dismissed as distorting natural processes.

In triumph, political economy gained scientific prestige on the grounds of 'disinfect[ing]' the market 'of intrusive moral imperatives' (Hont, 2005, p. 406). As for the economic suffering that ensued, political economy had an answer for that: just as nature's predator/prey relationships are not judged to be just or unjust, so too must economic conditions be judged not by the Magistrate but by the majesty of nature, free of moral sentiments and sanctions.[11]

Over time market naturalism's biological foundations were disposed of in favour of a more constructionist story of voluntary buying and selling, equilibrated by the law-like fulcrum of the price mechanism. But while biological foundations are not necessary to maintain the functional autonomy of the economy from government, what is necessary is a sustained commitment to some version of market naturalism. Without it, the idea of the market's benign system of incentives that operates freely without the exercise of power is implausible, as is the market's capacity to self-govern without politically imposed distortions and the self-regulative capacity of the price system. Absent political management, a 'free' market must be rooted in some kind of naturalistic ontology.[12] For that, *efficiency* is a perfectly serviceable modern replacement.

From market naturalism to market justice

What followed next was a remarkable act of epistemic cunning: having shifted the centre of ontological gravity away from the morality-laden coercions of government to the morally indifferent sphere of nature, political economy now smuggled in under the cloak of nature a *new metric of morality*, this one measured by *conformity to the laws of nature*. In a dizzying ethical and epistemic brain twister, the moral neutrality of nature laid the predicate for the invention of a new kind of justice, which I name as *market justice*. Market justice declares that as the site of the self-regulating force of nature, the market's adjudications by definition are just because they are uninfected by morality, unimpeded by human capriciousness, untouched by political power. The scientific privileging of morally neutral laws of nature was thus effortlessly – and by sleight of hand – converted to the moral privilege of markets.

Consider the conceptual gymnastics: market naturalism was endowed primacy not because it embodied a better system of values or because of the moral superiority of property rights. Rather, it was deemed superior to a government-managed economy because it was alleged to have dispensed entirely with morality and to be completely *free of values*, reflecting nothing more than the unbiased bloodless regularities of the natural world. It was the ice-cold laws of nature that conferred scientifically grounded privilege to the market, not loftier values, ethics, or morality. How then does the site of nonmorality transform into one of moral privilege? By sheer chicanery: *the market's adjudications become morally just precisely because unimpeded by morality*. Its claims to just deserts, meritocracy, and moral righteousness rest incoherently on its putative roots in moral *absence*.

Market justice's inequality regime

Market justice, with its roots in (and dependence upon) market naturalism, is the scaffolding of capitalism's moral economy, which in turn supports the *inequality regime* of modern market society.[13] Comprised of justifications for unequal market outcomes, mandates for appropriate structural arrangements, and policy blueprints for its own survival, market justice can be parsed into three of its most significant diktats.

The first diktat of market justice is the original justification for social exclusion and inequality, which in turn laid the predicate for modern economics' *marginal productivity theory*. As explained by Thomas Malthus ([1803] 1992), poverty and riches alike are the result of nature's distributional processes and thus cannot be subject to social, moral, or political judgement (Block & Somers, 2014, pp. 150–192). Precisely because market distribution is a product of natural, not human laws, the suffering of the hungry is morally unimpeachable and cannot be 'disobeyed' without enormous risk:

> A man who … cannot get subsistence … [because] society does not want his labour, has no claim of right to the smallest portion of food … At nature's

> mighty feast there is no vacant cover [seat]. She tells him to be gone, and will quickly execute her own orders. We disobey[ed] these laws at our peril
> (Malthus ([1803] 1992, p. 249; see also Somers, 2020b)

Decades later, Malthusianism found its echo in neoclassical economics' keystone principle of marginal productivity theory, which posits that because it is a self-equilibrating naturalistic system, the market's distributional incomes precisely reflect different degrees of effort and contribution. Thus John Bates Clark in 1899:

> It is the purpose of this work to show that the distribution of the income of society is controlled by *a natural law*, and that this law, if it worked without friction, would give to every agent of production the amount of wealth which that agent creates.
> (Clark, [1899] 2001)

With marginal productivity theory, the sleight of hand by which the moral neutrality of natural law becomes the backdoor route to a morally privileged theory of market justice reaches its specious apogee in an illogical amalgam of impersonal naturalism and voluntaristic meritocracy. On the one hand, because it is the result of 'natural law' shorn of the pity and perversities of human morality and passions, the existing distribution of income and wealth, however unequal, is morally just. At the same time, market outcomes are morally just because whatever the market produces in the way of income, wage, or wealth inequalities reflects 'the amount of wealth which that agent creates' (Clark, [1899] 2001) or what each person has contributed to total output, whether through labour or ownership of capital. Rewards are thus the product of *just deserts*; earnings are *deserved*.[14] It is desert achieved by naturalism's tautological fiat: inequality *must* fairly reflect desert because, qua Bates, the market is controlled by *natural law*.

In its potent blend of naturalism and marginal productivity, market justice issued in a new *political economy of moral worth* (Somers, 2017). More than a century later, little has changed with market justice: referring to the stagnant wages of American workers, corporate apologists explain it as 'the tough-but-fair result of market forces': 'People will get paid on how valuable they are to the enterprise', John Snow, the economist then serving as Treasury Secretary under President George W. Bush, explained in 2006 (*New York Times*, 2020). On this theory, thanks to new technologies and increased foreign competition, 'most Americans just aren't worth what they used to be' (*New York Times*, 2020). The conservative playbook thrives on this diktat, and even celebrates inequality for its fair reflection of merit-driven market justice, protected from the distortions of 'social justice' that are arbitrary and driven by envy of the rich. In a world of market justice, market naturalism endows moral worth.[15]

Redistribution as theft

From the first claim that market outcomes are morally just and deserved, the second condemns as theft efforts to alleviate need through redistributive social provisioning. Murphy and Nagel (2002) dub this 'everyday libertarianism' – the conceit that because pretax income is 'presumptively just' (reflects fair earnings), it is 'owned' by the earners and 'departures from that baseline' in the form of taxes entail nothing less than government larceny (Murphy & Nagel, 2002, p. 15). Market justice by definition makes government redistribution morally illegitimate.

When its beneficiaries are factored in, the crime of redistribution becomes even more odious to the inequality regime as it entails wrongly appropriating from the meritorious to give to the undeserving. And while it is empirically the case that over the last four decades, tax policy has overwhelmingly redistributed *from* the have-nots *upwards to* the highest earners (Saez & Zucman, 2019; Piketty, 2020), the language of redistribution is associated – and stigmatized – exclusively with the transfer of income from 'hard workers' to the 'lazy poor'. In the popular jargon of neoliberalism, the state illegitimately taxes the 'makers' to give to the 'takers' (Foroohar, 2016) and subjects property to the predatory excesses of unearned entitlement (Buchanan & Tullock, 1962).

Democracy as moral and mortal threat

The third diktat of the inequality regime demonizes and initially criminalizes popular sovereignty as moral and mortal threat to market justice. Since market justice was born of the conceit of naturalism's freedom from politics and power, democracy was a menacing source of political power. Whereas 17th- and 18th-century political liberals focused on protecting property from the tyranny of the Crown, 19th-century political economists and *economic* liberals were hell-bent on protecting their property and market freedom from The People. Statesmen used political economy to denounce democratic rights-claims as stealth designs to violate market justice by plundering private property. British Chartists were persecuted as moral outlaws and prosecuted as criminals (Somers, 1995, 1997). Polanyi writes: 'Inside and outside England, from Macaulay to Mises, from Spencer to Sumner, there was not a militant [economic] liberal who did not express his conviction that popular democracy was a danger to capitalism' (Polanyi, [1944] 2001, p. 233).[16]

Capitalism's legally enforced 'hatred of democracy' (Rancière, [2005] 2014) proved untenable over time. In the face of the need for the services of working people in war and industry, elites eventually conceded to a widening of the franchise, and outright criminalization gave way to scope restrictions, putting at the centre of debate contestation over how much elasticity in the sphere of economic distribution popular sovereignty would be permitted. The compromise was a *market-conforming democracy*, in which the actualization of popular preferences – whether through legislative or collective action – is legitimate only insofar as its scope is restricted to the public sphere and prohibited from touching the property regime. With the overriding goal of public policy protecting the economy from political 'interventions', a constricted market-conforming democracy preserves the veneer of market justice as impartial, apolitical, morally neutral, universally beneficial, and free of the 'special interests' of democratic constituencies (Crouch, 2004).

These precepts took on new prestige in the 1920s with von Mises's and von Hayek's injunctions that the preferences of voters in democratic politics must be ignored when they conflict with the requisites of market processes.[17] And despite a brief interlude from the New Deal to the Cold War hybrid of 'capitalist democracies', the diktat of a constricted market-conforming democracy came back turbocharged when in the 1970s centrist intellectuals sent out alarms that the 1960s had produced way too much democracy and not enough capitalism. Embodied in the Tri-Lateral Commission's (Crozier, Huntington & Watanuki, 1975) famous attack on 'an excess of rights', the fanfare over public choice theory (Buchanan & Tullock, 1962; MacLean, 2017), and the rise of Chicago's 'law and economics', the newly named 'crisis of democracy' (along with Great Society policies) was blamed for much that ailed the economy in the 1970s and early 1980s. Under the exigency to not 'politicize' the economy, neoliberalism endowed market efficiency with the privilege of trumping democratic efforts to address distributional inequity.[18] Increasingly deemed by the right as too troublesome to capitalism to endure, democracy retained its legitimacy only to the extent that it was a depleted and disempowered democracy of restriction, defined by its proscriptions rather than by substantive affirmative rights (Streeck, 2014, 2016).[19]

The power of predistribution: Denaturalizing market naturalism

Market naturalism is of course a complete fiction: the market has no laws, natural or otherwise; there is no market neutrality free of power and politics; unequal income and wealth do not reflect market justice, merit, or worth; nor is there any moral justification for restricting democratic practices to that of market-conformity. No matter; with market naturalism and justice political economy produced the most formidable ideational regime of the last two centuries, one which continues to give moral credit to the wealthy while shaming the poor for moral deficiencies; to condemn government efforts to alleviate the suffering of those in need; and to legally enhance and protect the power of capital over and against that of a democratic citizenry.

Against the metaphysics of market naturalism, Polanyi ([1944] 2001) challenged the assumptions that endowed market justice with the privilege of adjudicating moral worth. His method was to reverse engineer the epistemic sleight of hand by which the market was made morally privileged precisely because it was declared free of moral contamination and political interest. Since the entire edifice rested on the nominalist naturalism of the economy, he had only to dismantle this naturalist illusion and the moral code of market justice would collapse precipitously.

Polanyi (1957) developed an alternative institutionalist political economy based on the premise that all of social life is based on institutions, coercion, and power rather than nature, voluntarism, and neutrality, and that free markets do not exist in the wild but are engineered to appear as such. His most counterintuitive and paradigm-changing argument is that actual markets are constituted by the very power, coercion, and violence abhorred and repudiated by the market naturalist ideal. Free market doctrine claims an economy made efficient and free by its liberation from government interference, but Polanyi denies that markets and governments are separate and autonomous entities. Government action cannot 'interfere' in the economy; government rules, rights, and legal powers are what constitute the economy in the first place. The market is itself an allocative institution of power.

What appear to be free, natural, and autonomous markets are *politically* engineered in at least three ways: (1) predistributive legal and political power; (2) the power to extract social wealth and convert it to private gain; (3) the power to disempower democracy.

From the myth of the stateless market to predistributive political engineering

The concept of predistribution[20] conveys the Polanyian (1957) insight that primary market outcomes (wages, income, wealth), which appear to be the result of impersonal autonomous market forces (globalization, automation, the price mechanism), are in fact driven by government policies, legal coercions, and institutional powers. The concept plays on the contrast with the more familiar one of redistribution: whereas the latter focuses on government policies (especially taxation) *outside* the economy, predistribution exposes how government policies and legal powers actually shape the structure of markets *inside the economy* and influence primary market *pre*distribution. It upends the binary that attributes politics, power, and governance to the public sphere, and freedom *from* power to the private. By putting law and government engineering into the heart of the price mechanism, predistribution challenges the very idea of the economy as the 'private' sector separate from government and law and puts an end to the myth of the stateless market.[21]

Examples of predistributive governance that are treated as natural to markets include copyright and patent laws that favour Big Pharma and obstruct fair competition (intellectual property law); crippling anti-union judicial rulings that have created radical asymmetries of power in waged labour and in the workplace (contract law), vigorous disabling of anti-trust law since the 1970s, leading to massive corporate consolidation (monopolies and anti-trust); financial instruments that create wealth out of legal technologies; bankruptcy laws written by the financial sector (bankruptcy law); and defanged regulatory agencies (lack of enforcement).[22]

A key feature of predistributive practices is that they are designed to occlude the exercise of political or legal power inside the economy and to instead appear simply to be in the nature of things. Unlike redistribution, which is aggressively contested in the open realm of government policy and legislative debate, predistribution operates inside the black box of the market, and is fiercely shielded from public scrutiny. The result is that market outcomes continue to be perceived as reflecting impersonal natural market forces. Indeed, the very novelty and unfamiliarity of the term 'predistribution' testifies to the successful *depoliticization* of primary market inequalities, making the ever increasing levels of wealth that have moved upward to the rich and super rich appear nonpolitical and simply market driven rather than as the result of predistributive power.[23] Alas even much of the left tends to attribute decades of rising inequality to 'unfettered' and 'deregulated' markets rather than to politically and legally engineered ones.[24]

Predistribution, as a concept, echoes the pathbreaking insights of the legal realists (Block, 2013; Britton-Purdy et al., 2020; Fried, 1998; Hale, 1920, 1923, 1943; Rahman, 2016b) and American institutionalists (Novak, 2019; Veblen, 1904, 1936; Commons, 1924, 1934) who in the 1920s and 1930s argued that contra the laissez-faire free contract ideology of their day, the economy is constitutively enmeshed in legally administered coercions.[25] They demonstrated how those coercions underpinned all economic transactions through the rights and capacities allocated by law to market participants, which in turn explains the relative bargaining power of labour and employers, of renters and property owners, of consumers and firms, and so on (see also Woodruff, 2014). Like legal realism, predistribution exposes the deceit that attributes power and coercion exclusively to the state, while denying the power of political and legal engineering to effect market outcomes.

Social predistribution: Extracting wealth from the commons

The second form of predistributive power is what I dub social predistribution, which, despite the limited nature of their actual wealth-creating activity, allows businesses to accumulate great wealth by extracting value from what we today call the *social commons* and convert it into exclusively private gain. Alperovitz and Daly (2008) focus in particular on how companies and wealthy individuals extract for private gain the economic value of society's 'knowledge inheritance', especially that of accumulated social, scientific, and technological knowledge: '[The] great bulk of our prosperity is due not to our own efforts or genius, but to the efforts and knowledge accumulation of those who came before us' (Alperovitz & Daly, 2008, p. 158). Social predistribution explains how much private wealth is less the product of a firm's productivity and capital investment and more of unremunerated productivity, knowledge, skills, technology, and infrastructure – the value, in short, of 'a complex system of social cooperation' (Alperovitz & Daly, 2008, p. 157).

Warren Buffet, among the wealthiest men on the earth, implicitly recognized social predistribution: '[Society] is responsible for a very significant percentage of what I've earned' (Buffet, cited in Caulkin, 2013). Buffet was actually channelling Thomas Paine's *Agrarian Justice* ([1795/96] 2015), in which Paine lays out a plan for universal social insurance[26] based on his analysis of the foundations of economic value and private riches, a political economy that turns on its head the standard Lockean assumptions that property is the natural right of those who have 'mixed their labor with the soil' (Somers, 1995). Not when that soil is the property of the commons and of society as a whole, Paine avers, and not when those riches are the product of the wrongful private appropriation of society's much larger contributions:

> Personal property is the *effect of society*; and it is as impossible for an individual to acquire personal property without the aid of society, as it is for him to make land originally. Separate an individual from society, and give him an island or continent to possess, and he cannot acquire personal property … All accumulation, therefore, of personal property, beyond what a man's own hands produce, is derived to him by living in society.
>
> (Paine, [1795/96] 2015, p. 34)

Elizabeth Warren (2011) also captured the practice of social predistribution when she made her famous 'You didn't build that' speech, in which she explains that the rich get rich by freeloading off of societal value. It is no coincidence that Warren has directed her criticism in particular to the high-tech companies such as Amazon, Facebook, and Google, whose vast wealth has been vacuumed up from personal data provided by you and me, which they recycle into private gain by marketization (Fourcade & Gordon, 2020; Zuboff, 2019; Kapczynski, 2020). Arguably, Silicon Valley can only exist by appropriating government-funded technological knowledge and public university research, as well as the common stock of scientific knowledge developed over generations (Block & Keller, 2011; Mazzucato, 2015). Social predistribution accelerates inequality and the wealth of private capital because unlike labour, that which is created from social resources is treated as a private asset. Put succinctly, modern economies reward activities that extract value rather than create it (Mazzucato, 2019).

Social predistribution also captures Polanyi's most influential insight that market economies are built by organizing into commodity markets what he calls social substances: labour and land are 'no[ne] other than the human beings themselves of which every society consists and the natural surroundings in which it exists' (Polanyi, [1944] 2001, p. 75). Private capital deploys social predistribution to extract societal value by converting humans and nature into factors of production. The value of 'labor' derives from the vast amount of unpaid work in families, communities, schools, indeed the entire social environment that makes human society and human reproduction possible – none of which is returned to the commons (Federici, 2012; Folbre et al., 2013; Hester, 2018; Fraser, 2016). Polanyi best explains how markets extract from what he calls 'the reality of society' in the form of fictitious commodities: 'All along the line, *human society had become an accessory of the economic system*' (Polanyi, [1944] 2001, italics added, p. 79; see also Ferreras, 2017, 2020).

Predistributive dedemocratization: The power to constrict democracy

Although capitalism's long history of repressing democratic forces in the public sphere (voter suppression, Jim Crow, etc.) has always been the more conspicuous, *predistributive dedemocratization* is more effective as it hardwires – and naturalizes – dedemocratization into the economy itself and excludes ordinary citizens from exercising democratic influence over the economy. By instituting a firewall between economy and politics, it enforces and polices the boundaries of democracy by shielding market efficiency from political and moral considerations of equality and distribution.

Like other forms of predistribution, dedemocratization and the restrictions of market-conforming democracy are difficult to recognize as they have been so normalized as part of a free-market society that excluding citizens from having a voice in their own livelihoods appears to be simply in the nature of things. From the outset, the founders designed the US Constitution to institutionalize, and naturalize, a Rubicon-like divide between the economy and the polity, to structurally depoliticize the economy by isolating it from constitutional jurisdiction, and to give the public sector free rein only insofar as it was market-conforming. Thanks to the ideational regime of natural rights, constructing what Polanyi ([1944] 2001) called the 'only legally grounded market society in the world' appeared not as an act of affirmative power, but as if dividing up and protecting market processes from citizens was simply naming what was already given in nature. Notwithstanding an early and extensive white male franchise, even citizens with political rights were effectively powerless against the power of owners and employers (Polanyi, [1944] 2001, p. 234).

Under the rule of judicial review, the American judiciary has reiteratively enforced market-conforming democracy by swatting away legislative attempts to contest the absolute power embodied in property rights and freedom of contract.[27] In the early 20th century, Lochner-era courts notoriously and repeatedly struck down, in the name of freedom of contract, legislation that aimed to expand and protect the rights of workers.[28] It took three decades before New Deal economic policies were able to survive constitutional scrutiny, notably the 1935 NLRB (created the right to form unions) and the 1938 Fair Labor Standards Act (legalized minimum wages and maximum hours) (Fishkin & Forbath, 2014).[29] But notwithstanding a 30-year New Deal legal era and landmark civil rights victories under the Warren court in the 1950s and 1960s, since the 1970s we have seen the full-blown return of a neo-Lochnerian 'juristocracy' that polices with an iron fist the structural constraints of a market-conforming democracy,[30] not merely thwarting democratic efforts at regulation but also making creative use of unrelated constitutional rights to undermine the democratizing power of unions.[31]

Thanks to predistributive dedemocratization, when workers commute from home to work, where they have no voice over the conditions and practices that dominate their lives and livelihoods, they transform from rights-bearing citizens to rightless fictitious commodities. Rightlessness in the workplace is justified as a product of voluntary free contract in the private sphere, but it is the *political* nature of the firm and legal *predistribution* that makes the workplace the ultimate site of dedemocratization. As Anderson (2017, p. 54) explains: 'The state has established the constitution of government of the workplace: it is a form of *private government*' where employers' authority is 'sweeping, arbitrary, and unaccountable—not subject to notice, process, or appeal'. With legally orchestrated rightlessness in the workplace, predistributive dedemocratization turns citizenship into a very thin concept. The commodification of humans into labour explains why dedemocratization creates not just inequality, and not just unequal power, but the much greater affliction of *unfreedom*. As Polanyi ([1944] 2001, p. 74) explains, the 'commodity "labor power'' is actually the 'human individual who happens to be the bearer of this peculiar commodity' and because 'man's labor power' is one and the same thing as the 'physical, psychological, and moral entity "man' attached to that tag', it is not some fictional abstraction of 'labor' but the whole human being who is subjected to the silencing of dedemocratization and the unfreedom of servility that is a condition of employment (see also Ferreras, 2017).

The privatization of public goods is another mechanism of predistributive dedemocratization. Years of dismantling the social state have been justified by market efficiency, but motivating these conversions is not greater efficiency but the project of dedemocratization and the nullification of rights. When public goods are privatized, they are removed from the public sphere of democratic accountability and moved into the unaccountability of the private zone. Privatization means that efforts to exercise democratic voice over the distribution of social necessities are silenced for violating the firewall between efficiency and politics (Somers, 2017; Farrell, 2018).

Central banks hardwire dedemocratization into the heart of the economy. The outsized influence of the American Fed is virtually uncontestable because of its independence from – and unaccountability to – the legislature and public sphere. Completely unimpeded by democratic voices, it sets interest rates based on an obsessive focus on low inflation, which is guaranteed to keep unemployment rates high and labour's bargaining power low. Predistributive dedemocratization has been the very essence of the global economy (Slobodian, 2018). Fashioned to scale up to the global level the (fictional) self-regulating capacities of the domestic market, the gold standard has long given way to such bodies as the WTO, GATT, the IMF, the World Bank, and numerous international trade deals. In the absence of any comparable political bodies, they are even more cloistered from democratic input than are national markets, while at the same time legally enabled to impose policies and mandates to override democratically elected national legislative bodies (Braithwaite, 2008; Chang, 2002; Streeck, 2014; Slobodian, 2018).

After predistributive denaturalization: Deconstructing the inequality regime

By shattering the fabrications of market naturalism, predistributive analysis leaves exposed the moral trickery of market justice, whose claim to just deserts rests entirely on the economy's professed absence of power. Where does the denaturalized economy leave the diktats of market justice?

The truth about inequality and the political economy of moral worth

At the close of GT, Polanyi confronts the moral superiority and the smug indifference so often expressed toward the suffering of the vast numbers of unemployed in the 1930s:

> Neither voters, nor owners, neither producers, nor consumers [felt they] could be held responsible for such *brutal restrictions of freedom* as were involved in the occurrence of unemployment and destitution. Any decent individual could imagine himself free from all responsibility for acts of compulsion on the part of a state which he, *personally*, rejected; or for economic suffering in society from which he, *personally*, had not benefited. He was 'paying his way,' was 'in nobody's debt' ... His *lack of responsibility* for them seemed so evident that he *denied their reality* in the name of *his freedom*.
>
> (Polanyi, [1944] 2001, p. 266 italics added)

Polanyi here captures the self-righteousness – expressed in the language of personal responsibility, individual merit, and self-reliance – produced by the code of market justice, which allocates moral worth, blame, and responsibility according to the principles of just deserts and the stateless market. Regulated by the allegedly moral neutrality of marginal productivity, unemployment and social exclusion can only reflect merit and desert. 'Paying one's own way' and being in 'nobody's debt' put one beyond both moral reproach and responsibility for others' suffering. After all, if market justice makes unemployment and destitution the effect not of shared fate and social conditions but of moral deficits and nature's preferences, then our own good luck reflects our superior capacities, extraordinary productivity, and moral character.

But then with surgical precision, Polanyi tears away the veil of self-satisfaction: look closer and we'll see that market justice is a 'false Utopia' as it is in fact driven by underlying mechanisms of power and coercion:

> Liberal economy gave a false direction to our ideals. It seemed to approximate the fulfillment of intrinsically Utopian expectations. *No society is possible in which power and compulsion are absent, nor a world in which force has no function.* Vision was limited by the market which 'fragmented' life into the producers' sector that ended when his product reached the market, and the sector of the consumer for whom all goods sprang from the market. The one derived his income 'freely' from the market, the other spent it 'freely' there. Society as a whole remained invisible. The *power of the state was of no account* since the *less its power, the smoother the market mechanism would function*.
>
> (Polanyi, [1944] 2001, p. 266 italics added)[32]

The moral code of market justice, in short, is engineered by the exercise of power, not by the fiction of natural laws free of political domination. Earnings, income, and freedom itself reflect not merit and fairness but the coercions of asymmetrical power and commodification, just as corporate profits reflect not the equilibrium of the price mechanism but of government-protected monopolies, the legal suppression of unions, and the private appropriation of social wealth. The 'power of the state' makes the price mechanism not a neutral regulator but a function of the allocation of legal rights and capacities, just as the legally sanctioned maldistribution of bargaining power between workers and employers undermines the meritocratic and naturalistic claims of marginal productivity theory. The fairness, worth, and desert attributed to market distributions are reflections of power and coercion smuggled under nature's protective cover into the 'morality-free' economy. Power, not nature, ascribes economic status, and inequality is a problem of domination and unfreedom (Rahman, 2016a).

Today, four decades of rising inequality have likewise been explained by an incoherent mix of market forces – globalization, automation, and technology – combined with the voluntaristic self-congratulatory language of meritocracy (Markovits, 2019; Sandel, 2020). Just as Polanyi disposed handily of the specious political economy of moral worth in his time, a comparative international glance refutes it in ours: no advanced country comes even close to the levels of US inequality (see Alvaredo et al., 2018). It is not globalization that has driven up the enormous fortunes of Bill Gates, Big Pharma, and the top 1 per cent but, among other things, government-granted patent and copyright monopolies (Baker, 2016, 2018; Pistor, 2019, 2020; Kapczynski, 2014). Market justice would have us believe that oligopolies are so profitable and CEOs so overpaid because they are superbly managed, but the reality is that predistribution, not meritocracy, is occurring.[33] Their heightened profits reflect neoliberal judicial doctrine and practice that facilitate monopolies and oligopolies in the name of 'consumer welfare' (Crouch, 2011; Khan & Vaheesan, 2017; Piraino, 2007; Rahman, 2016a, b; Somers, 2012; Whitehouse, 2020).

Nor is it robots and automation that have stagnated wages for 40 years but far-reaching asymmetries of power inside the workplace, both the 'initial endowments' market participants bring to the labour contract as well as the rules of absolute dominion – 'employment at will' – those contracts enforce (Economic Policy Institute, 2020; Bagenstos, 2020). These are policies and laws that, under the formalist illusion of the free labour contract, overwhelmingly endow employers and high-level managers with vastly disproportionate power, while simultaneously restricting and constricting the rights and freedoms of the citizenry qua workers, both inside and outside the workplace (Anderson, 2017; Purdy, 2018a). Above all, much of today's extreme inequality can be attributed to anti-union judicial rulings that today's neo-Lochnerian juristocracy can count among its most shameful predistributive achievements (Cohen, 2020). The specious doctrine of equal bargaining power[34] in labour law has provided cover for the courts to prohibit collective labour litigation, while it has 'weaponized' the First Amendment to weaken and undermine unions (see Janus v. AFSCME, 2018; see also Purdy, 2018b; Tebbe, 2020).

In short, it is predistributive political and judicial engineering that has orchestrated the massive upward redistribution of wealth and income in US since the 1970s (Baker, 2016; Whitehouse, 2020). But because predistribution remains shrouded, four decades of rising inequality have been attributed to 'deregulated' markets rather than to capital's four-decade campaign redistributing wealth through predistributive practices. There is, of course, no such thing as deregulated markets, only *reregulated* ones – predistributive practices that switch from one beneficiary to another (Block & Somers, 2014). Viewed through the *alchemy of misrecognition*, 'deregulation' is simply the name used for unrecognized and unnamed predistributive practices that redistribute income and wealth upwards – 'naturally' (Somers, 2018).

The truth about redistributive justice

Justifying inequality by market justice leads inexorably to the claim that efforts to mitigate the suffering of those in need through redistributive taxation wrongfully steal from the deserving 'owners' of their income and give these 'stolen' unearned rewards to the undeserving. Social predistribution clarifies who is stealing from whom. In their *Myth of Ownership*, Murphy and Nagel (2002) challenge the premise that the pre-tax distribution of income and wealth should be taken as the 'presumptively given' – that is, fairly earned – baseline, which in turn challenges the idea that taxes are theft. Although taxes are generally deemed redistributive, they use predistributive reasoning to show that pre-tax earnings are not earned 'on one's own' but are dependent on the taxes that *precede* and *make feasible the possibility of any economic transactions at all*. It is taxes that sustain the legal system that defines property rights and the boundaries of their control; that support the legal and policing infrastructure that protects the rights to private property; that support the sites of capital accumulation through which goods and services are produced; and that sustain the financial system, the legal system of patents and copyrights, the vast infrastructure of transportation and telecommunications and all the other aspects of society that those from Thomas Paine ([1795/96] 2015) to Elizabeth Warren (2011) have documented as foundational to all wealth creation. Without taxes derived from society, there would be no market economy. In this sense, taxes can be predistributive.

Everyday libertarianism, like market justice, rests on the myth of the stateless and taxless market. What appears to be the market's natural distribution of income and wages is in great part the product of the *prior* predistributive power of taxes to create the conditions for markets in the first place. The idea that income is presumptively earned by one's own hands in the market, prior to and independently of any government or social support, is part of the 'myth of ownership' of pre-tax income.

Once everyday libertarianism has been punctured, so too must be its claim that redistribution benefits the 'undeserving', who are stigmatized as social parasites (Mazzucato, 2019). Social predistribution – the unearned wealth accumulated by those rich enough to extract value from society's present and past resources – also makes short shrift of the poisonous vocabulary of 'deserts' and the political economy of moral worth from which it derives. The real injustice is the outsized power that allows private capital to accumulate vast wealth by taking from society and giving nothing in return (other than the opportunity to buy more), not even the duly owed taxes which they lawlessly evade (Saez & Zucman, 2019). The World Inequality Lab's 2018 (Alvaredo et al., 2018) report analyzes how private capital and businesses appropriate enormous amounts of public wealth, creating state indebtedness and incapacitating governments. Social predistribution makes clear where the real theft takes place and who are the truly undeserving.

The truth about democracy and capitalism

The diktat of criminalizing and then radically constricting popular governance to that of market-conforming democracy was designed to contain the threat to property of the pitchforked masses. Predistributive analysis reveals that the true threat is the power of property and capital to democracy, rather than vice versa. Predistributive dedemocratization so efficiently escalates inequality that the plutocracy it nurtures effortlessly glides into becoming an occupying power in the public sphere where it neutralizes all but the formalities of democratic citizenship.

The end of market naturalism exposes the multiple deceptions market justice mobilizes to justify robbing the citizenry of their democratic rights. One is that democracy is a vehicle of 'special' interests and so threatens market justice's 'universality' – the claim that its wealth-maximizing efficiency makes everyone better off. The evidence against this is overwhelming. If the alarmist cries of the 1970s about the perils to capitalism of 'too much democracy' and an 'excess of rights' had any credibility, the preceding decades should have been years of stagnation. Instead, as is well known, the *trentes glorieuses* produced not only high growth rates but years of relatively high equality. By contrast, over the recent decades of neoliberalism, rather than benefitting the whole of society, almost every additional penny of growth has accrued to the top 0.01 per cent while leaving workers unremunerated for their productivity gains.[35] Contrary to public choice theory (Buchanan, 2000), not innocent property-owners but the public fisc is the real 'prey' in the market/democracy relationship (Block, 2018; Streeck, 2014, 2016; Hacker & Pierson, 2010, 2020; Gilens & Page, 2014).

In another deceptive claim, market justice is depicted as a morally disinterested process of unbiased nonpolitical 'horizontal' transactions among equals, entirely free of the coercions of 'vertical' domination characteristic of politics and power. Predistributive dedemocratization punctures this fiction by revealing the currency of the market economy to be power – the power to enforce a limited market-conforming democracy and to silence democratic voices in the workplace. The truth about this diktat is that democracy is encaged not because it is a threat to *la doux commerce* (Hirschman, [1977] 2013) but because it is a *competing* power. The difference between the two kinds of power is that the market's predistributive powers and coercions are occluded under the veil of the 'free market', whereas democratically articulated efforts to exercise power are fully visible and contestable in the public realm of legislative debate and collective action. The comparative advantage that accrues to market justice is that of *naming*: keeping workers in conditions of virtual servility in the workplace, prohibited from expressing their voices as citizens, is named as freedom of contract, while contesting these conditions in the effort to democratize the workplace is named as politicizing the economy. Predistributive analysis, by making explicit that the economy is already constitutively political, makes a mockery of this false dichotomy between neutral and power-driven (Somers, 2018; Block, 2018; Britton-Purdy et al., 2020).

A third deception that rationalizes the constriction of democracy derives from the edicts of public choice theory – that feckless politicians acting out of their own economic self-interest will succumb to popular predations upon defenceless property owners who will be left besieged and stripped of their wealth (Buchanan, 2000; MacLean, 2017). Four decades of neoliberalism have rendered ludicrous this narrative of helpless property owners under assault by a rapacious democratic mobocracy (Brown, 2019). On the contrary, predistributive dedemocratization has institutionalized structural bulwarks deep inside the market economy to completely bar the democratic citizenry from coming anywhere near the propertied elite and their wealth. From the constitutional firewall between politics and property, to the prohibition of workers' voices in 'private governments', to the judicial support of monopoly and monopsony, to the dedemocratized central banks and global financial organizations, naming the problem as 'too much democracy' is risible.

History, in fact, demonstrates the reverse – it has been the refusal of capital to tolerate even the mildest of economic reforms that precipitated not merely plutocratic control of governance but moves to eliminate democracy altogether. In GT, Polanyi argues that the triumph of fascism in Continental Europe in 1930s was triggered by an impasse between democracy and global capital – working-class led parliamentary efforts to democratically enact social protections against the extreme privations of mass unemployment, versus (or vs. if not enough room) the gold standard's dictum against 'distorting' national currencies through social spending. Defining the essence of fascism as using state power to save capitalism by extirpating democracy, Polanyi argues that economic elites' virulent antagonism to democracy was so overdetermining that it motivated them to ally with fascists to fortify capitalist power through a strong state: '[The] victory of fascism was made practically unavoidable by the [economic] liberals' obstruction of any reform involving planning, regulation, or control' (Polanyi, [1944] 2001, p. 265; Dale, 2016a, b).

Polanyi saw fascism's triumph as but the most virulent outbreak of capitalism's innate antidemocratic virus. Echoes of the calamitous fate of Europe in the 1930s are found in America's surging inequality and illiberal market authoritarianism today. The complicity between the Republican Party, a colluding judiciary, and the Trump presidency most clearly underlines the elective affinity between a plutocracy and authoritarianism (Whitehouse, 2020). Predistributive dedemocratization reveals that it is not market justice that is threatened by democracy, but – once again – democracy that is threatened by capital (Streeck, 2016).[36]

Toward a predistributive democracy

Market justice was born under the false flag of nature and the myth of the stateless market. Based on this fictional naturalism – unencumbered by the biased hands of power and social ideas of morality – political economy then attributed moral privilege to market outcomes. Predistribution – legal/political, social, and dedemocratizing – is a solvent; once it strips away the make-believe symmetry between the laws of nature and those of the market, it exposes market justice as empirically and morally bankrupt – it is neither true nor just. Where then does that leave us? Is there an alternative metric of justice?

Redistributive justice has been the traditional philosophy of compensating for unjust deserts, and redistributive social provisioning continues to be an essential element in a progressive political programme, especially in light of its decommodifying and democratizing effects (O'Neill, 2020; Esping-Andersen, 1990; Piketty, 2014, 2020; Klein, 2020). But by itself, redistribution is insufficient, as it 'comes too late' (Vogel, 2019). It primarily focuses on government *corrections* for market inequalities, while it deflects attention from the maldistributive *origins* in the market's asymmetrical powers of domination and dedemocratization. The solution, then, is not merely a redistribution of income, but a *redistribution of power* and *democratization* through what I dub as *predistributive democratization.*

The goal of a predistributive democracy is to hardwire justice and democracy into the structure of the market (Kennedy, 2019) by reappropriating the predistributive powers that currently advantage wealth and capital and reverse engineer them to egalitarian and democratic ends. This would eschew peddling the pretence of achieving a market free of power – or of the legal fiction of equal power, which amounts to the same thing. Once we have established that all markets are structured by power, we can also recognize the politically contingent nature of predistribution: it can either strengthen or weaken the bargaining power of workers, either bolster or tame corporate profits through antitrust and rules of monopoly, be calibrated either to skew income to the 1 per cent or to contribute to a more equitable wage and income structure. Whether predistribution will advantage wealth and capital or distribute income and wages in a more egalitarian direction depends almost entirely on the balance of power between capitalism and democracy.

With this in mind the goal of a predistributive democracy is to laser focus on the very predistributive policies that have been most instrumental in generating four decades of ever spiking inequality and dedemocratization and to mobilize *countervailing predistributive democratically driven powers* to undo and transcend them. Jacob Hacker (2011) explains the project clearly: predistribution 'focus[es] on market reforms that encourage a more equal distribution of economic power and rewards even before government collects taxes or pays out benefits'. Martin O'Neill (O'Neill & Williamson, 2012a), the philosopher who should be credited with most widely and effectively disseminating the concept, elaborates: 'Instead of equalizing unfair market outcomes through tax-and-spend or tax-and-transfer, we instead engineer markets at their internal structural level to create fairer outcomes from the beginning' (see also Vogel, 2019). Beyond just 'fairer outcomes', however, a predistributive democracy must confront the economic and political oligarchy that, in a vicious circle, is able to continuously reimpose inegalitarian policies and legal coercions to undermine not merely fair earnings but ultimately freedom and democracy itself (Bartels, 2008; Brown, 2019; Gilens & Page, 2014; Reich, 2015; Hacker & Pierson, 2020).

To dismantle the inequality regime produced by market justice requires an alternative institutionalist and power-centric political economy (Polanyi, 1957; Guinan & O'Neill, 2018; Somers & Block, 2020; Block & Somers, 2014; Fligstein & Vogel, 2020; Britton-Purdy et al., 2020) to that of social naturalism: (1) Market processes do not mimic the self-regulative laws of nature, always moving toward a default state of equilibrium. The currency of markets is power, not nature: all market participants are enmeshed in networks of power, and market outcomes reflect the market's infrastructural relations of power, specifically those of political/legal, social, and dedemocratizing predistributive power. (2) The stateless market is a myth, the economy is 'market-crafted' by the state (Vogel, 1996, 2018), and the market is an allocative institution of power predistributively designed to dedemocratize (Somers, 2020a). (3) Wealth is not produced exclusively by capital accumulation but by the predistributive powers of political power and law, the predistributive powers of capital to extract social and public value from the commons and the public fisc, and by the predistributive powers to structurally dedemocratize and restrict popular sovereignty to its market-conforming limits.

This political economy makes clear the solution to inequality and the moral crimes of market justice requires the countervailing powers of predistributive democratization. At the top of the agenda must be redressing the 'unjust deserts' (Alperovitz & Daly, 2008) by which private capital and owners engorge themselves on the social resources and inheritances they had little to do with creating. Recalling Thomas Paine's ([1795/96] 2015) manifesto, since private property is built on societal wealth, then justice requires returning that social wealth to the commons: '[He] owes on every principle of justice, of gratitude, and of civilization, a part of that accumulation back again to society from whence the whole came' (Paine, [1795/96] 2015, p. 34). Inspired by Paine, thinkers from Louis Bourgeois to Henry George, through Elizabeth Warren, have worked to elaborate this vision. Alperovitz and Daly (2008) argue that because so much capital accumulation is due not to individual efforts or merit but to exploiting social inheritance and the commons it follows that 'properly recognizing this gift establishes *a social claim to the wealth that it generates, a moral claim* that is presently largely unrecognized' (Alperovitz & Daly, 2008, italics added, p. 156).

Recognizing that so much wealth is a product of the extraction of social value compels us to discard the wrongheaded precepts of desert-based ideas of justice and substitute democratic ones. If market outcomes are shaped not by neutral market processes or merit, but by politics, rules, power, and the extraction of societal value, it is much easier to understand that wealth and property are not individually but collectively produced. Property, from this angle of vision, is a fictive private asset; its privileges must be subject to the democratic deconstruction of their illicit foundations. A citizen dividend, public wealth funds, new public utilities – these are just some of the ways this could happen (Guinan & O'Neill, 2019; O'Neill, 2019; Rahman, 2016b; Alperovitz, 2017; Alperovitz & Daly, 2008; Howard et al., 2020; Poole, 2020).

Perhaps the most important mandate of a predistributive democracy is to unbridle the encaged powers of democratic citizenship beyond the limits of a market-conforming democracy. Working people have been stripped of their full citizenship rights inside the firm under the doctrine of equal bargaining power and consent-based freedom of contract, which 'undermines freedom, fairness, and democracy' (Economic Policy Institute, 2020; Bagenstos, 2020). Rather than accept the ruse of an apolitical economy, it is critical to recognize there is a *citizenry* already inside the economy. A predistributive democracy aims to activate those democratic citizenship rights currently suppressed inside the economy, and for citizens to activate their rights in the polity beyond the emaciated rights of a market-conforming democracy.

Reviving union power is at the heart of a predistributive democracy. No less than Lawrence Summers (2020) now argues that strengthening the countervailing power of unions is the 'central and urgent priority' for combating inequality. But at stake in reviving unions is much more than income distribution: union power is democratic power. As Block and Sachs (2020) remind us: '[Without] unions … millions of lower-income Americans have lost their most effective voice in our democracy'. Unions are also critical vectors for decommodification, as democratization is the precondition for decommodification, which is itself the precondition for freedom (Polanyi, [1944] 2001; Ferreras, 2020).

Predistributive democracy thus aims to constrain the powers of economic and political domination by enlarging democratic citizenship at the structural level (Mackert, 2017; Rahman, 2018; Rahman & Russon, 2019; Somers, 2008; Somers & Roberts, 2008). Fourcade and Gordon (2020) argue for 'seeing like a citizen', while Forbath and Fishkin (2014, 2016) articulate a new political economy based on an 'anti-oligarchic constitution'. They argue that when the courts have disallowed on the grounds of contractual consent efforts to redress workplace imbalance of power, it is not enough to respond that the Constitution does not disallow these ameliorative acts. Because they read the Constitution as an 'equality of opportunity' and 'anti-oligarchy' document, the issue is not about what the Constitution 'allows' but what it *demands and requires* the legislature to do if it is to meet its primary goal of constructing an anti-oligarchic democratic republic with equal citizenship rights (Forbath, 2019; see also Sitaraman, 2016, 2017). To combat the hegemony of the neoliberal 'One Percent Constitution', McCluskey (2016, 2020) argues for a progressive 'structural constitutionalism' that aims to 're-order the distribution of power' away from a market-conforming democracy toward generating 'collective political economic power for an inclusive and democratic vision of "we the people"'. Rahman (2016b, d) also argues for a new 'constitutional political economy', but with less of an emphasis on the formal Constitution and more on the democratic moralities and structures that are necessary to 'constitute' a democratic egalitarian society.

Monopolization increasingly enriches the financial oligarchy and bolsters its ability to suppress the voices – and the wages – of an independent democratic citizenry. The 'New Brandeisians' and others (Lynn, 2010; Khan, 2018; Khan & Vaheesan, 2017; Teachout, 2020, Teachout & Khan, 2014; Rahman, 2016c;

Reich, 2015; Steinbaum, 2019; Vaheesan, 2020; Schneider & Vaheesan, 2019) focus on combating the law and economics doctrine of anti-anti-trust that predistributively coddles monopolies in the name of greater 'consumer welfare', efficiency, and growth, while prohibiting any consideration of democratically deliberated distributive equity.[37] While it was Lynn (2010) who first brought back to public attention the predatory politics of monopolization, the movement has quickly grown with Rahman (2016b) arguing that to oppose monopoly is to support an independent democratic citizenry against a financial autocracy, and Khan (2018, p. 131) writing: 'antimonopoly is a key tool and philosophical underpinning for structuring society on a democratic foundation'. In the same vein, Baker (2016) and Kapcynski (2014) challenge the system of patents and copyrights as a primary predistributive driver of inequality, while Reich (2015), Stiglitz (2015, 2019, 2020), Baker (2016), and Sitaraman (2019) all have developed extensive programmes for combating the government's multiple methods of predistributive market 'rigging' that drive wealth and income upwards to an ever more financially bloated plutocracy (Guinan & O'Neill, 2019; Rahman, 2017–2018).

A different angle of vision focuses on the structure of property itself. Ciepley (2020) focuses on the public and socialized nature of the corporation, reminding us that the corporation is not a private entity but constituted by a charter, granted by the state (see also Crouch, 2011). Even in a corporate-dominated economy not stockholders but the 'sovereignty of public authority' is the ultimate owner, which includes workers, consumers, the community, and the environment. Forcing the public nature of the corporation into the open has clear implications for democratizing the economy. Under the moniker of 'capital predistribution', from a different angle of vision Martin O'Neill (2017) argues that we should be 'worrying less about marginal tax rates and more about ownership and control of capital'. More important than the flow of income streams are 'the sources of wealth from which they came' – from ownership patterns increasingly structured to support a plutocracy. Capital predistribution would aim to 'change the nature of property rights such that wealth … would be dispersed across the population, with individual capital holdings for all viewed as *an entitlement of citizenship*'. Restructuring ownership toward a 'property-owning democracy' (O'Neill, 2017, pp. 363, 369) captures the essence of predistributive democracy, which recognizes the social foundations of wealth and property, and aims to redemocratize the value of that which has been privatized by the enclosure of the commons (see also O'Neill, 2020, 2021; Guinan & O'Neill, 2019; Alperovitz, 2017).

Conclusion

Although there are differences of emphasis, all these proposals contribute to envisioning the components of a predistributive democracy. They make clear that inequality is not merely a moral issue of deep injustice and harm – although it certainly is that; nor is it merely an economic issue of redistributing income – although income must indeed be redistributed. Rather, they clarify that the maldistribution of power and property, as well as the continuing violence of dedemocratization and human commodification, is both the cause and consequence of authoritarian oligarchy, making inequality a crisis of democracy and political freedom itself.

A Polanyian perspective explains this crisis not as the effect of deregulated market forces nor of the absence of morality, but of predistributive coercive powers, including those of an all-powerful juristocracy and the legal invention of wealth, the wrongful extraction of social wealth by capital, and the structural processes of dedemocratization. Market justice provided the original justification: because market outcomes, however cruel, reflect nature's own distributional mechanisms, they are the unbiased arbiters of livelihood and fate. This in turn produced a political economy of moral worth that righteously grafts stigmatizing blame onto the pain of exclusion, and self-congratulatory praise onto the comfort of wealth. An alternative predistributive political economy exposes market justice's moral crimes of justifying inequality, degrading the moral worth of the excluded, and nullifying democratic citizenship rights. Polanyi understood democracy to be the only thing standing between the crises wrought by market justice and full-blown fascism. He also taught us that discarding the false dichotomy of markets versus morals is a precondition to fashioning a democratic rather than an authoritarian response. Clearly, those who fail to reckon with the moral economy of the capitalist crowd will fail to understand its outsized powers. We can only build a predistributive democracy on the ruins of market justice.

Acknowledgements

Earlier versions of this chapter were presented at Princeton University's Belknap Global Workshop on the Moral Economy, 6–7April 2018; the University of Potsdam, Germany, International Conference on The Condition of Democracy and the Fate of Citizenship 11–13 July 2019; and at the Conference on *The Great Transformation* at 75, Bennington College, 25–27 October 2019. I'm appreciative of the many comments I received in those settings. As always, Fred Block gave invaluable feedback on previous drafts.

Notes

1 It would take an average Amazon worker *3.8 million years*, working full time, to earn what CEO Jeff Bezos now possesses. And the country's wealthiest 20 people own more wealth than half of the nation combined – 20 people with more wealth than 152 million others. See https://inequality.org/facts/income-inequality/. Alvaredo et al. (2018), Roser & Ortiz-Ospina (2016).

2 In 'En route to autocracy in America', Masha Gessen argues that United States is in the first stage of an autocratic transformation. See Heffner (2020).

3 The term 'moral economy' famously comes from E.P. Thompson (1971). On the influence of Polanyi on Thompson, see Block and Somers (2014, pp. 44–72).

4 This would hardly surprise those familiar with 40 years of revisionist scholarship on Adam Smith. Polanyi, however, attributes classical political economy not to Smith but to Malthus and Ricardo.

5 There is an elective affinity between market justice and meritocracy, see Markovits (2019) and Sandel (2020), but they are not the same. The latter addresses individual input and outcomes whereas market justice, while it has implications for micro justification or 'just deserts', is a macro-generated normative claim about structural market forces.

6 Rather than an exegesis on his work, this chapter uses a Polanyian conceptual vocabulary Fred Block and I have abstracted from his writings (Block & Somers, 2014).

7 The accusation of moral invidiousness was based on Joseph Townsend's and Malthus's claims that providing poor relief presented a moral hazard, inducing laziness and more poverty (Block & Somers, 2014, pp. 150–192; Somers, 2020b).

8 This and several of the following paragraphs are revised from Somers (2020a).

9 On theoretical realism in economics, see Somers (1998).

10 On naturalism, see Polanyi ([1944] 2001). On social and market naturalism, see Block and Somers (2014, pp. 150–192) and Somers (2008, pp. 254–288). On the history of economic naturalism, see Harcourt (2011) and Grewal (2017).

11 Thus Polanyi: 'Essentially, economic society was founded on the grim realities of Nature. If man disobeyed the laws which ruled that society, the fell executioner would strangle the offspring of the improvident. *The laws of a competitive society were put under the sanction of the jungle*' (Polanyi, [1944] 2001, p. 131 - italics added).

12 Lest anyone be tempted to think the crude discourse of market naturalism has been surpassed, consider the recent thoughts of President Bill Clinton: globalization is 'the economic equivalent of a force of nature, like wind or water', see https://www.economist.com/books-and-arts/2016/11/19/the-third-wave-of-globalisation-may-be-the-hardest, or former Prime Minister Tony Blair, regarding the globalization debate: 'You might as well debate whether autumn should follow summer', see https://www.theguardian.com/uk/2005/sep/27/labourconference.speeches.

13 Piketty (2020) uses the same concept of an inequality regime but with very different substantive content.

14 In its crudest version, that CEOs receive 500 times that of each individual worker in his/her firm simply reflects a remarkably talented corporate elite.

15 On how this moral code shapes modern social policy, see Somers (2017).

16 Dale (2016b, pp. 55–79) masterfully reconstructs Polanyi's thesis on the basic incompatibility of capitalism and democracy. See especially Streeck (2014) to understand the fundamental conflict between democracy and capitalism.

17 Hayek's strenuous anti-democratic injunctions continued through his life's work, see von Hayek ([1939] 1980), Mirowski and Plehwe (2009), Burgin (2012), Stedman Jones (2012), Streeck (2014).

18 On law and economics, see Harcourt (2011), Crouch (2011), Britton-Purdy et al. (2020), Teles (2012), Posner (1983).

19 See Krugman (2014), 'American politicians don't dare say outright that only the wealthy should have political rights—at least not yet but if you follow the currents of thought now prevalent on the political right to their logical conclusion, that's where you end up'. Thus, Steven Moore, one of the leading pundits of conservative economics: 'Capitalism is a lot more important than democracy, I'm not even a big believer in democracy. I always say that democracy can be two wolves and a sheep deciding what to have for dinner' (Harwood, 2019).

20 The term predistribution was coined by political scientist Jacob Hacker (2011), and put into currency by Ed Miliband in 2012, then leader of the UK's Labour Party. See also O'Neill and Williamson (2012a, b), O'Neill (2020), Thomas (2017), Somers (2018), Vogel (1996, 2018, 2019). Predistribution should not be confused with the more familiar concept of embeddedness, which is used most commonly to suggest that social and political institutions modify markets rather than structure their mechanisms (e.g. price system) of distribution. For analyses of the Polanyian roots of predistribution, see Somers (2018), Somers and Block (2020).

21 For a discussion of how Polanyi's theory of market utopianism lays the groundwork for the modern concept of predistribution, see Somers (2018).

22 Reich, 2015; Baker, 2016; Bagenstos, 2013, 2020; Block and Somers, 2014; Stiglitz, 2015; Pistor, 2019, 2020.

23 Although he does not use the term predistribution, few have done more than Baker (especially 2016) to convey that it is government policy and law, not the 'free market', that are responsible for driving incomes upwards over the recent decades.
24 But see Somers (2008) and Stiglitz (2020): 'But, of course, the neoliberal deregulation agenda was never really about deregulation per se. The point has always been to regulate in a way that will advance certain interests at the expense of others'.
25 Although Polanyi's work has strong elective affinities with legal realism (as well as with American economic institutionalists, such as Veblen and Commons), it was the structuralist anthropologists, especially R.C. Thurnwald and B. Malinowski, the German historical school, especially G. Schmoller and C. Bücher, the English historical economists, especially W. Ashley and W. Cunningham, and E. Heckscher, who most influenced his historical institutionalist thinking in *The Great Transformation* (pp. 269–303; Polanyi, 2014; Somers, 1990; Koot, 1987). Although, see Dale (2016a, b) for the definitive discussion of Polanyi's intellectual influences.
26 Both *Agrarian Justice* and the plan are currently featured on the US government's official Social Security website http://www.ssa.gov/history/paine4.html. See also socialsecurityworks.org.
27 The apparent exception to this rule was the 1890 Sherman Anti-Trust Act, which, perhaps not surprisingly, was justified entirely by its stated purpose of using law to strengthen the competitive nature of capitalism. Indeed, while on its surface it appeared to use the law to 'interfere' in free trade, in reality it was at first used almost exclusively to 'interfere' with the creation of labor unions, the primary vector of democratic influence in the interest of expanding the rights of working people.
28 Lochner v. New York. 198 U.S. 45 (1905).
29 Although, see Taft-Hartley (1947).
30 Law and economics has provided the intellectual fodder, see Teles (2012), Harcourt (2011), Phillips-Fein (2010), Britton-Purdy et al. (2020), Kapczynski (2018).
31 Janus v. AFSCME 138 S. Ct. 2448 (2018), and see Cohen (2020).
32 Thanks to David Woodruff for reminding me of the importance of these paragraphs for my analysis.
33 Piketty (2014) empirically and handily undermines CEO claims to meritocratically justified 'super salaries'.
34 On the deadly effects of the doctrine of equal bargaining power in labor law, see Bagenstos (2020), and EPI (2020).
35 Recent estimates suggest that the annual sum that has shifted from workers to owners now tops $1 trillion. Every American worker who is not in the top 10 per cent of the income ladder is in effect sending an annual check for $12,000 to a richer person in the top 10 per cent (*New York Times*, 2020). The World Inequality Lab's 2018 report reveals that the global top 1 per cent of wage earners captured twice as much economic growth as the bottom 50 per cent between 1980 and 2016.
36 Hence Stiglitz (2020): 'In America, self-interested wealthy elites who want to secure their position at the top have formed a de facto unholy alliance with extremists (including white supremacists and neo-Nazis). By manipulating the political system and supporting measures to disenfranchise and suppress voters, they have effectively replaced American democracy with minority rule'.
37 The Democratic Party now has a strong programme for combating monopoly: https://prospect.org/power/house-antitrust-big-tech-report-not-about-big-tech/.

References

Alperovitz, G. (2017). *Principles of a pluralist commonwealth*. Retrieved from https://thenextsystem.org/principles.

Alperovitz, G., & Daly, L. (2008). *Unjust deserts*. New York: The New Press.

Alvaredo, F., Chancel, L., Piketty, T., Saez, E., & Zucman, G. (2018). *World inequality report*. Cambridge: Harvard University Press. Retrieved from https://wir2018.wid.world/files/download/wir2018-summary-english.pdf.
Anderson, E. (2017). *Private government*. Princeton: Princeton University Press.
Bagenstos, S. (2020). Lochner lives on. *Economic Policy Institute*. October 7. Retrieved from https://www.epi.org/publication/lochner-undermines-constitution-law-workplace-protections/.
Bagenstos, S.R. (2013). Employment law and social equality. *Michigan Law Review*, *112*(2), 225–273.
Baker, D. (2016). *Rigged: How globalization and the rules of the modern economy were structured to make the rich richer*. Washington, DC: Center for Economic and Policy Research.
Baker, D. (2018). Is intellectual property the root of all evil? Patents, copyrights, and inequality. CEPR Working Paper. October 2018. Retrieved from https://www.cepr.net/images/stories/reports/ip-2018-10.pdf.
Bartels, L.M. (2008). *Unequal democracy: The political economy of the new gilded age*. New York: Russell Sage Foundation and Princeton University Press.
Block, F. (2013). Relational work and the law: Recapturing the legal realist critique of market fundamentalism. *Journal of Law and Society*, *40*(1), 27–48.
Block, F. (2018). *Capitalism: The future of an illusion*. Berkeley: University of California.
Block, F., & Keller, M. (2011). *The state of innovation*. Boulder: Paradigm.
Block, F., & Somers, M.R. (2014). *The power of market fundamentalism: Karl Polanyi's critique*. Cambridge: Harvard University Press.
Block, S., & Sachs, B. (2020). A clean slate: Reforming law to empower workers. *Canadian Law of Work Forum*. March 4. Retrieved from https://www.cleanslateworkerpower.org/.
Braithewaite, J. (2008). *Regulatory capitalism*. Cheltenham: Edward Elgar.
Britton-Purdy, J., Singh Grewal, D., Kapczynski, A., & Rahman, K.S. (2020). Building a law-and-political-economy framework: Beyond the twentieth-century synthesis. *The Yale Law Journal*, *129*(6), 1784–1832.
Brown, W. (2019). *In the ruins of neoliberalism: The rise of antidemocratic politics in the West*. New York: Columbia University Press.
Buchanan, J.M. (2000). *The politics of public choice*. Indianapolis: Liberty Fund.
Buchanan, J.M., & Tullock, G. (1962). *The calculus of consent: Logical foundations of constitutional democracy*. Ann Arbor: University of Michigan Press.
Burgin, A. (2012). *The great persuasion: Reinventing free markets since the depression*. Cambridge: Harvard University Press.
Caulkin, S. (2013). What Warren Buffett can teach us all. *Financial Times*. May 12. Retrieved from https://www.ft.com/content/2a9be5ca-ae83-11e2-8316-00144feabdc0.
Chang, H.-J. (2002). *Kicking away the ladder*. London: Anthem.
Ciepley, D. (2020). Privatizing sovereignty, socializing property: What economics doesn't teach you about the corporation. LPE Project. February 18. Retrieved from https://lpeproject.org/blog/privatizing-sovereignty-socializing-property-what-economics-doesnt-teach-you-about-the-corporation/.
Clark, J.B. [1899] (2001). *The distribution of wealth: A theory of wages, interest and profits*. Library of Economics and Liberty. New York: The Macmillan Company. Retrieved from https://www.econlib.org/library/Clark/clkDW.html.
Cohen, A. (2020). *Supreme inequality: The Supreme Court's fifty-year battle for a more unjust America*. New York: Penguin.

Commons, J.R. (1924). *The legal foundations of capitalism*. New York: The MacMillan Company.

Commons, J.R. (1934). *Institutional economics: Its place in political economy*. New York: MacMillan.

Crouch, C. (2004). *Post-democracy*. Cambridge: Polity.

Crouch, C. (2011). *The strange non-death of neoliberalism*. Malden: Polity.

Crozier, M., Huntington, S.P., & Watanuki, J. (Eds.) (1975). *The crisis of democracy: Report on the governability of democracies to the trilateral commission*. New York: New York University Press.

Dale, G. (2016a). *Karl Polanyi: A life on the left*. New York: Columbia University Press.

Dale, G. (2016b). *Reconstructing Karl Polanyi*. London: Pluto Press.

Economic Policy Institute (EPI). (2020). *Unequal power*. Retrieved from https://www.epi.org/unequalpower/.

Esping-Andersen, G. (1990). *The three worlds of welfare capitalism*. Princeton: Princeton University Press.

Farrell, H. (2018). *Privatization as state transformation*. University Press Scholarship Online. Retrieved from doi:10.18574/nyu/9781479842933.003.0008.

Federici, S. (2012). The reproduction of labor power in the global economy and the unfinished feminist revolution. In S. Federici (Ed.), *Revolution at point zero: Housework, reproduction, and feminist struggle* (pp. 101–122). Oakland: PM Press.

Ferreras, I. (2017). *Firms as political entities: Saving democracy through economic bicameralism*. New York: Cambridge University Press.

Ferreras, I. (2020). Work: Democratize, decommodify, remediate. 29 October. Retrieved from https://democratizingwork.org/.

Fishkin, J., & Forbath, W.E. (2014). The anti-oligarchy constitution. *Boston University Law Review*, *94*(671). Research Paper No. 561. Retrieved from SSRN: https://ssrn.com/abstract=2431255.

Fishkin, J., & Forbath, W.E. (2015–2016). Reclaiming constitutional political economy: An introduction to the symposium on the constitution and economic inequality. *Texas Law Review*, *94*, 1287–1299.

Fligstein, N., &Vogel, S. (2020). Political economy after neoliberalism. *Boston Review*. October 6. Retrieved from https://bostonreview.net/class-inequality/neil-fligstein-steven-vogel-political-economy-after-neoliberalism.

Folbre, N., Gornick, J.C., Connolly, H., & Munzi, T. (2013). Women's employment, unpaid work, and economic inequality. In J.C. Gornik & M. Jäntti (Eds.), *Income inequality: Economic disparities and the middle class in affluent countries* (pp. 234–260). Stanford: Stanford University Press

Forbath, W. (2019). A political economy the constitution requires. *LPE Blog*. October 23. Retrieved from https://lpeproject.org/blog/title-tk/#more-2944.

Foroohar, R. (2016). *Makers and takers: The rise of finance and the fall of American business*. New York: Crown Business.

Fourcade, M., & Gordon, J. (2020). Learning like a state: Statecraft in the digital age. *Journal of Law and Political Economy*, *1*(1), 78–108.

Fraser, N. (2016). Contradictions of capitalism and care. *New Left Review*, *100*, 99–117.

Fried, B.H. (1998). *The progressive assault on laissez faire: Robert Hale and the first law and economics movement*. Cambridge: Harvard University Press.

Gilens, M., & Page, B.I. (2014). Testing theories of American politics: Elites, interest groups, and average citizens. *Perspectives on Politics*, *12*(3), 564–581.

Grewal, D.S. (2017). The legal constitution of capitalism. In H. Boushey, J.B. DeLong, & M. Steinbaum (Eds.), *After Piketty: The agenda for economics and inequality* (pp. 471–490). Cambridge: Harvard University Press.
Guinan, J., & O'Neill, M. (2018). The institutional turn: Labour's new political economy. *Renewal: A Journal of Labour Politics*, *26*(2), 5–16.
Guinan, J., & O'Neill, M. (2019). *The case for community wealth building*. Cambridge: Polity Press.
Hacker, J. (2011).The institutional foundations of middle-class democracy. *Policy Network*, *6*(5). Retrieved from http://www.policy-network.net/pno_detail.aspx?ID=3998&title=The-institutional-foundations-of-middle-class-democracy.
Hacker, J., & Pierson, P. (2020). *Let them eat tweets: How the right rules in an age of extreme inequality*. New York: Liveright Publishing Corp.
Hacker, J.S., & Pierson, P. (2010). *Winner-take-all politics: How Washington made the rich richer—and turned its back on the middle class*. New York: Simon & Schuster.
Hale, R.L. (1920). Law making by unofficial minorities. *Columbia Law Review*, *20*(4), 451–456.
Hale, R.L. (1923). Coercion and distribution in a supposedly non-coercive state. *Political Science Quarterly*, *38*(3), 470–494.
Hale, R.L. (1943). Bargaining, duress, and economic liberty. *Columbia Law Review*, *43*(5), 603–628.
Harcourt, B. (2011). *The illusion of free markets*. Cambridge: Harvard University Press.
Harwood, J. (2019). The GOP is attacking socialism, but Trump Fed pick Stephen Moore pits capitalism against democracy. *CNBC*. April 18. Retrieved from https://www.cnbc.com/2019/04/18/capitalism-trumps-democracy-for-trump-fed-pick-stephen-moore.html.
Heffner, A. (2020). En route to autocracy in America. *The American Prospect*. October 11. Retrieved from https://prospect.org/politics/en-route-to-autocracy-in-america/.
Hester, H. (2018). Care under capitalism: The crisis of "women's work". *IPPR Progressive Review*. Retrieved from https://onlinelibrary.wiley.com/doi/full/10.1111/newe.12074.
Hirschman, A.O. [1977] (2013). *The passions and the interests: Political arguments for capitalism before its triumph*. Princeton: Princeton University Press.
Hont, I. (2005). *Jealousy of trade*. Cambridge: Harvard University Press.
Howard, T., Galvin, R., Guinan, J., & Kelly, M. (2020). Owning our future after COVID-19. *Democracy Collaborative*. Retrieved from https://democracycollaborative.org/.
Janus v. Am. Fed'n of State, Cty., & Mun. Employees. (2018). Council 31, 138 S. Ct. 2448, 2501 (Kagan, J., dissenting).
Kapczynski, A. (2014). Intellectual property's leviathan. *Law and Contemporary Problems*, *77*(4), 131–145.
Kapczynski, A. (2018). The Lochnerized First Amendment and the FDA: Toward a more democratic political economy. *Columbia Law Review Online*, *118*. Retrieved from https://columbialawreview.org/content/the-lochnerized-first-amendment-and-the-fda-toward-a-more-democratic-political-economy/.
Kapczynski, A. (2020). The law of informational capitalism. *The Yale Law Journal*, *129*(5), 1276–1599.
Kennedy, L. (2019). Inequality: From redistribution to predistribution and beyond? *Social Europe*. May 2. Retrieved from https://www.socialeurope.eu/inequality-socialisation.
Khan, L. (2018). The new Brandeis movement: America's antimonopoly debate. *Journal of European Competition Law & Practice*, *9*(3), 131–132.

Khan, L., & Vaheesan, S. (2017). Market power and inequality: The antitrust counterrevolution and its discontents. *Harvard Law & Policy Review*. Retrieved from https://ssrn-com.proxy.lib.umich.edu/abstract=2769132.
Klein, S. (2020). *The work of politics: Making a democratic welfare state*. Cambridge: Cambridge University Press.
Koot, G.M. (1987). *English historical economics*. Cambridge: Cambridge University Press.
Krugman, P. (2014). Plutocrats against democracy. *New York Times*. October 23. Retrieved from https://www.nytimes.com/2014/10/24/opinion/paul-krugman-plutocrats-against-democracy.html.
Lynn, B. (2010). *Cornered: The new monopoly capitalism and the economics of destruction*. Hoboken: John Wiley & Sons.
Mackert, J. (2017). Why we need a new political economy of citizenship. Neo-liberalism, the bank crisis and the 'Panama Papers'. In J. Mackert & B.S. Turner (Eds.), *The transformation of citizenship. Vol. 1. Political economy* (pp. 99–117). London: Routledge.
MacLean, N. (2017). *Democracy in chains: The deep history of the radical right's stealth plan for America*. New York: Viking.
Malthus, T.R. [1803] (1992). *An essay on the principle of population*. Edited by D. Winch. Cambridge: Cambridge University Press.
Markovits, D. (2019). *The meritocracy trap: How America's foundational myth feeds inequality, dismantles the middle class, and devours the elite*. New York: Penguin.
Mazzucato, M. (2015). *The entrepreneurial state: Debunking public vs. private sector myths*. New York: Public Affairs.
Mazzucato, M. (2019). *The value of everything: Making and taking in the global economy*. New York: Penguin.
McCluskey, M. (2016). Constitutional economic justice: Structural power for 'We the people'. *Yale Law & Policy Review*, *35*(1), 271–296.
McCluskey, M. (2020). Countering the neoliberal structural constitution. *LPE Blog*. September 15. Retrieved from https://lpeproject.org/blog/countering-the-neoliberal-structural-constitution/.
Mirowski, P., & Plehwe, D. (2009). *The road from Mont Pèlerin*. Cambridge: Harvard University Press.
Murphy, L., & Nagel, T. (2002). *The myth of ownership: Taxes and justice*. New York: Oxford University Press.
New York Times. (2020). The jobs we need. *Editorial Board*, June 24. Retrieved from https://www.nytimes.com/2020/06/24/opinion/sunday/income-wealth-inequality america.html.
Novak, W. (2019). Institutional economics and the progressive movement for the social control of American business. *Business History Review*, *93*(4), 665–696.
O'Neill, M. (2017). Philosophy and public policy after Piketty. *Journal of Political Philosophy*, *25*(3), 343–375.
O'Neill, M. (2019). James Meade, public ownership, and the idea of a citizens' trust (with S. White). *International Journal of Public Policy*, *15*(1–2), 21–37.
O'Neill, M. (2020). Power, predistribution, and social justice. *Philosophy*, *95*(1), 63–91.
O'Neill, M. (2021). Social justice and economic systems: On Rawls, democratic socialism, and alternatives to capitalism. *Philosophical Topics*, *49*(1) (forthcoming). http://eprints.whiterose.ac.uk/165444/.
O'Neill, M., & Williamson, T. (2012a). The promise of predistribution. *Policy Network*. September 28. Retrieved from http://www.policy-network.net/pno_detail.aspx?ID=4262&title=The-Promise-of-Pre-distribution.

O'Neill, M., & Williamson, T. (Eds.) (2012b). *Property-owning democracy: Rawls and beyond*. Boston: Wiley-Blackwell.

Paine, T. [1795/6] (2015). *Agrarian justice*. Foreword by N.J. Altman. Washington: Social Security Works Education Fund.

Phillips-Fein, K. (2010). *Invisible hands*. New York: W. W. Norton & Company.

Piketty, T. (2014). *Capital in the twenty-first century*. Cambridge: Harvard University Press.

Piketty, T. (2020). *Capital and ideology*. Cambridge: Harvard University Press.

Piraino, T.A. Jr. (2007). Reconciling the Harvard and Chicago schools: A new antitrust approach for the 21st century. *Indiana Law Journal*, *82*(2), 346–409.

Pistor, K. (2019). *The code of capital*. Princeton: Princeton University Press.

Pistor, K. (2020). The value of law. *Theory and Society*, *49*(2), 165–186.

Polanyi, K. [1944] (2001). *The great transformation: The political and economic origins of our time*. Boston: Beacon Press.

Polanyi, K. (1957). The economy as instituted process. In K. Polanyi, C.M. Arensberg & W. Pearson (Eds.), *Trade and market in the early empires* (pp. 243–270). Chicago: University of Chicago.

Polanyi, K. (2014). *For a new West*. Edited by G. Resta & M. Catanzariti. Cambridge: Polity Press.

Poole, I. (2020). The popular mandate for a democratic economy in 2020. *The Next System Project*. November 3. Retrieved from https://thenextsystem.org/.

Posner, R. (1983). *The economics of justice*. Cambridge: Harvard University Press.

Purdy, J. (2018a). The left's guide to reclaiming the constitution. *New York Times*. September 10. Retrieved from https://www.nytimes.com/2018/09/10/opinion/brett-kavanaugh-supreme-court-constitution-democrats-.html.

Purdy, J. (2018b). Beyond the bosses' constitution: The First Amendment and class entrenchment. *Columbia Law Review*, *118*(7), 2159–2184.

Rahman, K.S. (2016a). *Democracy against domination*. New York: Oxford.

Rahman, K.S. (2016b). Domination, democracy, and constitutional political economy in the new gilded age: Towards a fourth wave of legal realism?, *Texas Law Review*, *94*(7), 1329–1359.

Rahman, K. S, (2016c). Challenging the new curse of bigness. *The American Prospect*. Retrieved from https://prospect.org/economy/challenging-new-curse-bigness/

Rahman, K.S. (2016d). From economic inequality to economic freedom: Constitutional political economy in the new gilded age. *Yale Law & Policy Review*, *35*(1), 321–336.

Rahman, K.S. (2017–18). Policymaking as power-building. *Southern California Interdisciplinary Law Journal*, *27*(2), 315–377.

Rahman, K. (2018). Constructing citizenship: Exclusion and inclusion through the governance of basic necessities. *Columbia Law Review*, *118*(8), 2447–2503.

Rahman, K.S., & Russon, H. (2019). *Civic power: Building American democracy in an era of Crisis*. Cambridge: Cambridge University Press.

Rancière, J. [2005] 2014). *Hatred of democracy*. New York: Verso.

Reich, R.B. (2015). *Saving capitalism: For the many, not the few*. New York: Knopf.

Roser, M., & Ortiz-Ospina, E. (2016). Income inequality: *Our world in data*. October. Retrieved from https://ourworldindata.org/income-inequality.

Saez, E., & Zucman, G. (2019). *The triumph of injustice: How the rich dodge taxes and how to make them pay*. New York: W. W. Norton & Company.

Sandel, M. (2020). *The tyranny of merit: What's become of the common good?* New York: Farrar, Straus and Giroux.

Schneider, N., & Vaheesan, S. (2019). There's more than one way to fight a monopoly. *The Atlantic*. August 11. Retrieved from https://www.theatlantic.com/ideas/archive/2019/08/fighting-monopoly-will-require-collective-power/595729.

Sitaraman, G. (2016). The puzzling absence of economic power in constitutional theory. *Cornell Law Review*, *101*(6), 1445–1532.

Sitaraman, G. (2017). *The crisis of the middle-class constitution*. New York: Vintage.

Sitaraman, G. (2019). *The great democracy: How to fix our politics, unrig the economy, and unite America*. New York: Basic Books.

Slobodian, Q. (2018). *Globalists: The end of empire and the birth of neoliberalism*. Cambridge: Harvard University Press.

Somers, M.R. (1990). Polanyi's intellectual legacy. In K. Polanyi-Levitt (Ed.), *The life and work of Karl Polanyi* (pp. 152–160). Montreal: Black Rose Books.

Somers, M.R. (1995). The 'mysteries' of property: Relationality, families, and community in Chartist narratives of political rights. In J. Brewer & S. Staves (Eds.), *Early modern conceptions of property* (pp. 62–92). London and New York: Routledge.

Somers, M.R. (1997). Deconstructing and reconstructing class formation theory: Narrativity, relational analysis, and social theory. In J.R. Hall (Ed.), *Reworking class* (pp. 73–106). Ithaca: Cornell University Press.

Somers, M.R. (1998). We're no angels: Realism, rational choice, and relationality in social science. *American Journal of Sociology*, *104*(3), 722–784.

Somers, M.R. (2008). *Genealogies of citizenship: Markets, statelessness, and the right to have rights*. Cambridge: Cambridge University Press.

Somers, M.R. (2012). Zombie entanglements: How corporate power stalks among us. *Socio-Economic Review*, *10*(3): 617–623.

Somers, M.R. (2017). How grandpa became a welfare queen: Social insurance, the economisation of citizenship, and a new political economy of moral worth. In J. Mackert & B.S. Turner (Eds.), *The transformation of citizenship. Vol. 1. Political Economy* (pp. 76–98). London: Routledge.

Somers, M.R. (2018). Utopianism and the reality of society: Decoding Polanyi's socialism, freedom, and the alchemy of misrecognition. In M. Brie & C. Thomasberger (Eds.), *Karl Polanyi's vision of a socialist transformation* (pp. 91–109). Montreal: Black Rose Books.

Somers, M.R. (2020a). The moral economy of the capitalist crowd: Utopianism, the reality of society, and the market as a morally instituted process in Karl Polanyi's The Great Transformation. *Humanity: An International Journal of Human Rights, Humanitarianism, and Development*, *11*(2), 227–234. Retrieved from doi.10.1353/hum.2020.0017.

Somers, M.R. (2020b). Even the Republican 'skinny' relief bill failed. How is such unnecessary suffering justified? *The Guardian*. September 14. Retrieved from https://www.theguardian.com/commentisfree/2020/sep/14/republican-skinny-coronavirus-relief-mitch-mcconnell?CMP=Share_iOSApp_Other.

Somers, M.R., & Block, F. (2020). Polanyi's democratic socialist vision: Piketty through the lens of Polanyi. In R. Desai & K. Polanyi Levitt (Eds.), *Karl Polanyi and twenty-first century capitalism* (pp. 211–230). Manchester: University of Manchester Press.

Somers, M.R., & Roberts, C.N. (2008). Toward a new sociology of rights: A genealogy of 'buried bodies' of citizenship and human rights. *Annual Review of Law and Social Science*, *4*, 385–425.

Stedman Jones, D. (2012). *Masters of the universe*. Princeton: Princeton University Press.

Steinbaum, M. (2019). Antitrust, the gig economy, and labor market power. *Law & Contemporary Problems*, *82*(3), 45–64.

Stiglitz, J.E. (2015). *Rewriting the rules of the American economy: An agenda for growth and shared prosperity*. New York: Norton.

Stiglitz, J.E. (2019). *People, power and profits: Progressive capitalism for an age of discontent*. New York and London: W. W. Norton & Company.

Stiglitz, J.E. (2020). Solidarity now. *Project Syndicate*. February 28. Retrieved from https://www.project-syndicate.org/onpoint/abandoning-neoliberalism-reforming-capitalism-globalization-by-joseph-e-stiglitz-2020-02.

Streeck, W. (2014). *Buying time: The delayed crisis of democratic capitalism*. New York: Verso.

Streeck, W. (2016). *How will capitalism end?* New York: Verso.

Summers, L. (2020). U.S. workers need more power. *The Washington Post*. June 28. Retrieved from https://www.washingtonpost.com/opinions/2020/06/28/us-workers-need-more-power/.

Teachout, Z. (2020). *Break 'em up: Recovering our freedom from Big Ag*, Big Tech, and Big Money. New York: All Points Books.

Teachout, Z., & Khan, L. (2014). Market structure and political law: A taxonomy of power. *Duke Journal of Constitutional Law and Public Policy*, *9*(1), 38–74.

Tebbe, N. (2020). A democratic political economy for the First Amendment. *Cornell Law Review*, *105*(3), 959–1021.

Teles, S. (2012). *The rise of the conservative legal movement: The battle for control of the law*. Princeton: Princeton University Press.

Thomas, A. (2017). *Republic of equals: Predistribution and property-owning democracy*. Oxford: Oxford University Press.

Thompson, E.P. (1971). The moral economy of the English crowd in the eighteenth century. *Past & Present*, *50*(1), 76–136.

Vaheesan, S. (2020). Privileging consolidation and proscribing cooperation: The perversity of contemporary antitrust law. *Journal of Law and Political Economy*, *28*(1), 28–45.

Veblen, T. (1904). *Theory of Business Enterprise*. New York: Charles Sribner & Sons.

Veblen, T. (1936). The preconceptions of economic science. In Wesley C. Mitchell (Ed.), *What Veblen Taught: Selected writings of Thorstein Veblen* (pp. 39–150). New York: The Viking Press.

Vogel, S. (1996). *Freer markets, more rules*. Ithaca: Cornell University Press.

Vogel, S. (2018). *Marketcraft: How governments make markets work*. New York: Oxford University Press.

Vogel, S. (2019). Elizabeth Warren wants to stop inequality before it starts. *The New York Times*. 3 January. Retrieved from https://www.nytimes.com/2019/01/03/opinion/elizabeth-warren-economic-policy-democrats.html.

Von Hayek, F.A. [1939] (1980). The economic conditions of interstate federalism. In F.A. von Hayek (Ed.), *Individual and economic order* (pp. 255–572). Chicago: University of Chicago Press.

Warren, E. (2011). In Lucy Madison: 'Elizabeth Warren: "There is nobody in this country who got rich on his own"'. *CBS News*. September 22. Retrieved from https://www.cbsnews.com/news/elizabeth-warren-there-is-nobody-in-this-country-who-got-rich-on-his-own/.

Whitehouse, S. (2020). America's captured courts. *Project Syndicate*. November 25. Retrieved from https://www.project-syndicate.org/commentary/dark-money-federalist-society-captured-us-courts-by-sheldon-whitehouse-2020-11.

Woodruff, D. (2014). Commons, Hale, Polanyi, and, naturally, Piketty. *Political Economy in Public*. July 4. Retrieved from http://politicaleconomyinpublic.blogspot.com/2014/07/commons-hale-polanyi-and-naturally.html?m=1.

World Inequality Lab. (2018). World inequality report. Retrieved from https://wir2018.wid.world/.

Zuboff, S. (2019). *The age of surveillance capitalism: The fight for a human future at the new frontier of power*. New York: Public Affairs.

4 The politics of bailing-out the rich

The role of 'systemic importance' within the European Banking Union

Andreas Kallert

Introduction

More than ten years ago, the financial crisis was at its peak: based on, among other things, over-accumulation and low profit rates, huge debt-financed spending, and new financial instruments, the crisis affected almost all banks and other financial institutions (Friedman, 2011; Krugman, 2009; Roubini & Mihm, 2011). Consequently, this global financial crisis (GFC) led to a number of impending failures of large banks that were considered *too big to fail*. Confronted with these imminent insolvencies, national governments rescued most of the banks through large-scale public bail-outs. The main argument was the proclaimed systemic risk proceeding from major banks, hence the danger of crisis spreading from one bank to another and/or from the financial system to the real economy. Small savings and even rents were at stake, according to the many supporters of state interventions.

As a result, the immense costs of bank failure were shifted from the shareholders and creditors to the public budgets and finally to the taxpayers. Hence, in the aftermath of these state interventions, state debt levels reached new peaks. For some EU countries like Spain, Greece, or Portugal, the (re-)financing of sovereign bonds became increasingly expensive or even impossible (Lapavitsas, 2012). Subsequently, democratically contested austerity policies were imposed on broad parts of these societies (Hadjimichalis, 2018). The euro-system was on the brink of collapsing and was only ensured through a security umbrella provided by the EU member states and the European Central Bank (Bieling, 2013). These uncoordinated, ad-hoc bail-outs showed the lack of a common and functioning financial regulation on a European level (Howarth & Quaglia, 2015) and, generally, the need for macroprudential supervision ensuring financial stability (Baker, 2013; Borio, 2011; Helleiner, 2014; Hellwig, 2015). Subsequently, the European Union's regulatory response tries to harmonize banking supervision and resolution in order to minimize public risks in cases of imminent failure – thus bailing-in instead of bailing-out creditors and shareholders. But the Banking Union (BU) as a European supervisory authority directly covers only systemically important financial institutions (SIFIs). For this purpose, the BU strongly relies on a definition of SIFIs, wherefore some criteria like size, complexity, or substitutability are matched to a bench-marking of systemic importance. These definitions suggest an objectivity of systemic importance and consequently an improvement of financial regulation.

Against this, the paper argues that systemic importance serves rather as a means to socialize private losses whereas the previous profits are privatized. Therefore, the perspective of a cultural political economy is adopted as a productive and critical research approach. Consequently, a critique of systemic importance and concepts relating to this feature is necessary. For this, the integration of systemic importance into the BU is briefly illustrated – starting from the bail-outs during the GFC and moving to the institutionalization of the complex bail-in cascade within the BU. The financial status of holders of bail-in-able capital is analyzed with a special focus on Italian bank bonds. Subsequently, the paper aims to criticize and to discuss the first implementation under the new regulatory framework. The case of the Italian Monte dei Paschi (MPS) shows: despite the rules of the BU, taxpayers' money is still used to recover domestic banks and to bail-out their creditors promoted by a broad coalition of financial capital, affected national governments, and experts. The discursive strategies of systemic importance and financial stability under the pretext of saving small savers succeed in avoiding consequent bail-ins of financial capital by shifting risks and losses to public finances even under the new regulations. Hence, the paper contributes to the existing literature some first results of hegemony (re-)production in the area of finance following the GFC.

Cultural political economy as a critical research approach to hegemonial struggles

To investigate the mechanisms of the ongoing socialization of private losses in the banking sector, the perspective of a cultural political economy (CPE) promises to be a helpful approach for insights into this task. CPE as a synthesis of regulationist, state-theoretical, and discourse-analytic concepts navigates between constructivism and structuralism taking into account both the roles of ideas, discourses, culture and those of capitalist 'iron laws', market forces, and forms (Jessop & Scherrer, 2015; Jessop & Sum, 2006). Concerning the latter, bank rescues and the role of systemic importance in them have to be put into the greater context of financialization including the development of new articulations of financial capital. Thereby, the structural limitations and selectivity as a consequence thereof can be comprehended (Sum & Jessop, 2015). Within these structural limits, the discursive modus of the generalization of particular interests needs to be understood (Caterina, 2017). What are the main arguments in favour of public bail-out and against private bail-in? What are the 'powerful narratives' (Best, 2009, p. 461) tending to bail-out instead of bail-in?

A CPE analysis conducts 'an ideological critique that exposes the socially constructed nature of hegemonies and dominations in which discourses and social practices produce strategic logics that legitimize the sectional interests of particular groups at the expense of others' (Sum & Jessop, 2014, p. 230). The discursive strategies of various fractions form causal stories through which certain crisis phenomena are highlighted and causations are attributed in specific ways (Kutter & Jessop, 2015; Stone, 1989). But not every social actor is able to obtain access in the same way to shape such causal stories. Different levels of interpretative power allow us to construe which crisis is happening to whom and to predict large impacts to broad society in order to mobilize (popular) support for a specific crisis response (Heinrich & Jessop, 2015). All in all, CPE is interested in the struggles from social construal to social construction to hegemony and, hence, the contested generalization of particular interests.

Regarding the empirical study on bank rescues within the BU, the paper conducts a context analysis which is followed by an analysis of the (discursive) strategies (Kannankulam & Georgi, 2014). The context analysis introduces the BU and the resolution mechanisms by emphasizing the impact of systemic importance for the bail-in system and by critically putting it into the greater context of financialization. Subsequently, the participation rate and asset situation of (bank) bond holders are discussed. Also, the first implementation under the new rules of the BU is presented: the prevented collapse of the Italian MPS in 2016. Afterwards, the actor analysis is based on a critical discourse analysis (Jäger & Jäger, 2007) of the financial reporting on the investigated societal conflict in the leading newspaper the *Financial Times*.

By doing this, the recent bail-outs can be examined, drawing on specific discursive strategies like financial stability or systemic risk. This CPE approach provides 'historically sensitive conceptual frameworks for understanding real capitalism with its characteristic crisis-tendencies and improbable social regularization, but with an explicit commitment to analysing the level of the concrete as well as the dimension of semiosis' (Belfrage & Hauf, 2015, p. 328).

That means: a CPE-inspired analysis questions how banks and their creditors succeed in establishing themselves as systemic and subsequently avoid being bailed-in. The socialization of private losses (and vice versa the previous privatization of profits) and hence the redistribution and shifting of taxpayers' money into private hands is considered a highly political struggle. Therefore, it's essential to understand *how* the financial sector succeeds in establishing itself as of general interest – which the paper shows by using the example of MPS's rescue in 2016.

Bank bail-outs: Systemic importance since the global financial crisis

The global financial crisis (GFC) evolved quite slowly with stagnating or even falling prices for private houses in the USA in the middle of 2006 – after skyrocketing prices in the preceding years (Financial Crisis Inquiry Commission, 2011; Kessler, 2011). Long before the famous fall of Lehman Brothers in September 2008, financial institutions like New Century, Bear Stearns, Northern Rock, and IKB ran into problems and subsequently went bankrupt, were absorbed by rival companies, or received public subsidies. However, these imminent insolvencies were handled employing ad-hoc negotiations between governmental departments, regulatory boards, and financial institutions mostly without fixed methods of decision-making. But it was only in the aftermath of Lehman, that the G-7 governments agreed to rescue all then so-called systemically important financial institutions.

Like other countries, the German government imposed a legal framework in favour of domestic banks with a volume of almost half a trillion euro. To get some of the subsidies, German banks had to be systemically important without closer definition of this feature despite taking into account liabilities, risks, deposits, and cross-linkages (FMStFG, 2008). This quite loose criterion implied that even very small financial institutions like Aareal Bank got fresh equity and guarantees from state funds (FMSA, 2015). This state-run support of domestic banks wasn't specific to Germany but to almost all countries affected by the crisis (Grossman & Woll, 2014). Extensive sums were spent on financial institutions: whereas the USA alone mobilized $3.6 trillion, Ireland raised $613 billion and therewith more than double its GDP (European Commission Competition, 2011; Woll, 2011).

Although large amounts of public money were spent, even after the crisis some banks especially in southern euro countries still faced problems with nonperforming loans (NPLs), low profitability, and lack of equity. Together with rising government debt levels, these increasing and persistent imbalances on a sovereign and private level menaced a new crisis on the financial markets, possibly spreading to other countries and to the real economy. The necessity for common financial regulation in the EU was growing given the ongoing crisis despite the national subsidies for banks (Ferran, 2014). It became clear that, especially in a monetary union like the euro area, imbalances caused by close links between public sector finances and the banking sector can easily spill over national borders and cause financial problems in other EU countries (Howarth & Quaglia, 2016b; Rynck, 2015). Therefore, the European Commission proposed common mechanisms for supervision, resolution, and deposit guarantee – the Banking Union (BU). Referring to the structural power of large banks, Culpepper and Tesche (2019) argue that the diverging (strategic) interests between small and big banks within a broader intergovernmental setting were central in pushing forward the BU: the large and widely internationalized banks benefit from the BU and, hence, bolster their competitive positions against smaller rivals.

The BU consists of three pillars of which two are already implemented and fully activated (Castañeda, Mayes & Wood, 2016; Howarth & Quaglia, 2016a). The Single Supervisory Mechanism (SSM) as the first pillar is the new system of banking supervision for Europe. It comprises the European Central Bank (ECB) and the national supervisory authorities of the participating countries and became effective in November 2014.

The second pillar contains the resolution of SIFIs and went into full force in the beginning of 2016. The proclaimed main purpose of this Single Resolution Mechanism (SRM) is to ensure the efficient resolution of failing banks with both minimal costs for taxpayers and minimal impact on financial stability and the (real) economy (Single Resolution Board, 2016). Thereby, according to the new rules the creditors and investors have to bear the losses of banking default (i.e. bail-in) instead of public money being used to refinance financial institutions (i.e. bail-out) (Tröger, 2017b). As a supervisor, the ECB plays an important role in deciding whether a bank is failing or is likely to fail. A Single Resolution Board (SRB) ensures swift decision-making procedures in case of failing or likely to fail banks and, if no private sector measures are available, to restore the bank to viability: resolution in the event of public interest or otherwise being liquidated under normal insolvency proceedings. Subsequently, it enables resolution authorities within a complex bail-in regime to write down and convert liabilities (like bank bonds) into equity – in line with the hierarchy of creditors starting with the riskiest junior bonds and proceeding to the senior bonds. Lastly, even deposits above €100,000 can be bailed-in.

The third pillar, still in legislative procedures, contains the European deposit insurance scheme (EDIS). Thereby, the national guarantee schemes are to be harmonized but there is still strong opposition especially by Germany (Howarth & Quaglia, 2018).

For both supervision and resolution, the more or less systemic importance of a financial institution makes a big difference. The grade of systemic importance is now an integral part of the mode of financial regulation in the current accumulation regime – both on a European and a global level such as global SIFIs (Financial Stability Board, 2018; Kranke & Yarrow, 2018). If a bank is labelled systemically important, European supervision and resolution authorities are responsible; if not, the respective national authorities stay in charge but under the new regulations of the BU. Whereas during the financial crisis, no common definition for systemic importance existed. There are now fixed and transparent criteria for this classification. Determining criteria are size (>€30 billion), (relative) economic importance, cross-border activities, direct public financial assistance, and the fact of being one of the three most significant credit institutions in a state (Regulation EU, 2014).

These definitions suggest an objectivity estimation of systemic importance and consequently an improvement in financial regulation regarding transparency (Mügge & Perry, 2014). In case of failure, SIFI banks fall within the remit of the stricter rules of the SRM rather than national measurements and insolvency procedures. Besides, decisions regarding failing financial institutions are withdrawn from domestic politics and their influencers and shifted to, on paper, a more technocratic, supra-national level. In theory, these newly implemented financial regulations seem to work quite well. Compared with the high public costs following the bail-outs during the GFC, there is now a detailed framework that should prevent bail-outs at the expense of taxpayers' money.

But the concept of systemic importance comes along with the goal of ensuring financial stability, accordingly avoiding systemic risks which is seen as indispensable for economic growth. Hence, the fall of a SIFI endangers the stability of the financial markets (Barth & Wihlborg, 2016). However, defining stability in a capitalist economic system in which crisis are immanent is a strongly political task (Aglietta, 2000; Kindleberger & Aliber, 2011). Especially in a finance-led accumulation regime, the hazard for crisis is higher compared to the Fordist regime up to the 1970s (Sablowski, 2011; Stockhammer, 2014). In particular the financial markets in neoliberalism are vulnerable to ups and downs in rapid succession.

Likewise, it is necessary to take into consideration the processes of financialization which refer to the increasing importance of financial markets, motives, institutions, and elites in economy, society, and the state apparatus (Epstein, 2005; Heires & Nölke, 2014; Mader, Mertens & van der Zwan, 2020). Poulantzas conceptualized the modern, capitalist state as 'a relationship of forces, or more precisely the material condensation of such a relationship among classes and class fractions, such as this is expressed within the state in a necessarily specific form' (Poulantzas, 1978, p. 129). Therefore, with growing financialization the interests of financial capital are better able to prevail against other particular interests and are reflected accordingly in public policy, including financial regulation – among other things due to the immanent 'structural selectivity of the state' (Jessop, 1999). Financialization embraces not only financial institutions but also the everyday life of more and more citizens: private pensions, insurances in various circumstances, the expansion of consumer credits, student loans, or housing mortgages (Mertens & Meyer-Eppler, 2014). The rationality of financing has found its way into our thinking in a more concrete and tangible modus. Consequently, the probability for policies in favour of ensuring capital investments – such as bail-outs or moderate regulations – is rising with the scale of financialization.

Who holds (bank) bonds?

To break the complexity of bail-in-able investments down to concrete numbers and participation rates, the following section approaches the distribution of bond holders (governmental, corporate, banks, and others) in the euro area with special focus on Italy. Generally, only a small fraction of households owns bonds (4.6 per cent) which can be bailed-in according to the resolution scheme. In addition to this, the lower deciles of total financial asset portfolios hold almost no risky financial assets (mutual funds, shares, bonds) whereas the participation rate for the highest decile is 64.5 per cent. The smaller the financial asset portfolios are, the higher is the share of deposits and with it the lower the share of risky financial assets. By contrast, the top 10 per cent of financial portfolios (more than €102,900) consists of 26.2 per cent risky assets (European Central Bank, 2016).

For Italy, the figures differ a bit: the number of households owning bonds (13 per cent) is above the euro area average whereas the number for shares is below (3.7 per cent). All in all, the participation rate in risky assets for Italian households is almost the same: 22.8 per cent in the euro area compared to the Italian 22.6 per cent. Unsurprisingly, the total financial assets of the lower deciles are very small: the lowest four Italian deciles own between €0 and €4,900 in total financial assets whereas the conditional median for Italian households holding bonds is €25,000 (European Central Bank, 2017).

Focusing on bank bonds which are generally bail-in-able, Lindner and Redak (2017) have shown the bias towards wealthy and high-income households. Only very few Italian households (5.4 per cent) own bank bonds (16.4 per cent of the top 10 per cent wealthy families vs. 4.2 per cent of the bottom 90 per cent). On average, these households hold €49,300 (conditional median €30,000) in bank bonds. Their mean income is almost twice that of all households (€60,200 vs. €33,400) and their mean net wealth exceeds that of all households by a factor of 2.3 (€518,000 vs. €226,400).

That implies that any potential losses from bank bond investments affect only very few households in the lower 90 per cent (regarding net wealth) and even in the top 10 per cent only a small minority is affected which is anyway more affluent in terms of income. Extending this bank bond perspective by deposits above €100,000 and investment funds, the households potentially affected by a bail-in are even more dominated by rich people. In Italy, only 6.8 per cent of the bottom 90 per cent of households (regarding gross wealth) owns bail-in-able assets compared to 32.1 per cent of the top 10 per cent of households. These households holding bail-in-able assets have a mean and median net wealth of €539,800 and €369,700 (all Italian households €226,400 and €146,200). Their median share of bail-in-able assets in relation to gross wealth stands at 9.1 per cent (Lindner & Redak, 2017).

It has to be added that these riskier assets in particular have much higher yields than more conservative investments or, in contrast, the categorical impossibility of participating in any investments because of the lack of any (money) capital at all. In addition to these numbers which do not differentiate between senior and junior bank bonds, the *Financial Times* (11.7.2016) reported on the holders of subordinated bonds issued by Italian banks: accordingly, between a half and a third of the €60 billion of these Italian junior bonds are in the hands of just 60,000 retail investors who alone own €5 billion of MPS bonds. This implies that retail investors would hold a mean investment between €333,000 and €500,000 of these especially risky and high-yielding debt securities which are prior to bail-in in the resolution schema of the BU.[1]

All in all, Italian households with bail-in-able assets are affluent in terms of wealth and income on an aggregated level. Hence, they have high financial resilience to absorb shocks from asset devaluation and receive large interest payments. The other way around, the vast majority of Italian households are not affected by a potential bail-in because they don't hold any bail-in-able assets. That doesn't mean that there aren't any less wealthy bank bond holders who would potentially lose big portions of their financial assets in cases of bail-in. But these relatively poor retail investors holding bank bonds are exceptions.

The crisis of Italian Monte dei Paschi: The politics of bailing-out the rich under the pretext of saving the poor

As stated above, the BU tries to respond to some of the critique through more efficient supervision and resolution – according to the new rules for resolution, investors' and creditors' money is to be used instead of taxpayers' money to ensure the continuity of critical banking functions (Binder, 2016). But there are exceptions: before a minimum bail-in of investors amounting to at least 8 per cent of total liabilities has occurred, government money can only be injected in emergency cases to remedy a serious disturbance in the economy and to preserve financial stability (Götz, Krahnen & Tröger, 2017). However, the scope for interpreting the outcome of a bank insolvency ex ante as a serious economic disturbance and danger for financial stability is immense. Hence, high (governmental and/or finance-led) interpretative power and authority (Heinrich & Jessop, 2015) facilitate the rating of such events as a potential or probable crisis – opposition, parliament, civil society, and academics are often not able to counter these interpretations in the hurry of resolution decisions and under the circumstances of ever-present business secrets.

The case of Monte dei Paschi di Siena (MPS) illustrates this bias towards the executive power and the powerful narratives arguing in favour of public bail-out. MPS is ranked as the oldest bank in the world and, after UniCredit and Intesa Sanpaolo, the third biggest Italian bank. Ahead of the GFC, MPS undertook an expansive policy with high-priced acquisitions and new business activity especially related to (hidden) derivatives. With the beginning of the Italian sovereign-debt crisis (2011), MPS sustained huge losses on bonds and derivatives, the share price was dropping, and a first governmental bail-out by the Bank of Italy of over €3.9 billion was implemented. Even after more recapitalizations, further losses vaporized parts of the equity, and MPS failed the ECB banking stress test in 2014 (European Banking Authority, 2014). But the bank still suffered considerably from NPLs. Various attempts to sell NPLs via securitization didn't meet enough private demand – with the packing of bad loans into securitized debt obligations, the same techniques from before 2008 were applied, shifting risks from one actor to another. In the middle of 2016, MPS stood as the worst performer in the EU-wide stress test with negative equity as a result of the adverse stress test scenario (European Banking Authority, 2016). One final effort to raise five billion euro of private equity was cancelled in December 2016 despite several pre-underwriting agreements of global banks. MPS was still afflicted with NPLs easily surpassing the equity – therefore, at the end of 2016 the bank was close to both insolvency and illiquidity.

As a bank ranked as SIFI and supervised by the ECB, according to the resolution rules of the BU, bail-in-able capital up to 8 per cent ('the private sector involvement') had to be used before any public money may be spent (Tröger, 2017a). Hence, the Italian government pushed the European Commission to allow an exemption: so-called 'precautionary recapitalization' to avoid serious economic disturbance and preserve financial stability. Albeit, this instrument shall be confined to solvent institutions unable to raise capital privately in markets (Mesnard, Margerit & Magnus, 2017). Finally, on 23 December 2016 the Italian government passed a decree to bail-out MPS drawing on precautionary recapitalization. After long negotiations between the Commission and the Italian authorities, the precautionary recapitalization was approved on 4 July 2017. The total sum of capital injected amounts to €8.1 billion which includes the contribution of MPS's shareholders and junior bondholders in the amount of €4.3 billion (i.e. bail-in) as well as a capital injection of €3.9 billion by Italy (i.e. bail-out). Out of the bailed-in money, Italy will pay €1.5 billion to compensate the retail bondholders supposed to be victims of mis-selling (European Commission, 2017). Taken together, the Italian government again rescued one of its domestic banks with €5.4 billion of public money by avoiding the trigger of an ordinary resolution scheme which would have forced all bail-in-able liabilities into bail-in.

In the following actor analysis, it is illustrated how this generalization of particular interests was achieved, employing various discursive strategies and alliances. Therefore, the *Financial Times* reporting on BU and resolution in general as well as the case of MPS in particular is analysed. The entire discourse corpus consists of some 650 articles of the daily newspaper the *Financial Times* (printed European edition) between 1 January 2016 and 16 September 2018, which were selected through keyword search.[2] Subsequently, some first results are presented in a compact way and summarized in Table 4.1.

'The imperative of financial stability'

At the beginning of 2016, the stricter bail-in rules regarding resolution and state-aid for stumbling banks were activated. Financial capital groups like PIMCO (asset manager) and Moody's (rating agency) appreciated these regulatory steps but, from the start, they showed the way for one future strategic debate concerning the bail-in of bank bondholders: 'The broad distinction is between retail and wholesale investors' (*Financial Times*, 15.1.16). In the first half of 2016, the NPLs of MPS were increasingly addressed by discussing (financial) industry- or public-led equity contributions and the corresponding role of bail-in of MPS's shareholders and bondholders. At this time, EU institutions like the Commission or the SRB insisted on observing the new rules and received support especially from German officials. Hence, the German Chancellor Merkel rebuffed demands for exceptions to the bail-in rules in the case of MPS: 'We cannot change them [the rules] every two years' (*Financial Times*, 1.7.16). But the overall narrative was already shifting towards a causal chain in which the bail-in of MPS's bondholders was linked with contagion (Italian Finance Minister Padoan), financial stability (Italian insurer Generali), and even systemic crisis (journalists). MPS was considered as a major risk to Italian financial stability and as 'too big to fail' and was consequently called 'the elephant in the room' (*Financial Times*, 11.4.16). There was talk of the (relatively) weak European financial system and extra-ordinary times (particularly Brexit) in which a more anti-EU atmosphere could be sparked by 'telling pappa and mama their savings are being written down due to a letter from Brussels' (*Financial Times*, 16.7.16). Thus, exemptions (PIMCO) to the bail-in rules and flexibility (Padoan) were postulated. For example, the world's biggest asset manager BlackRock argued that state debt as a result of bail-out should not count anymore for EU fiscal rules in these times interpreted by various actors as a crisis. Accordingly, the French government adopted these interpretations and considered it its 'duty to show solidarity with the Italian government' and to 'apply the rules in an intelligent manner' (*Financial Times*, 12.7.16).

Table 4.1 Summarized results of actor analysis concerning the rescue of Monte dei Paschi in 2016

Relevant social fractions	*Discursive strategies*	*Causal stories and narratives*	*Preferred solutions*
Capital groups (e.g. asset manager, bank, insurer)	Weak European banks; presence of large numbers of retail investors; financial stability; too big to fail; flexibility in BU ('don't break the rules but problem of interpretation'); distinction between retail and wholesale investors	Bail-in → financial stability and economic growth in danger ('chain reaction', 'panic') Bail-in → raising borrowing costs for sovereign debt	NPLs → securitization (business opportunity); state-led equity contributions; Exemptions to bail-in rules in times of impending financial instability
European Commission	State aid rules; search for exemptions; rejection of Italian bad bank	Allowing state-aid under certain conditions → securing stability and pro-EU atmosphere	Allowing precautionary recapitalization and bail-in but: compensation of 'mis-sold' retail investors; securitization of NPLs
European Central Bank (incl. Single Resolution Board)	Fulfilling bail-in rules; Italy missed opportunity to establish public bad banks in 2012	Up from middle of 2016: bail-out is a matter of public interest → stabilizing European banking market	Use of exemptions in BU rules but generally pro completing BU (EDIS)
Italian government	Large numbers of retail investors; mis-sold retail investors; need for flexibility in BU; extra-ordinary times	Bail-in of retail investors → 'disaster for credibility and confidence'; bail-in leads to contagion	Public bail-out and reimbursement; precautionary recapitalization
Other governments (especially Germany/ France)	Germany: insisting on BU rules France: showing solidarity with Italy; need for flexibility	Germany: complying with the rules → precondition for completing BU Bail-in → danger of anti-EU atmosphere	Germany: reducing NPLs France: completing BU (EDIS); exemptions to bail-in rules
Organic intellectuals (academics, journalists)	Emphasizing pensioner suicide; MPS as major risk and too big to fail	Bail-in → 'social disaster', affects 'small guys' Bail-in → political and systemic risk	Avoiding bail-in of retail investors; bail-in as worthy aim for the future; completing BU (EDIS)

All this shows that concepts of systemic risk or financial stability relating to systemic importance in general are not definable in an objective way. Albeit, these concepts are critical for the rulebook of the BU and especially for exceptions within this rulebook. An Italian banker illustrated that point strikingly: 'Italy is not asking to suspend or break the rules but it's clear there is a problem of interpretation' (*Financial Times*, 12.7.16). Accordingly, different social actors can refer to financial stability and the postulated danger of it which than shapes the possible policy answers to that situation. Hence, the 'imperative of financial stability demands that the state be the backstop' (*Financial Times*, 6.12.16). Therefore, there is a powerful alliance of the Italian and French governments, organic intellectuals (analysts, academics, journalists), the Commission (finally allowing public recapitalization), and the international financial capital which follows the causal story: a bail-in of MPS's bonds may cause a 'chain reaction across the European banking system' (*Financial Times*, 16.4.16) and set off 'panic among investors and depositors' (*Financial Times*, 2.5.16) and, consequently, a state-backed bail-out of MPS is essential. Ultimately, the long opposing and in financial analysis mighty ECB is also moving towards bail-out in 'exceptional circumstances' (ECB President Draghi (*Financial Times*, 22.7.16)).

Bail-in as 'social disaster' for the 'small guys'

There is one omnipresent narrative behind the dominant bail-out positions despite the new regulations in which state-aid is mandatorily linked to bail-in: the involvement of retail investors and depositors, meaning alleged small savers according to the discourse of the financial press. From the beginning of the analyzed crisis of MPS, various actors argued that these small savers should be protected against the losses of their savings and therefore the bail-out would be a matter of public interest. The presence of large numbers of retail investors in Italy was emphasized to give further weight to this urgency. Accordingly, the bailing-in of such assets would be a 'disaster for credibility and confidence' as maintained by Italian Prime Minister Renzi (*Financial Times*, 4.8.16). Even losses for the riskiest bonds were ruled out because of the 'severe loss of political capital' and the danger to financial stability (*Financial Times*, 15.7.16). Just a couple of days later, asset manager PIMCO agreed with that reading and added that a 'broad bail-in' also posed steep risks to economic growth (*Financial Times*, 19.7.16). Furthermore, the narrative of mis-sold retail investors was adopted to underline the unfair results of a bail-in. Therefore, the suicide of a pensioner whose Banca Etruria bond of €100,000 was wiped out during the state-backed rescue of four small Italian banks in 2015 was used in quite a cynical way: 'If we bail in subordinated debt, people will not be able to live' (*Financial Times*, 11.7.16). Consequently, a professor of commercial law called a bail-in a 'social disaster': 'The people who will get hurt are the small guys' (*Financial Times*, 24.11.16). Finally, the Italian government and the Commission agreed to compensate retail investors holding bailed-in subordinated bonds with high yields.

The combination of mis-sold and small savers in a situation generally interpreted as a crisis is fundamental to achieve broad consent to the public bail-out of a private bank. It helps to legitimize the political project of bailing-out financial capital and the rich. For this, the reimbursement of retail investors can be seen as a compensation to stabilize a hegemonial configuration in which the tax-paid socialization of private losses is of general interest – despite BU rules in order to prevent exactly that. Especially in a finance-led accumulation regime with high dependency on financial markets – as is the case in privatized pension systems – the probability of policies in favour of financial capital is high. The multiple remarks on the suicide of a pensioner as a result of a bail-in can take full effect in supporting public reimbursements of retail investors.

In contrast, a counter-narrative criticizing this ongoing socialization is not able to become established. The strategically postulated consequences of a bail-in for ordinary depositors and bond holders as a social disaster and damaging for both financial stability and economic growth are promoted by all social fractions from organic intellectuals to politicians to financial capital. They hold discursive positions from which to define possible outcomes and to shape appropriate policy answers (Scherrer, 2011). Albeit, the narrative of the mis-sold and small retail investors could be easily deconstructed bearing in mind the aggregated asset situation of bank bond holders. This makes the image of the small saver at least questionable and points rather to quite wealthy people having profited from the high interest of principally bail-in-able assets that are now being bailed-out.

Summarized, the exception to the new European rules on bail-out is justified by the danger of both systemic risk and financial instability and with the protection of small savers – but again, just as during the GFC (Kallert, 2017), this reasoning is highly controversial. Once more, narratives and causal stories promoted by a broad and powerful alliance are able to establish a hegemonial configuration supporting the generalization of the particular interests of the very few households potentially affected by bail-in. But the strategic menace of financial instability affecting everyone is very mighty, leading to an (implicit) consent to the described bail out policy – although especially wealthy people are profiting from it. As shown, the financial resilience of bank bondholders to absorb shocks from asset devaluation is high, which means that direct risks to current financial stability stemming from the bail-in of household assets are very low (Lindner & Redak, 2017). But despite these insights, once again, it's taxpayers' money that is used to save the investments of people who tend to be richer than others.

Conclusion

What can we learn from these insights into the first implementation of the new financial regulation in Europe? First of all, there isn't any objective definition of either systemic importance or financial stability. Although some progress has been made towards a more concrete and transparent assignment of SIFIs compared to the GFC, systemic importance and financial stability still serve as empty signifiers. The BU tries to define systemic importance in a hegemonial attempt but this is impossible: different actors in various social conflicts can refer to such empty signifiers without knowing what they exactly mean. Hence, the concepts of systemic importance and financial stability aren't neutral features but highly political and contested categories. After the first implementations of (non-)resolutions, the urgent problem is how banks and the capital behind these financial institutions still succeed in socializing private losses whereas the foregoing profits are privatized (and often barely taxed) – while, according to the BU, taxpayers' money shouldn't be spent anymore or only exceptionally for bail-outs. Therefore, the indefinable concepts of systemic importance serve as a necessary means to enforce particular interests. The growing power of financial capital in the more finance-led accumulation regime tends to privilege policies which protect money capital under the pretext of financial stability in crises of capitalism – that means bail-out instead of bail-in. Due to the structural selectivities of the (capitalist) state such policies are more likely (Kannankulam & Georgi, 2014). At the same time, the relative autonomy of the state is diminishing in favour of an authoritarian statism (Kannankulam, 2010; Sandbeck & Schneider, 2014) when the individual interests of specific financial capitals are directly shared by the state apparatus – as happened during the GFC as well as recently within the framework of the BU.

Ex-ante, it is not possible to determine one single financial institution as systemically important without further analysis of social power relations and the purpose of the definition including the final rating decisions. Only the credit system as a whole is systemic and indispensable for accumulation and social reproduction in capitalism. Therefore, we need a critique of systemic importance and concepts relating to this feature.

Even the Financial Stability Board et al. (2009, p. 8) had to admit that the 'nature of the assessment [of systemic risk or SIFIs] may be conditioned by its purpose'. Following these considerations, there are different kinds of systemic importance – depending on the purpose, may it be the rescue of domestic banks or investors, the guarantee of small savings and pensions, the reduction of wealth inequality, or the regulation of the *too big to fail* doctrine. Furthermore, both the quantitative thresholds of the assessments as SIFI and its weighting factors are arbitrary and part of controversies between the supervisors and the supervised entities (Kranke & Yarrow, 2018).[3] Consequently, the measurement of systemic importance can imply a 'false sense of precision', and therefore, according to the Financial Stability Board et al. (2009, p. 12), 'distinguishing between systemic and non systemic entities would involve additional and highly judgmental analysis'. These problems in determining systemic importance allow for a wide range of interpretations that are prone to intervention by powerful (capital) factions and their discursive narratives. Thus, shadow financial institutions like asset managers (for example BlackRock) are still able to evade stricter supervision with regard to financial stability. Likewise, wealthy (retail) investors manage to receive reimbursements for the losses on their investments in bank bonds which were yielding the years before.

Currently, a new Italian bank called *illimity* is buying NPLs in huge amounts from domestic banks and forming securitized products out of these bad loans. These financial innovations are planned to be sold to 200,000 retail investors, laying the ground for the next bail-out (*Financial Times*, 24.7.2018). Without a fundamental critique of these developments and the reasoning behind those within the contemporary mode of accumulation, the socialization of private losses will proceed without any lessons being learned.

Notes

1 For an impression of the high interest paid from such junior bonds: a Banco Popular Espanol bond was priced with interest of 11.5 per cent (2013), and one of Bank of Cyprus with 12.5 per cent (2017). In 2017, euro-zone banks sold €106 billion of subordinated bonds at an average 4.9 per cent yield compared to €132 billion at an average yield of 9.2 per cent in 2013 (Ramnarayan & Gledhill, 2018). Compared to these vast profit rates, the interest for normal and low-risk deposits in the euro area is (close to) zero for a couple of years.

2 Keyword for banks: *Monte dei Paschi, Banco Popular, Veneto Banca, Banca Popolare di Vicenza*; for Banking Union: *Single Resolution Board, Banking Union, Single Resolution Mechanism*; for concepts of systemic importance: *systemic risk, SIFI, systemically important institutions, systemically important banks, too big to fail, bail-in.*

3 The US insurer MetLife got rid of the SIFI label by winning a court battle with the US authorities: the designation as SIFI had been ‘arbitrary and capricious’ (Lambert, 2016). Furthermore, after intense lobbying the US congress raised the threshold for the designation as SIFI from $50 billion to $250 billion.

References

Aglietta, M. (2000). *A theory of capitalist regulation: the US experience*. London: Verso.

Baker, A. (2013). The new political economy of the macroprudential ideational shift. *New Political Economy*, *18*(1), 112–139.

Barth, J.R., & Wihlborg, C. (2016). Too big to fail and too big to save: dilemmas for banking reform. *National Institute Economic Review*, *235*(1), R27–R39.

Belfrage, C.A., & Hauf, F. (2015). Operationalizing cultural political economy: towards critical grounded theory. *Journal of Organizational Ethnography*, *4*(3), 324–340.

Best, J. (2009). How to make a bubble: towards a cultural political economy of the financial crisis. *International Political Sociology*, *3*(4), 461–465.

Bieling, H.-J. (2013). Das Projekt der Euro-Rettung und die Widersprüche des europäischen Krisenkonstitutionalismus. *Zeitschrift für Internationale Beziehungen*, *20*(1), 89–103.

Binder, J.-H. (2016). Resolution: concepts, requirements, and tools. In J.-H. Binder & D. Singh (Eds.), *Bank resolution: the European regime* (pp. 25–59). Oxford: Oxford University Press.

Borio, C. (2011). Implementing a macroprudential framework: blending boldness and realism. *Capitalism and Society*, *6*(1), 1–23.

Castañeda, J.E., Mayes, D.G., & Wood, G. (2016). *European banking union: prospects and challenges*. Abingdon & New York: Routledge.

Caterina, D. (2017). Investigating hegemony struggles: transdisciplinary considerations on the role of a critical discourse analysis of practical argumentation. *Critical Discourse Studies*, *15*(3), 211–227.

Culpepper, P.D., & Tesche, T. (2019). Death in Veneto? European banking union and the structural power of large banks (EUI working papers No. 2019/04). Cadmus, European University Institute Research Repository. Retrieved from https://cadmus.eui.eu/handle/1814/60426.

De Rynck, S. (2015). Banking on a union: the politics of changing Eurozone banking supervision. *Journal of European Public Policy*, *23*(1), 119–135.

Epstein, G.A. (2005). *Financialization and the world economy*. Cheltenham: Elgar.

European Banking Authority. (2014). *Results of 2014 EU-wide stress test: aggregate results*. London: European Banking Authority.

European Banking Authority. (2016). *2016 EU-wide stress test: results, 29 July*. London: European Banking Authority.

European Central Bank. (2016). *The household finance and consumption survey: results from the second wave* (statistics paper series No. 18). Frankfurt a.M.: European Central Bank.

European Central Bank. (2017). *The household finance and consumption survey: wave 2—statistical tables*. Frankfurt a.M.: European Central Bank.

European Commission. (2017). *State aid: commission authorises precautionary recapitalisation of Italian bank Monte dei Paschi di Siena*. Brussels: European Commission.

European Commission Competition. (2011). *The effects of temporary state aid rules adopted in the context of the financial and economic crisis: commission staff working paper*. Brussels: European Commission.

Ferran, E. (2014). European banking union: imperfect, but it can work (University of Cambridge Faculty of Law research paper No. 30/2014). *Legal Studies Research* Paper Series. Retrieved from https://papers.ssrn.com/sol3/papers.cfm?abstract_id=2426247.

Financial Crisis Inquiry Commission. (2011). CDO charts. *Financial Crisis Inquiry Commission*. Retrieved from http://fcic.law.stanford.edu/resource/staff-data-projects/cdo-charts.

Financial Stability Board. (2018). *Implementation and effects of the G20 financial regulatory reforms: fourth annual report*. Basel: Financial Stability Board.

Financial Stability Board, International Monetary Fund, & Bank for International Settlements. (2009). Guidance to assess the systemic importance of financial institutions, markets and instruments: initial considerations: Report to G20 finance ministers and governors. International Monetary Fund. Retrieved from https://www.imf.org/external/np/g20/pdf/100109.pdf.

Financial Times. (15.1.2016). Capital markets. Rating agencies warn over bank bail-in rules, p. 22.

Financial Times. (11.4.2016). Fiscal strategy. Italy pushes for bank rescue fund, p. 2.

Financial Times. (16.4.2016). Rescue mission. When the country's bankers were summoned to meet the finance minister they knew what was at stake. They either agreed to stump up more than €4bn or face the consequences of one of their own failing, p. 10.

Financial Times. (2.5.2016). Italian fund Atlante in first bailout after capital call fail, p. 15.

Financial Times. (1.7.2016). Bailout fund. Italy rescues lender after Renzi plea fails, p. 2.

Financial Times. (11.7.2016). Essential repairs. Shares in Italian banks have fallen by a third since the UK voted to quit the EU, p. 5.

Financial Times. (12.7.2016). Eurogroup meeting. Brussels warns Italy against breaking strict bank rescue rules, p. 2.

Financial Times. (15.7.2016). Italy's retail investors are in a bind over bank debt exposure, p. 20.

Financial Times. (16.7.2016). EU regulation. Banking crisis. Exploiting the fine print to save Italy's lenders, p. 11.

Financial Times. (19.7.2016). European banks' crisis of earnings cries out for a quick Italian job, p. 22.

Financial Times. (22.7.2016). State support. Draghi backs public bailout of Italy's ailing banks. ECB president says such a move could be done in exceptional circumstances, p. 4.

Financial Times. (4.8.2016). Siena adjusts to a bleaker future after 500 years of Monte dei Paschi largesse. Tuscan town's handouts dry up now that charitable foundation owns only 1.49% of struggling Italian bank, p. 3.

Financial Times. (24.11.2016). End of the embrace. Cosy lending practices in the country's Veneto region—one of the richest parts of Europe—added to the country's banking crisis, p. 11.

Financial Times. (6.12.2016). Italian state must act as backstop to bolster ailing banking system, p. 14.

Financial Times. (24.7.2018). Veteran banker returns to the fray in Italy, p. 12.

FMSA—Bundesanstalt für Finanzmarktstabilisierung. (2015). Historischer Überblick über die Maßnahmen des SoFFin. *FMSA*. Retrieved from https://media.frag-den-staat.de/files/foi/31511/20150706_Historischerberblick.pdf.

FMStFG—Gesetz zur Errichtung eines Finanzmarkt- und eines Wirtschaftsstabilisierungsfonds (Stabilisierungsfondsgesetz). (2008). *Bundesministerium der Justiz und für Verbraucherschutz*. Retrieved from http://www.gesetze-im-internet.de/fmstfg/BJNR198210008.html.

Friedman, J. (2011). *What caused the financial crisis*. Philadelphia: University Press.

Götz, M.G., Krahnen, J.P., & Tröger, T.H. (2017). *Taking bail-in seriously—the looming risks for banking policy in the rescue of Monte Paschi di Siena* (SAFE policy letter No. 54). Frankfurt a.M.: SAFE Policy Center.

Grossman, E., & Woll, C. (2014). Saving the banks. *Comparative Political Studies*, *47*(4), 574–600.

Hadjimichalis, C.M. (2018). *Crisis spaces: structures, struggles and solidarity in Southern Europe*. London: Routledge.

Heinrich, M., & Jessop, B. (2015). Interpretations of the EU crisis and their policy implementation. In B. Jessop, B. Young, & C. Scherrer (Eds.), *Financial cultures and crisis dynamics* (pp. 278–293). New York: Routledge.

Heires, M., & Nölke, A. (2014). *Politische Ökonomie der Finanzialisierung*. Wiesbaden: Springer.

Helleiner, E. (2014). *The status quo crisis: global financial governance after the 2008 meltdown*. New York: Oxford University Press.

Hellwig, M. (2015). *Financial stability and monetary policy* (reprints of the Max Planck Institute for research on collective goods No. 10). Bonn: Max-Planck-Institut für Gesellschaftsforschung.

Howarth, D., & Quaglia, L. (2015). Die Bankenunion als Krönung der Wirtschafts- und Währungsunion?. *Integration*, *38*(1), 44–59.

Howarth, D., & Quaglia, L. (2016a). Internationalised banking, alternative banks and the single supervisory mechanism. *West European Politics*, *39*(3), 438–461.

Howarth, D., & Quaglia, L. (2016b). *The political economy of European banking union*. Oxford: Oxford University Press.

Howarth, D., & Quaglia, L. (2018). The difficult construction of a European deposit insurance scheme: a step too far in banking union? *Journal of Economic Policy Reform*, *21*(3), 190–209.

Jäger, M., & Jäger, S. (2007). *Medien—Kultur—Kommunikation: Deutungskämpfe: Theorie und Praxis kritischer Diskursanalyse*. Wiesbaden: VS-Verlag.

Jessop, B. (1999). The strategic selectivity of the state: reflections on a theme of Poulantzas. *Journal of the Hellenic Diaspora*, *25*(1–2), 41–77.

Jessop, B., & Scherrer, C. (2015). Introduction. In B. Jessop, B. Young, & C. Scherrer (Eds.), *Financial cultures and crisis dynamics* (pp. 1–23). New York: Routledge.

Jessop, B., & Sum, N.-L. (2006). *Beyond the regulation approach: putting capitalist economies in their place*. Cheltenham: Edward Elgar.

Kallert, A. (2017). *Die Bankenrettungen während der Finanzkrise* 2007–2009 *in Deutschland: Zur Kritik der Systemrelevanz*. Münster: Westfälisches Dampfboot.

Kannankulam, J. (2010). Autoritärer Etatismus: elemente eines staats- und krisentheoretischen Konzepts von Nicos Poulantzas. In A. Demirović, S. Adolphs, & S. Karakayali (Eds.), *Das Staatsverständnis von Nicos Poulantzas: Der Staat als gesellschaftliches Verhältnis* (pp. 223–239). Baden-Baden: Nomos.

Kannankulam, J., & Georgi, F. (2014). Varieties of capitalism or varieties of relationships of forces? Outlines of a historical materialist policy analysis. *Capital & Class*, *38*(1), 59–71.

Kessler, O. (2011). *Globale politische Ökonomie: Die Internationale Politische Ökonomie der Weltfinanzkrise*. Wiesbaden: VS Verlag.

Kindleberger, C.P., & Aliber, R.Z. (2011). *Manias, panics and crashes: a history of financial crises* (6th edition). New York: Palgrave Macmillan.

Kranke, M., & Yarrow, D. (2018). The global governance of systemic risk: how measurement practices tame macroprudential politics. *New Political Economy*, *13*(2), 1–17.

Krugman, P.R. (2009). *The return of depression economics and the crisis of 2008*. New York: Norton.

Kutter, A., & Jessop, B. (2015). Culture as discursive practice: combining cultural political economy and discursive political studies in investigations of the financial crisis. In B. Jessop, B. Young & C. Scherrer (Eds.), *Financial cultures and crisis dynamics* (pp. 64–82). New York: Routledge.

Lambert, L. (2016). MetLife's 'too big to fail' tag is 'arbitrary, capricious': U.S. judge. Reuters. Retrieved from https://www.reuters.com/article/us-usa-metlife-appeal-idUSKCN0X42GM.

Lapavitsas, C. (2012). *Crisis in the Eurozone*. London: Verso.

Lindner, P., & Redak, V. (2017). The resilience of households in bank bail-ins. *Financial Stability Report*, *33*, 88–101.

Mader, P., Mertens, D., & van der Zwan, N. (2020). *The Routledge international handbook of financialization*. Abingdon: Routledge.

Mertens, D., & Meyer-Eppler, R. (2014). Pensionsfonds-Kapitalismus und privatisierter Keynesianismus. In M. Heires & A. Nölke (Eds.), *Politische Ökonomie der Finanzialisierung* (pp. 259–274). Wiesbaden: Springer.

Mesnard, B., Margerit, A., & Magnus, M. (2017). *Precautionary recapitalisations under the Bank recovery and resolution directive: conditionality and case practice. Briefing for European Parliament*. Brussels: European Union.

Mügge, D., & Perry, J. (2014). The flaws of fragmented financial standard setting. *Politics & Society*, *42*(2), 194–222.

Poulantzas, N. (1978). *State, power, socialism*. London: Verso.

Ramnarayan, A., & Gledhill, A. (2018). High-risk euro bank bonds find buyers as crisis memories fade. Reuters. Retrieved from https://www.reuters.com/article/us-europe-banks-bonds-analysis/high-risk-euro-bank-bonds-find-buyers-as-crisis-memories-fade-idUSKCN1G524V.

Regulation EU. (2014). 468/2014 of the ECB of 16 April 2014. *Official Journal of the European Union*. Retrieved from https://www.ecb.europa.eu/ecb/legal/pdf/celex_32014r0468_en_txt.pdf.

Roubini, N., & Mihm, S. (2011). *Crisis economics: a crash course in the future of finance*. London: Penguin Books.

Sablowski, T. (2011). Krise und Kontinuität des finanzdominierten Akkumulationsregimes. *Zeitschrift für Wirtschaftsgeographie*, *55*(1–2), 50–64.

Sandbeck, S., & Schneider, E. (2014). From the sovereign debt crisis to authoritarian statism: contradictions of the European state project. *New Political Economy*, *19*(6), 847–871.

Scherrer, C. (2011). Reproducing hegemony: US finance capital and the 2008 crisis. *Critical Policy Studies*, *5*(3), 219–246.

Single Resolution Board. (2016). *The single resolution mechanism: introduction to resolution planning*. Brussels: Single Resolution Board.

Stockhammer, E. (2014). Financialization, income distribution and the crisis. In S. Fadda & P. Tridico (Eds.), *Financial crisis, labour markets and institutions* (pp. 98–119). London: Routledge.

Stone, D.A. (1989). Causal stories and the formation of policy agendas. *Political Science Quarterly*, *104*(2), 281–300.

Sum, N.L., & Jessop, B. (2014). *Towards a cultural political economy: putting culture in its place in political economy*. Cheltenham: Edward Elgar Publishing.

Sum, N.-L., & Jessop, B. (2015). Sense- and meaning-making in the critique of political economy. In B. Jessop, B. Young, & C. Scherrer (Eds.), *Financial cultures and crisis dynamics* (pp. 27–43). New York: Routledge.

Tröger, T.H. (2017a). Too complex to work: a critical assessment of the bail-in tool under the European bank recovery and resolution regime (SAFE working paper No. 179). SAFE Working Paper Series. Retrieved from https://papers.ssrn.com/sol3/papers.cfm?abstract_id=3023184##.

Woll, C. (2011). Wer rettet die Banken? Staatliche Nothilfe im internationalen Vergleich. In Max-Planck-Institut für Gesellschaftsforschung (Ed.), *MPIfG Jahrbuch 2011–2012* (pp. 19–26). Köln: Max-Planck-Institut für Gesellschaftsforschung.

5 Democratization or politicization?

The changing face of political-economic expertise in European expert groups, 1966–2017

Christian Schmidt-Wellenburg

Introduction

Consulting and following the advice of experts when creating policies has been part and parcel of European Union (EU) politics right from the outset. The same applies to the passionate debates on the functions, meaning, and legitimacy of expertise in EU policymaking in which political agents engage as eagerly as academics (European Ombudsman, 2015; Sabido, 2013; Vassalos, 2008). Two main positions can be identified in these debates. On the one hand, there are warnings that experts contribute to the technocratic and bureaucratic nature of EU politics (Habermas, 2015; Sanchez-Cuenca, 2017; Wiesner, 2019a) and increase the influence of lobbyists (Courty & Michel, 2013; Laurens, 2018). These assessments tend to view the involvement of experts in policy process and, more generally, the evolution of EU politics as a challenge to democratic ideals that turns democracy into expertocracy. On the other hand, high hopes are linked to the involvement of experts in EU policy process emphasizing the democratizing (Commission of the European Communities, 2001; Fischer, 2009; Quittkat & Finke, 2008), politicizing (Scicluna, 2014; Statham & Trenz, 2015), and rationalizing (Majone, 1999; Schmidt, 2012; Sunstein, 2016) effects of the engagement of academics, interest groups, civil society actors, and other stakeholders. This controversy has triggered a vast body of research, most recently into the diversity of experts involved in EU policy processes (Bajenova, 2019; Büttner et al., 2015; Christensen, 2015; Góra et al., 2018), providing detailed accounts of the diversity of expertise and its workings. In most cases, the aim is to ascertain empirically or using normative theory either the claim of democratic benefit or technocratic threat, without taking into account that this controversy is itself part of the political struggle over the face of EU politics, a struggle that draws heavily on research produced in EU studies and positions argued by EU experts.

In recent years, a prominent battlefield in this struggle has been EU expert groups (Gornitzka & Sverdrup, 2011, 2015; Krick & Gornitzka, 2019; Larsson, 2003; Metz, 2015; Moodie, 2016; Robert, 2012). Here, the normative democratic challenge is posed most notably by NGOs from a civil society background such as the Alliance for Lobbying Transparency and Ethics Regulation (ALTER-EU), Members of the European Parliament (MEP), and the European Ombudsman and directed at the European Commission. The assessment voiced by the Commission that expertise in EU politics has a democratizing effect is a reaction to these normative challenges, based on a more functional and bureaucratic view of politics that sees experts as part of institutional checks and balances. As I will argue below, the current outcome of this struggle is neither the democratization of expertise desired nor the bureaucratization and scientization feared but rather a gradual politicization of expertise. The contribution traces this process of politicization in three steps (see Wiesner, 2019b).

First, an analytical framework is constructed that allows us to conceptualize different forms of expertise as effects of a political field and its relationship to other fields, drawing on recent field analytical work on the EU and transnational fields (Bigo, 2017; Georgakakis & Rowell, 2013; Kauppi, 2018; Schmidt-Wellenburg & Bernhard, 2020b). This opens up the opportunity to locate experts in their specific socio-historical contexts and to understand the differences between various forms of expertise and sources of authority that they utilize in conjunction with these contexts. With regard to the field of EU politics, the hypothesis can be put forward that changes in expertise over time and policy area are field effects directly related to the socio-historical state of field struggles at a given moment. Hence, the questions of who is seen as legitimately engaging in politics as an expert on the basis of which background and why are directly connected to the state of EU integration and the legitimatory struggles over the EU's autonomy and normative validity.

Second, the theoretical framework is used to study the changing professional backgrounds of members of EU expert groups in the areas of monetary integration, market integration, and political-economic governance between 1966 and 2017. It can be demonstrated that over time fewer members of EU expert groups have an academic or scientific background and an increasing number are associated with financial market politics and regulation as well as the financial industry and business. Results are interpreted as a de-scientization and, at the same time, politicization of expertise in this policy area: professional stakeholders are increasingly seen as legitimate experts engaged in contentious politics of professionalized interest representation.

Third, drawing on the analytical framework outlined above and the empirical insights generated, an initial tentative explanation of the politicization in this area of EU expertise is developed. Special emphasis is placed on the debates that succeeded the resignation of the Santer Commission, the Kinnock reforms, and the Commission's White Book on European Governance in 2001 and that turned into a controversy over how access to EU expert groups should be regulated. It will be argued that calls for democratization have ultimately led to developments of 'de-scientization' and 'politicization' in this area of EU politics.

Experts in EU politics

EU politics as a field

From a field analytical perspective, European integration is conceived as the outcome of a political struggle over the autonomy of the EU field of politics vis à vis national political fields in which agents draw on varying sources of authority derived from diverse contexts. Over decades, this conflictual relationship has shaped how a specific 'European' political practice looks, transforming it from diplomacy involving agents deeply rooted in their nationally framed political fields (Caporaso, 1998) into an international organization in terms of IR research (Moravcsik, 1993) and recently into Eurocracy as part of a European political field (Georgakakis, 2013; Kauppi, 2018). Experts and their expertise have played a decisive role in this process. In transaction with other political agents, they have shaped this highly contested project of creating a new form of transnational political field unlike nation-state political fields (Schmidt-Wellenburg, 2017; McNamara, 2018). Hence, to understand their shifting role, we need to analyze their relationships with other political agents and their position within this specific political practice.

Like any other political practice, European political practice is understood as 'a game in which the stakes are the legitimate imposition of the principles of vision and division of the social world' (Bourdieu, 2001, pp. 54–55). In this game, visions of Europe are created and implemented in the everyday governing of 'the social', drawing on the legitimate use of physical violence – as Weber (1978) put it – and much more of symbolic violence in the form of law – as Bourdieu (2014) emphasises. In this interpretation, politics goes beyond the mere exertion of power, even of direct governance or legitimate domination. It is also the struggle over the content of and ability to define and enforce commonly acceptable views of social behaviour, subjects, and meaning by realizing the 'common good' understood as naming and implementing a 'good' order and 'good' government (Bourdieu, 2001, pp. 51, 81; Bourdieu, 1991). This necessarily includes imagining communities for which a certain 'good' is sought (Anderson, 1983) and political practice applies, leading to different 'scopes' of political fields, with the nation state's scope being most prominent and in a contested relationship not only with European but also local and international politics (Schmidt-Wellenburg & Bernhard, 2020a).

Aimed at realizing the 'common good' by determining and implementing legitimate visions and divisions of the world, political practice takes on two dimensions (see Eyal, 2019, p. 37; Radaelli, 1999, p. 763; Schudson, 2006, p. 494). First, politics involves the exertion of violence, albeit not as uninhibited exercise of power but in the form of authority. Hence, political practices as aspects of governing are structured by legitimate forms of domination. This dimension of force is closely linked to a legitimatory discourse feeding on two ideal types of democracy (Habermas, 1998, pp. 239–244; see also Crouch, 2004). In its republican form, it stresses that political action is legitimate if it is the outcome of a process of mutual communication, thus closing the gap between governing oneself and being governed by others through understanding and reason. In its liberal form, the gap is closed by the contentious aggregation of plural interests into collective goals through majority institutions. At the same time, both discourses are grounded in ethics of self-government and see equality as a key prerequisite for legitimate political action.

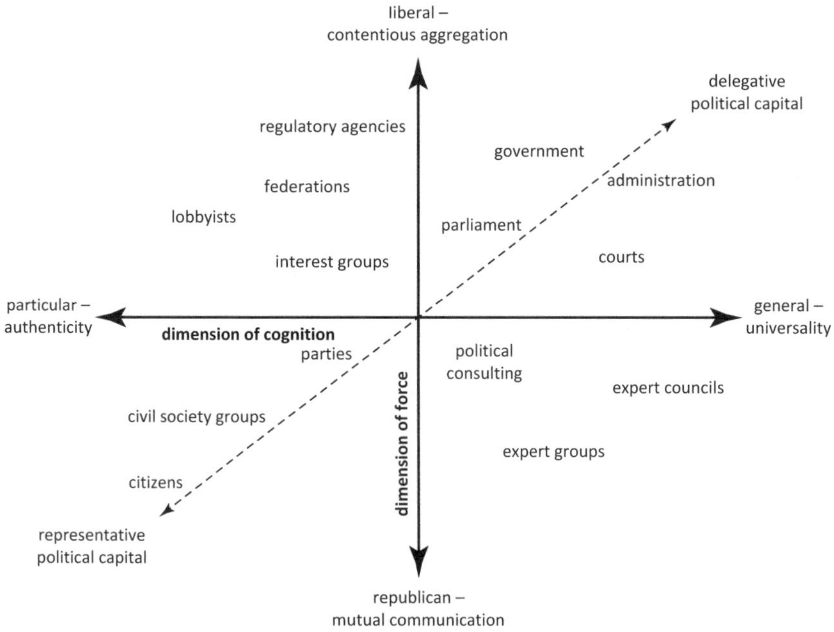

Figure 5.1 Two-dimensional space of political practice, schematic presentation.

Second, political practice is structured by knowledge of the current and desired future state of affairs, of what is to be governed effectively and efficiently, how, and to what end. This dimension of cognition is closely linked to two diametrically opposed conceptions of objectifying knowledge from experience, thus linking the universality and particularity of experience (Reckwitz, 2020). In its particularizing version, direct and unfettered perception guarantees the validity of knowledge due to its authenticity and 'a mutuality of experience' (Giddens, 1990, p. 95). Related legitimatory discourses emphasize first-hand experience by an individual or others as well as the positionality of world views when producing authentic statements on reality. In its generalizing version, specialized perception guarantees the validity of knowledge due to its methodologically controlled isolation of universal facts and is linked to 'an attitude of respect for most technical specialism' (Giddens, 1990, p. 89). Associated legitimatory discourses stress the role of scientific methods and competitive academic research to achieve universality when producing valid statements on reality.

Since it is structured by both dimensions, political practice also draws on democratic and epistemic authority (Turner, 2001, p. 129; Strassheim, 2015). Different practices and subjectivities involved in governing and being governed can then be distinguished according to their interlinking of these dimensions, creating socio-historically specific power/knowledge practices (Foucault, 2007, 2009) that differentiate politics. Voting and campaigning, policymaking, administering and enforcing the law, litigating and rendering verdicts, consulting, and counselling are all practices that create specific roles and corresponding institutions such as those of citizens, civil society movements, interest groups, parties, parliamentarians, government, bureaucrats, judges, and courts.

The opportunity to engage in these practices depends on agents' habitual capabilities acknowledged and objectified in legitimate forms of political capital. It might be understood as specialized social capital, 'a durable network of more or less institutionalized relationships of mutual acquaintance and recognition – or in other words, to membership in a group – which provides each of the members with the backing of the collectively-owned capital' (Bourdieu, 1986, p. 249) that may be mobilized in struggles over 'the common good'. Political capital works along two lines of logic already inherent in social capital: the representation of citizens' authentic preferences (speaking for the group) and the effectiveness of delegation, of achieving goals envisioned, through efficient bureaucracy (acting on the group's behalf) (see Scharpf, 1997, p. 19).

In the case of representation, political capital stems from the eligibility to speak about the authentic experiences of others and, at the same time, to call the multitude to physical presence if necessary, be it in the form of a call to arms, strikes, or votes, depending on which imagined group is represented, citizens, the people, workers, the unachieving, company shareholders, or the hard-working (Bourdieu, 1991). In the case of delegation, it is the ability to draw on formalized technical knowledge of governing and collecting information about the imagined group who are to govern, be it the people, court, parish, church, army, economy, or society at large, as well as the belief in the contentious mechanisms of aggregating majorities and enforcing their rule (Bourdieu, 1994).

Experts, expertise, and EU expert groups

All political practices, positions, and forms of capital are linked to knowledge claims about reality, although some are better at creating shared world perceptions, definitions of urgent problems that push for political action and require solutions, such as parliamentary policy processes, juries and commissions, scientific advisory boards of bureaucratic institutions, expert groups, or citizens' round tables (s.a. Collins & Evans, 2007; Turner, 2014). Agents engaging in these practices mainly reference certain forms of epistemic rather than democratic authority, especially when challenged, thus highlighting their involvement as experts, be it due to particularistic or universal virtues. They use their experience and knowledge gained in fields such as the scientific or economic field as a basis for representation or delegation, thereby transforming other forms of capital into political capital. To do so, experts have to 'know their way' round a specific field of politics: they need to have the discursive and tacit knowledge of how to manoeuvre in this context. These abilities are acquired throughout a career, frequently by seeking out positions in different areas of political and related fields, taking revolving doors between think tanks, research institutes, companies, and bureaucracies (Bajenova, 2019; Courty & Michel, 2013; Tansey, 2014).

This field theoretical take on expertise allows us to make sense of the three major groups of experts in EU politics: 'scientific experts, societal interests and national governments' (Gornitzka & Sverdrup, 2011). In the case of the scientists, the authority of expertise is created by referencing the nomos of the scientific field as a legitimate form of objectifying knowledge, independent of political interests, and is an asset to governmental effectiveness in the political field. In the case of societal interests, the authority of expertise is derived from authentic first-hand experience of citizens and classical social interest groups or business and regional communities, reinforced by the appeal of representing part of the demos. In the case of national governments and, in recent years, also international organizations, bureaucratic experts are bolstered by the authority of their first-hand governmental experience and its reflection that nourishes hopes of increasing the effectiveness and efficiency of governing.

The idea of expertise as a switchyard of capital and authority from different sources into and out of political fields is of particular importance when attempting to understand the motivation of agents to engage in the evolving process of European integration. For agents located in national fields, be they economic, political, or academic, an evolving transnational political field opens up the opportunity not only to make their voices heard and perhaps even to influence national policy setting via transnational politics but also to gain recognition and authority in their own field. Conversely, agents located mainly in the evolving field of European politics use their expertise to define policy deficits and problems, to seek new challenges that require attention and old ones that need to be seen in a new European light, to imagine constituencies in Europe not yet represented, or at least not adequately. Expertise can be used to assert the need for European politics.

Three more historical developments also account for the prominence of experts in the field of European politics. First, compared to other administrations with similar tasks and responsibilities, the size of the Commission, its Directorates-General (DG), and the European Parliament (EP) is relatively small. Consequently, the demand for manpower and skills from outside EU institutions to support policy development, provision of regulations, and their implementation is arguably huge and served by a plethora of agents, groups, and organizations (Christensen, 2015, p. 653). Second, the EU's institutional arrangement for policymaking needs more coordination than other governance systems, leading the EU comitology to flourish. Expert groups are part of this '"auxiliary" policy-making structure' (Krick & Gornitzka, 2019, p. 105) that allows European institutions to gather information and learn from either direct or scientifically objectified experience (Krick, 2015). Third, EU institutions are in competition with nation state institutions over jurisdictions of policy areas. Following the increased use of the Open Method of Coordination in areas where neither the classical community method nor intergovernmental integration is used has created demand for 'impartial' knowledge, benchmarks, and policy learning mechanisms since Lisbon, a demand eagerly met by experts. Mobilizing experts and their non-political sources of authority, EU political agents have managed to sidestep direct challenges to nation-state agents and sovereignty while furthering EU integration at the same time (Bernhard, 2011).

Historically, this has led to a threefold classification of the EU's committee system as Council working parties and committees, comitology committees, and expert groups (Gornitzka & Severdrup, 2008, p. 727). Comitology committees are integrated into the policy process and serve to deliberate on and coordinate different EU institutions and member states. As part of the Council preparatory body, Council working parties are fora to assist and coordinate Council and member state interests. Commission expert groups are the most 'autonomous' of the three types since the Commission is in full control of their composition, and they serve a purely consultative function, advising the Commission on legislative proposals and policy initiatives (Larsson & Murk, 2007, p. 70). EU expert groups are the ideal research object for observing changes over time in the form of expertise sought by the Commission because they are not fully enmeshed in the European Union's comitology, less concerned with internal coordination, and hence open to draw on non-political sources of authority deemed appropriate at a particular moment in time (Krick & Gornitzka, 2019, p. 105).

The changing face of European experts

To trace changes in expertise in European expert groups over time, 21 expert groups with 261 members initiated by either the Commission, the Commission on behalf of the Council, or one of the Commission's DGs in the policy areas of monetary integration, market integration, and political-economic governance between 1966 and 2017 were studied, excluding groups mainly involved with technical tasks such as industry standard creation and alignment. It has to be taken into account that all insights generated apply only to this specific form of groups and cannot be simply generalized to all expert groups, many of which are anchored in different socio-historical contexts of EU politics. Expertise – what makes members experts – is understood as being composed of different forms of capital. Indicators for the amount and type of capital that experts have were derived from CVs published online and complemented by other publicly accessible information.

In a first analytical step, information from CVs was coded using grounded theory methodology (Corbin & Strauss, 2008), creating categories describing the commonalities and differences in individuals' professional experience, backgrounds, and trajectories (Schmidt-Wellenburg, 2019, p. 216). In a second quantifying step, the data generated was analyzed using multiple correspondence analysis (MCA) (Blasius, 1987; Le Roux & Rouanet, 2004). This enables us to construct a multidimensional cloud of individuals' characteristics that allows us to represent their relationships as geometric distances and to statistically discern the main structures in this group using techniques of dimensional reduction (Le Roux & Rouanet, 2004). MCA ideally complements grounded theory methodology because it also follows an inductive and reconstructive logic. Since the main research interest lies in differences or similarities in expertise in various groups over time, individuals were weighted according to the number of individuals in the relevant expert group in relation to all groups in order to prevent an overrepresentation of one group in the construction of the relational space.

The multidimensional space constructed is transhistorical and allows us to address research questions on historical processes viewed in retrospective using a common 'scale', despite not having ever existed at one moment in time. The first, second, and third axes of this space, together accounting for 80.4% of variance in the data when corrected using Bencécri's method, are interpreted using individual characteristics that contribute at least one and a half times the mean contribution (0.85%) to axis orientations (Le Roux & Rouanet, 2004, pp. 200–201, 209). The main structure of expertise reconstructed makes it possible to observe structural shifts over time and can subsequently be used to understand agents' strategies and position-takings in more recent struggles over the form and legitimacy of EU expert groups.

The first axis in Figure 5.2 accounts for 48.9% of the overall variance and contrasts 'classic' academic experts engaged in consulting politics with lobbying experts associated with the financial industry, particularly investment companies. On the left-hand side, careers can be found that normally require a degree in management or business studies (Man 1.4%) and include positions on executive boards (ExBoard, 2.5%) or as CEO (1.7%) most probably with an investment company (InvCom, 1.7%) or with financial service think tanks (Fintt, 1.3%). On the right-hand side, characteristics such as holding a PhD (2.4%), being a professor (Prof, 4.6%) being a member (natRInst, 6.2%) or the president (Pres, 3.6%) of a national research institute, holding a degree in economics (Econ, 2.1%), being a member of a national (natEconAss, 3.9%) or international economics association (intEcoAss, 3.3%), or working for national research councils (natRC, 2.1%) are listed. This academic background is also associated with consulting political institutions (PolCon 3.1%) such as national government and the ministry of state (StMin, 3.6%) or other ministries (Minother, 1.7%) and national administrations (natAdmin, 2.5%) also via national policy think tanks (natPoltt 2.1%) or experience as an economic advisor (EconAd 1.7%). Political consulting for transnational institutions such as the European Commission (EUCom, 1.8%) and related EU policy think tanks (tnEUtt 2.0%) or the UN (2.6%) and OECD (4.0%) are included here, too.

The second axis in Figure 5.2 accounts for 21.2% of the overall variance and distinguishes between two different political backgrounds. At the top, properties

Table 5.1 Variance rates (eigenvalue λ) and modified variance rates

Axis	*Eigen value (λ)*	*Variance rates modified %*
1	0.093	48.9
2	0.067	21.2
3	0.052	10.3
4	0.039	4.2
5	0.038	3.8

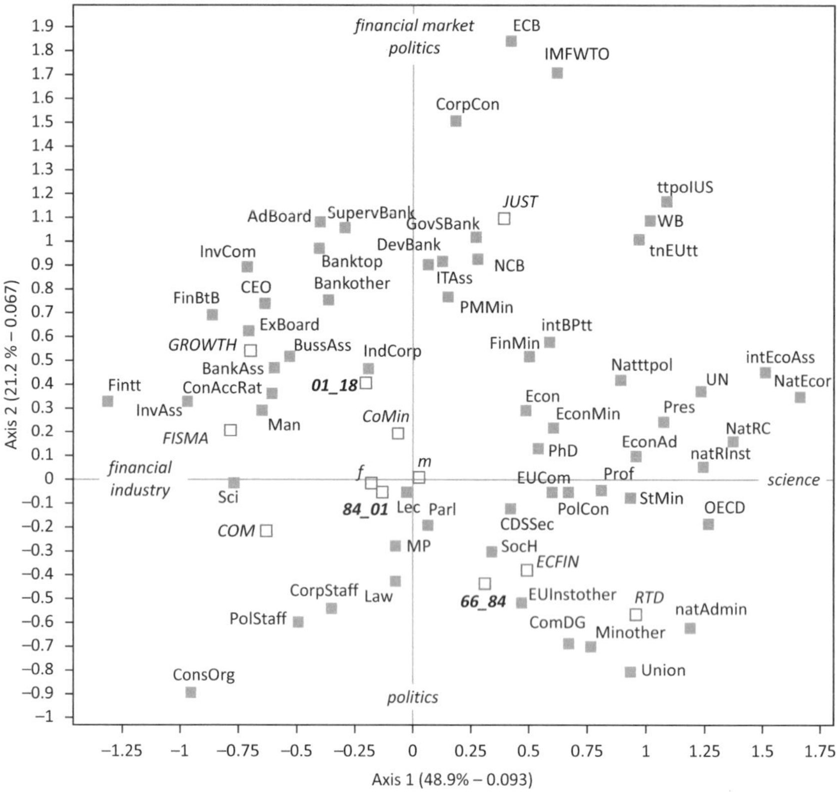

Figure 5.2 Plane 1_2 space of properties, passive categories in italic.

associated with financial market politics and infrastructure are shown, constituting a powerful pole, influencing the regulation and supervision of financial markets. In the top right-hand corner, we see affiliation with transnational European (2.9%) and US (2.0%) policy think tanks as well as positions in international financial institutions such as the World Bank (1.6%). Further down, we see connections to finance ministries (1.7%) or, further up, the IMF and the WTO (8.9%) or the ECB (6.5%). Near the top, consulting corporations or serving as chief economist (CorpCon, 3.1%) are plotted; slightly further down we see being governor of a state-owned bank (GovSBank, 4.6%), such as various development banks (DevBank 3.0%), and working for national central banks (NCB, 5.6%). Further to the left towards the financial industry pole, working for top banks (1.9%) (e.g. JP Morgan, Goldman Sachs, or BNP) and other banks (4.2%) is plotted in close proximity to working for one of the banking supervision authorities (SupervBank 2.5%). Further to the left, we find more associations with investment companies (InvCom, 3.6%), e.g. sitting on advisory boards (6.5%) or executive boards (2.7%) or being a CEO (3.1%). On the opposite side of the axis is a disciplinary background in law (1.1%) and working or consulting for other ministries (1.9%), political practices that are relatively far removed from financial market politics. Other less powerful practices that do not load high are also plotted here: positions of ordinary political or corporate staff and working for consumer organizations, unions, or national administrative bodies.

The third axis (see Figure 5.3) accounts for 10.3% of the overall variance and distinguishes backgrounds in democratic politics predominantly of national anchoring from academic and financial industry backgrounds associated with transnational linkages. At the bottom, we see being a member of parliament (MP, 9.1%), prime minister or minister (PMMin, 8.9%), and governor of a state bank

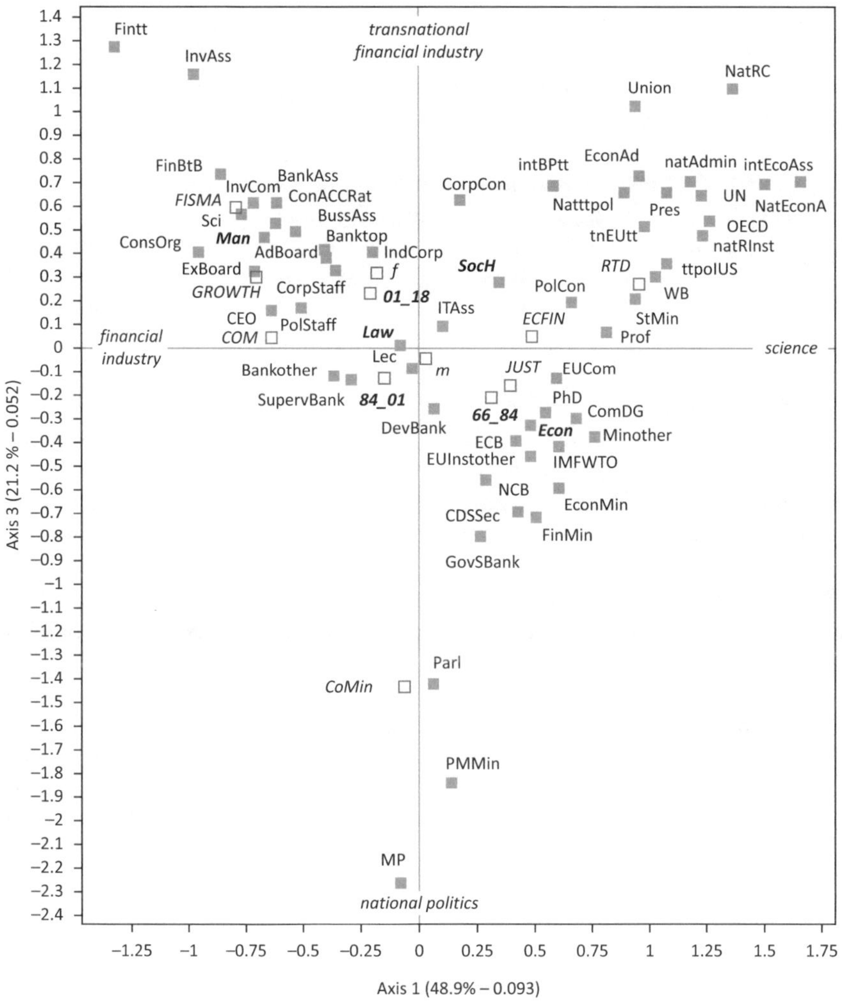

Figure 5.3 Plane 1_3 space of properties, passive categories in italic.

(3.6%), working in or for parliament (4.8%), ministries of finance (4.0%) and economy (2.1%), or central banks (NCB, 2.5%), serving as a state secretary or as a diplomat (CDSSec, 2.4%), and having a background in economics (Econ, 1.7%). The properties shown here appear to indicate traditional political careers in national political and, to a lesser degree, bureaucratic institutions with a European outlook. At the top, we see characteristics that generally also loaded highly on the first axis. To the left we have characteristics that describe a career in finance industry lobbying such as working for a finance industry association (InvAss, 2.9%) or for finance industry think tanks (2.1%), further down, for investment companies (InvCom, 2.3%), engaging in consulting, accounting, and rating (ConAccRat, 1.6%), and having a background in management studies (Man, 1.3%). To the right, we see characteristics that tend to lead to careers on the interface between academic economics and political consulting, such as working for the national research council (2.4%) and national research institutes (1.7%), being a member of a national (1.3%) or international (1.3%) economics association, and being president of a research institute (Pres, 2.5%). These careers often involve becoming a national economic advisor to the government (1.8%), consulting national administration (1.6%) or international institutions such as the UN (1.3%) and OECD (1.3%), and being associated with policy think tanks (2.1%) and unions (2.0%), and further to the left, we have business think tanks (1.7%). The interpretations of the second and third axes correspond to two different conceptions of political capital over time with the second axis stressing today's political power in financial market regulation and supervision and the third axis emphasizing a former more international political and diplomatic power pole of the EU's economic and market integration.

Each of the expert groups is initiated and administered either directly by the Commission (COM), by one of the Commission DGs (JUST, GROWTH, FISMA, ECFIN, or RTD), or by the Commission on behalf of the Council of Ministers (CoMin). Since each of these institutions is responsible for a certain policy area, being a member of an expert group affiliated with one of these institutions can be used to determine whether certain forms of expertise correspond with certain thematic content. When we look at the plane of axes 1 and 2 in the space of properties we see that these institutions (see Figure 5.2, all in italics) differ considerably from the barycentre, allowing the hypothesis that the structure of the expertise objectified in the first plane corresponds to differences between the groups according to who initiated them: DGs, COM, and CoMin are spread out in the plane with deviations between GROWTH and FISMA (0.34) and COM and FISMA (0.45) being deemed small, all others exceeding 0.5 and so seen as notable or when located at the other side of the plane such as ECFIN and GROWTH (1.5) as large (Le Roux & Rouanet, 2010, p. 59).

The one group initiated in 2013 by DG JUST, Expert Group on a Debt Redemption Fund and Eurobills, is the most diverse in terms of its experts' backgrounds and the only one located in the first quadrant in plane 1_2 and in the second quadrant in 1_3, close to bureaucratic and political backgrounds. FISMA, again only represented by one group, the High-Level Expert Group on

Sustainable Finance initiated in 2018, is much more focused on specific expertise and located in the fourth quadrant close to backgrounds in the financial industry, again in both planes. The same applies to the only group initiated by RTD, High Level Economic Expert Group 'Innovation for Growth – i4g' in 2013, that draws heavily on academic/scientific expertise located to the right of the first axis.

Two initiatives by the Council, the *Report to the Council and the Commission on the realization by stages of economic and monetary union in the Community* in 1970 and the Committee for the Study of Economic and Monetary Union in 1989, are much more political in their areas of expertise: on the second axis located on the top and on the third axis at the bottom, they draw heavily on nationally anchored political and administrative backgrounds. Conversely, the two groups initiated by the Commission on financial markets integration, The Development of a European Capital Market in 1966 and Improving European Corporate Bond Markets in 2017, are much less academic and more closely associated with the financial industry on the first axis as well as much less closely associated with nationally anchored democratic politics on the third axis. When taking a look at the two Commission groups separately (not shown here), we see a shift towards drawing on professional backgrounds and stakeholders addressed by the policy issue. A similar shift can be observed in the case of the two groups on monetary union initiated by the Council (also not shown here), towards financial market politics and infrastructure on the second axis and away from general national politics on the third axis, again indicating specialized backgrounds.

This leaves us with the two DGs that account for most of the expert groups observed: ECFIN with nine expert groups and GROWTH (formerly MARKT) with five. Each occupies a distinct area of expertise in both planes. Members of groups initiated by ECFIN have a more academic background, whereas members of groups initiated by GROWTH have more of a background in the financial industry and financial market politics and infrastructure (see Figure 5.2). This also corresponds to the historical location of the groups observed. In the 1970s, ECFIN initiated five groups on the subjects of economic and monetary union, problems of inflation, socio-economic development, and public finance, two on industrial policy and development of the economic system in the 1980s, one on the transition to the single currency in the 1990s, and one on GROWTH in 2003. It should be noted that most economic policy issues covered by ECFIN groups focus on initiating the economic and monetary integration of the EU in at least the 1970s and 1980s. Conversely, GROWTH's first group observed here was initiated in 1997 on the issue of banking charges for conversion to the euro, followed by two groups in 2006 on private equity and investment fund market efficiency. After the world economic crisis, GROWTH initiated groups tackling crisis issues: the High-Level Group on Financial Supervision in the EU in 2009 and the High-Level Expert Group on reforming the structure of the EU banking sector in 2012. The policy issues addressed by these groups are geared more towards the financial market and its infrastructure and appear to require a financial industry background rather than an academic background.

It should be taken into account that revamping financial markets and increasing their efficiency in the 1990s and 2000s only become possible due to previous economic and monetary EU integration. Consequently, the expert specialization observed is as much linked to a certain moment in time as to a specific policy issue examined. The general shift from academic and nationally anchored general political backgrounds towards financial market politics and infrastructure as well as finance industry backgrounds is well illustrated by the location of three periods in both planes (see Figures 5.3 and 5.4): groups initiated before the first Delors Commission (1966–1984), between the first Delors Commission and the resignation of the Santer Commission (1984–2001), and after the Santer Commission (2001–2018). When again observing the distances in the space of categories between the first and last period, we see a large overall deviation (1.0, Figure 5.2), mainly along the second axis (0.86, also Figure 5.2) that is inverted on the third axis (0.44, Figure 5.3). Hence, an increase in the importance of expertise located at the pole of financial markets and administrative regulatory politics is evident over time, as is a decrease in the importance of traditional democratic and international political expertise.

The movement over three periods observed from the bottom right to upper left on the first plane also corresponds to changes in the disciplinary background of experts. Social sciences and humanities (SocH) is located in the fourth quadrant close to the centre of gravity of the first period, whereas management (Man) is in

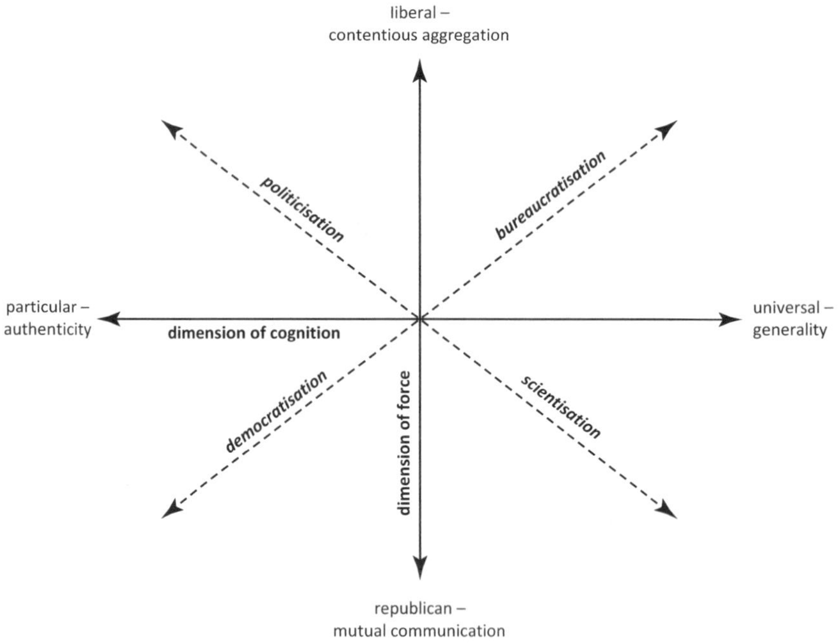

Figure 5.4 Dynamics of professionalization in the space of political practice, schematic presentation.

the second quadrant closer to the third period. Traditional degrees grouped under SocH are philosophy, politics, and economics read at Oxford or Cambridge, and political sciences at SciencePo in Paris or ENA in Strasbourg and Paris, as well as philosophy and history at University College Dublin or various German universities. Degrees subsumed under Man are often MBAs taken at international business schools such as INSEA, ESSEC, or Harvard as well as various Écoles Superieures de Commerce in the francophone context. Economics is located in the first quadrant, not close to any of the periods, and has been present throughout as part of academic expertise. Law is located in the third quadrant and is the only discipline loading (1.5%) on the second axis, meaning that the increasing distance over the three periods can be interpreted as a decline in experts' law backgrounds. The shift in experts' disciplinary backgrounds observed supports the earlier hypothesis that the importance of experts with a professional background in financial market issues as either stakeholders or regulators has increased, at the same time leading to a decline in experts with academic or general political backgrounds. Finally, it can be shown that over time more women are recruited to EU expert groups, although gender equality has by no means been achieved, with women still being underrepresented in the last period (with a ratio of men to women of 27.2% to 72.8%).

Politicization of EU expert groups and calls for legitimacy as investments in Europe

The specific space of EU expert groups' particular expertise reconstructed here shows at least three distinct changes over time and associated subjects. First, we see an increase in the importance of backgrounds in financial market politics and infrastructure regulation. It is a shift towards organized interests and interest brokering (see Gornitzka & Krick, 2018, p. 65) combined with a growing significance of regulative agencies. This leads to a politicization of expertise since it stresses the legitimacy of particularistic cognitive stances and sees political decisions as legitimate if interested parties played a part in their contentious formation. This leads to an increase in the salience of issues discussed, a wider range of backgrounds of agents involved, and a polarization of agents' communication, the three main features of politicization (de Wilde, 2011; Hutter & Grande, 2016). Here, politicization is understood as the act of not only making something political, but of making this claim with a reference to practices of contentious aggregation between contested particular standpoints that draw on authenticity: 'turning something a priori not contested, politically unmarked, devoid of struggle and disagreement, into something disputable or at least discussable, involving different perspectives and interests' (Kauppi & Trenz, 2019, p. 265).

Second, the opposite of politicization is not simply de(politicization) but more specifically either a countermovement of 'leaving it to the discretionary power of government and administration' (Palonen, 2019, p. 251) or to science and its search for objective facts and solutions. As the analysis has shown, the development observed is linked to a shift away from scientific backgrounds and the predominance of academic consulting. This 'de-scientization' of expertise is a counter-tendency to scientization observed in other areas of EU expertise (Krick et al., 2019). In addition, a shift away from general and mostly nationally anchored politics and associated diplomacy occurs, documenting the closure and increased autonomy of the field of EU politics (Georgakakis, 2013). This change can be interpreted as de-bureaucratization, albeit only with reference to national and not transnational bureaucracies, at least in this specific area of expertise.

Third, an increase in the importance of management and business backgrounds is observed (see Chalmers, 2014; Georgakakis, 2017), whereas the importance of civic society backgrounds as well as bureaucratic backgrounds remains virtually the same at a low level, a situation that can hardly be described as a surge towards democratization. Taken together, this development can best be understood as the politicization of expertise in the area of political-economic governance, one of four forms of potential professionalization in the schematic space of political practices shown here (see Figure 5.4) (see Turner, 2014, p. 32).

This development has been noted in the EU political field itself and has, at least in the last 20 years, sparked a heated controversy over the legitimacy of EU expert groups between MEPs, civic society groups such as ALTER-EU, and the Commission (Larsson, 2003; Radaelli, 1999, 2002). Starting with the *EU White Paper on European Governance* (Commission of the European Communities, 2001), the Commission discussed and subsequently issued new horizontal guidelines for establishing and running expert groups as well as initiating a public register as one measure of EU governance reform (Commission of the European Communities, 2005). Here, non-business interest groups have so far attempted to change what they see as inadequate access to the European policy process, that stems partly from the historical predominance of economic policy issues in European integration and partly from the amount of resources (financial as well as manpower and experience) that business interest representatives hold.

In their quest for democratization and transparency, they were joined by MEPs mainly drawing on representative political capital, also not located at the powerful pole of the reconstructed space and also typically outnumbered when it comes to EU expert group membership. Following the Lisbon Treaty, MEPs took the opportunity to test and use their extended powers to argue for further changes, hoping to tilt the prevailing power relationships with the Commission somewhat in their favour. The Commission in turn picked up the challenge for more democratic legitimacy, hoping to improve its battered symbolic stance, while at the same time taking care to maintain its autonomy in the legislative process vis à vis the EP and Council. This led to the development of a specific legitimatory narrative emphasizing the engagement of experts and expertise as one form of generating democratic legitimacy, a true investment in the field of EU politics (Georgakakis & Lasalle, 2012). Overall, the democratic challenge launched to change the rules of summoning experts in the EU context has not so much changed EU expert groups or tipped the scales in favour of the challengers but rather altered the legitimate discourse on EU experts that accompanies the politicization of expert backgrounds, as the following short summary shows.

Preliminary changes in 2005 barely restricted the freedom to appoint anyone the Commission or one of its DGs saw fit to consult on a specific issue. This did not appease the critics, whose main concerns were with transparency regarding membership and minutes of meetings, the overrepresentation of industry and business interests, and the incomplete and outdated register (Haar et al., 2009). In 2010, horizontal rules were again revised to place an emphasis on the mere consultative role of expert groups in aiding the Commission to draw up legislative proposals and policy initiatives, in preparing delegated acts, and in implementing existing EU legislation. Rules now specified more clearly who could be summoned as a member and named a wide range of possible organizations, took common interests held by stakeholders into account in a balanced manner, prevented conflicts of interest by having those appointed in a common interest not represent individual stakeholders, and stated that 'public calls for applications [should] be used as far as reasonably practicable' and that the EP should be informed exactly like member states and was allowed to send experts to attend meetings (European Commission, 2010, pp. 10, 12–13). As regards transparency, the rules required individual members to be named if appointed in their personal capacity or by member states' authorities and organizations as permanent members, which does not include all those representing an institution or organization in a non-personal capacity. How members were selected as well as activities undertaken by the expert group also now have to be made public in the register (European Commission, 2010, pp. 13–14).

Nevertheless, there was no easing of pressure on the Commission from the EP, which had in November 2011 (Moodie, 2016, p. 233) voted for a moratorium on any further funding of the Commission's expert groups and did so again in October 2014 (Holst & Moodie, 2015, p. 37), from the European Ombudsman, who initiated an investigation (European Ombudsman, 2015), or from ALTER-EU, which kept public attention high (Sabido, 2013). There were demands for public consultations, a balance in particular between business and non-business members, a broadened concept of conflict of interest, and more transparency about how groups worked (ALTER-EU, 2016a, b).

In 2016, subsequent changes took some of the demands into account, but not all. The new framework now makes the selection of members by means of public calls for tender a general rule, and requests that members appointed for a commonly shared interest by stakeholders or organizations (particularly those working as consultants) are registered in the transparency register as well as in the register of expert groups to be revised. In addition, the rules now demand a balanced composition, not only in terms of gender but also geography, knowhow, and areas of interest (but they do not make any further specifications). Conflicts of interest now have to be laid out in the form of a public declaration. Still, the Commission's autonomy in selecting members is preserved at least in principle, for example, with formulations like 'as far as possible' concerning the balance of groups (European Commission, 2016, p. 7).

This development shows a certain resemblance to how the Commission generally reacts to criticism of the community method: expert consultations are increased and hailed as sources of legitimacy; these have been part of EU institutions' legitimacy-seeking strategies since the late 1990s (Moodie, 2016, p. 230; Saurugger, 2010). Here, the emphasis is not on legitimacy that derives from democratic representation or input legitimacy. Instead, in line with popular concepts in EU studies of the time (Scharpf, 1997; Schmidt, 2012), the Commission stresses that the participation of experts and expertise in the policy process builds up throughput and output legitimacy. Whereas throughput legitimacy is created by involving stakeholders whose interests are affected by unintended and intended policy consequences and costs in the policy process, thus counteracting the predominance of administrative agents, output legitimacy depends on effectiveness and efficiency of policies, highlighting the importance of expertise and professionalization in order to achieve working policy solutions that serve the people and will create support for political processes (Krick & Gornitzka, 2019, pp. 104–105). Hence, it could be said that the Commission's use of experts and expertise has shifted 'from "consultation" (1960s/70s) to "partnership" (1980/1990) and "participation" (1990s/2000)' (Quittkat & Finke, 2008, p. 184). EU expert groups now seem to play a role as suppliers of sources of not only epistemic but increasingly of democratic authority – although one that feeds into a politicization of expertise.

The Commission's response to its critics has taken a democratic twist, arguing that the professionalization of stakeholder interest representation in the policy process is itself a democratic necessity to balance bureaucratic administrative powers (Georgakakis, 2017). In doing so, it seems to have become a 'normalised' bureaucracy in the sense that it reacts to legitimacy challenges fuelled by the arguments of democratic representation but does so by emphasizing in its own narrative balanced access to policy processes and efficiency of government as legitimation standards. Here, the 'normal' field mechanisms of a democratic political field are at work, diverting democratization challenges towards politicization, thereby safeguarding their bureaucratic stakes, albeit this time not in a national but rather in the European context (Wille, 2013).

Conclusion

Over a time span of 50 years, experts recruited by the Commission to EU expert groups in the areas of monetary integration, market integration, and political-economic governance have changed considerably. They have become less academic, closer to the financial industry and institutions associated with financial market supervision and regulation, and less anchored in national politics. At the same time, this has not made them any lesser 'experts', although it has triggered controversies over the validity of their cognitive claims and the legitimacy of their political power. Both developments – the changing face of expertise and its contestation – have to be seen as the outcome of struggles in the field of EU politics, with the direct involvement of political agents such as members of the Commission, MEPs, civil society groups, business lobbyists, and national politicians as well as EU studies researchers (often as experts). Together they have pushed a development that has led to the politicization of expert groups. Today, the authority of EU expert groups depends more on the authentic particularistic cognitive stances of members and the participation of relevant stakeholders that have proven themselves in contentious aggregation, be it in markets or in the political assertion of interests.

The documented politicization of EU expert groups in one specific area raises interesting questions along at least three dimensions that call for further research. First, empirical questions on the proliferation of politicization in the field of EU politics arise: in what context can these processes be observed, who is involved, and what legitimatory discourses are linked to these developments? Second, there are theoretical questions on the relationship of democratization to politicization, scientization, and bureaucratization, all forms of professionalization of political practices: why is it that calls for more democracy in Europe seem to have the paradoxical effect of increased specialization and the closure of political practices, thus provoking ever more challenges by nationally anchored populist movements from both the left and right? Third, we have methodological questions on researching fields from a historical perspective: what research designs, methods, and data allow us to conceptualize EU expertise and its professionalization as effects of an emerging political field in contested relations to other national and transnational fields, experts as multi-positioned agents in political, academic, and economic fields, and practices as historically conditioned structures shaping political action? In order to answer these questions, we need to further develop a relational and reflexive political sociology of expertise that acknowledges that the 'traditional' academic expert is merely one specific socio-historical form of expert, albeit one in the limelight and at times highly glorified, particularly by certain disciplines of social science which are themselves so heavily involved in constituting political expertise.

References

ALTER-EU. (2016a). *Follow up letter to Timmermans on expert groups*. Retrieved from https://www.alter-eu.org/documents/2016/04/an-open-letter-to-vice-president-timmermans.

ALTER-EU. (2016b). *Open letter to commission on expert groups*. Retrieved from https://www.alter-eu.org/documents/2016/02/ngos-demand-consultation-on-new-rules-for-expert-group.

Anderson, B. (1983). *Imagined communities: Reflections on the origin and spread of nationalism*. London: Verso.

Bajenova, T. (2019). Rescaling expertise in EU policy-making: European think tanks and their reliance on symbolic, political and network capital. *Globalisation, Societies and Education*, *17*(1), 61–77.

Bernhard, S. (2011). Beyond constructivism—the political sociology of an EU policy field. *International Political Sociology*, *5*(4), 426–445.

Bigo, D. (2017). International political sociology: Rethinking the international through dynamics of power. In T. Basaran (Ed.), *International political sociology* (pp. 24–48). Oxon and New York: Routledge.

Blasius, J. (1987). Korrespondenzanalyse: ein multivariates Verfahren zur Analyse qualitativer Daten. *Historical Social Research*, *12*(2/3), 172–189.

Bourdieu, P. (1986). The forms of capital. In J.G. Richardson (Ed.), *Handbook of theory and research in the sociology of education* (pp. 241–258). New York and London: Greenwood Press.

Bourdieu, P. (1991). Political representation: Elements for a theory of the political field. In John B. Thompson & P. Bourdieu (Eds.), *Language and symbolic power* (pp. 171–202). Cambridge: Harvard University Press.

Bourdieu, P. (1994). Rethinking the state: Genesis and structure of the bureaucratic field. *Sociological Theory*, *12*(1), 1–18.

Bourdieu, P. (2001). *Das politische Feld: Zur Kritik der politischen Vernunft*. Konstanz: Universitätsverlag Konstanz.

Bourdieu, P. (2014). *On the state: Lectures at the Collège de France, 1989–1992*. Cambridge: Polity Press.

Büttner, S.M., Leopold, L., Mau, S., & Posvic, M. (2015). Professionalization in EU policy-making? The typology of the transnational Field of EU affairs. *European Societies*, 17(4), 569–592.

Caporaso, J.A. (1998). Regional integration theory: Understanding our past and anticipating our future. *Journal of European Public Policy*, *5*(1), 1–16.

Chalmers, A.W. (2014). Getting a seat at the table: Capital capture and expert groups in the European Union. *West European Politics*, *37*(5), 976–992.

Christensen, J. (2015). The organization of professional expertise in the European Commission. *Politics and Governance*, *3*(1), 13–25.

Collins, H., & Evans, R. (2007). *Rethinking expertise*. Chicago: University of Chicago Press.

Commission of the European Communities. (2001). European Governance—a white paper. *COM(2001) 428 final (2001/C 287/01)*.

Commission of the European Communities. (2005). Framework for commission's expert groups: Horizontal rules and public rester. Communication from the President to the Commission in agreement with the Vice-President responsible for administrative affairs and the Member of the Commission responsible for financial programming and budget {SEC(2005)1004, 27.7.2005, C(2005)2817.

Corbin, J., & Strauss, A.L. (2008). *Basics of qualitative research: Techniques and procedures for developing grounded theory*. Los Angeles, London, New Delhi and Singapore: Sage.

Courty, G., & Michel, H. (2013). Interest groups and lobbyists in the European political space: The permanent Eurocrats. In D. Georgakakis & J. Rowell (Eds.), *The field of Eurocracy: Mapping the EU actors and professionals* (pp. 166–187). Houndmills: Palgrave Macmillan.

Crouch, C. (2004). *Post-democracy*. Cambridge: Polity Press.

De Wilde, P. (2011). No polity for old politics? A framework for analyzing the politicization of European integration. *Journal of European Integration*, *33*(5), 559–575.

European Commission. (2010). Communication from the President of the comission—framework for commission expert groups: Horizontal rules and public register SEC(2010) 1360, 10.11.2010, C(2010) 7649 final.

European Commission. (2016). Commission decision establishing horizontal rules on the creation and operation of Commission expert groups, 30.5.2016, C(2016) 3301 final.

European Ombudsman. (2015). Letter to the European Commission requesting an opinion in the European Ombudsman's own-initiative inquiry OI/6/2014/NF concerning the composition of Commission expert groups. Retrieved from https://www.ombudsman.europa.eu/en/correspondence/en/58861.

Eyal, G. (2019). *The crisis of expertise*. Cambridge: Polity Press.

Fischer, F. (2009). *Democracy and expertise: Reorienting policy analysis*. Oxford: Oxford University Press.

Foucault, M. (2007). *Security, territory, population: Lectures at the Collège de France 1977–1978*. Basingstoke: Palgrave Macmillan.

Foucault, M. (2009). *The birth of biopolitics: Lectures at the Collège de France, 1978–1979*. Basingstoke: Palgrave Macmillan.

Georgakakis, D. (2013). Conclusion: The field of Eurocracy: A new map for new research horizons. In D. Georgakakis & J. Rowell (Eds.), *The field of Eurocracy: Mapping the EU actors and professionals* (pp. 226–247). London: Palgrave Macmillan.

Georgakakis, D. (2017). *European civil service in (times of) crisis: A political sociology of the changing power of Eurocrats*. Cham: Palgrave Macmillan.

Georgakakis, D., & Lasalle, M. de (Eds.). (2012). *The political uses of European governance: Studying a EU white paper*. Opladen, Berlin and Toronto: Barbara Budrich Publishers.

Georgakakis, D., & Rowell, J. (Eds.). (2013). *The field of Eurocracy: Mapping the EU actors and professionals*. Houndsmill: Palgrave Macmillan.

Giddens, A. (1990). *Consequences of modernity*. Cambridge: Polity Press.

Góra, M., Holst, C., & Warat, M. (Eds.). (2018). *Expertisation and democracy in Europe*. London: Routledge.

Gornitzka, Å., & Krick, E. (2018). Stakeholder involvement in EU policy making. In M. Góra, C. Holst & M. Warat (Eds.), *Expertisation and democracy in Europe* (pp. 51–70). London: Routledge.

Gornitzka, Å., & Severdrup, U. (2008). Who consults? The configuration of expert groups in the European Union. *West European Politics*, *31*(4), 725–750.

Gornitzka, Å., & Sverdrup, U. (2011). Access of experts: Information and EU decision-making. *West European Politics*, *34*(1), 48–70.

Gornitzka, Å. & Sverdrup, U. (2015). Societal inclusion in expert venues: Participation of interest groups and business in the European commission expert groups. *Politics and Governance*, *3*(1), 151–164.

Haar, K., Pohl, C., Rowell, A., & Vassalos, Y. (2009). *A captive commission—the role of the financial industry in shaping EU regulation*. Brussels: The Alliance for Lobbying Transparency and Ethics Regulation in the European Union (ALTER-EU).

Habermas, J. (1998). *The inclusion of the other: Studies in political theory*. Cambridge: The MIT Press.

Habermas, J. (2015). *The lure of technocracy*. Cambridge: Polity Press.

Holst, C., & Moodie, J.R. (2015). Cynical or deliberative? An analysis of the European Commission's public communication on its use of expertise in policy-making. *Politics and Governance*, *3*(1), 37–48.

Hutter, S., & Grande, E. (2016). Introduction: European integration and the challange of politicization. In S. Hutter, E. Grande & H. Kriesi (Eds.), *Politicising Europe: Integration and mass politics* (pp. 3–31). Cambridge: Cambridge University Press.

Kauppi, N. (2018). *Toward a reflexive political sociology of the European Union: Fields, intellectuals and politicians*. Cham: Palgrave Macmillan.

Kauppi, N., & Trenz, H.-J. (2019). Notes on the politics of de(politicisation). *Contemporary Political Theory*, *18*(2), 263–268.

Krick, E. (2015). Negotiated expertise in policy-making: How governments use hybrid avisory committees. *Science and Public Policy*, *42*(4), 487–500.

Krick, E., Christensen, J., & Holst, C. (2019). Between 'scientisation' and a 'partizipatory turn'. Tracing shifts in the governance of policy advice. *Science and Public Policy*, *46*(6), 927–939.

Krick, E., & Gornitzka, Å. (2019). The governance of expertise production in the EU Commission's 'high level groups': Tracing expertisation tendencies in the expert group system. In M. Bevir & R. Phillips (Eds.), *Decentering European governance* (pp. 102–120). London and New York: Routledge.

Larsson, T. (2003). *Precooking in the European Union—the world of expert groups, Rep. Ds2003:16*. Stockholm. Retrieved from www.grondweteuropa.nl/9310000/d/europa/zwedneso.pdf.

Larsson, T. & Murk, J. (2007). The Commission's relations with expert advisory groups. In T. Christiansen & T. Larsson (Eds.), *The role of committees in the policy-process of the European Union: Legislation, implementation and deliberation* (pp. 64–95). Cheltenham: Edward Elgar.

Laurens, S. (2018). *Lobbyists and bureaucrats in Brussels: Capitalism's brokers*. Oxon: Routledge.

Le Roux, B., & Rouanet, H. (2004). *Geometric data analysis: From correspondence analysis to structural data analysis*. Dordrecht, Boston and London: Kluwer Academic Publishers.

Le Roux, B., & Rouanet, H. (2010). *Multiple correspondence analysis*. Thousand Oaks: Sage.

Majone, G. (1999). The regulatory state and its legitimacy problems. *West European Politics*, *22*(1), 1–24.

McNamara, K.R. (2018). Authority under construction: The European Union in comparative political perspective. *Journal of Common Market Studies*, *56*(7), 1510–1525.

Metz, J. (2015). *The European Commission, expert groups, and the policy process*. Basingstoke: Palgrave Macmillan.

Moodie, J.R. (2016). Resistant to change? The European Commission and expert group reform. *West European Politics*, *29*(2), 229–256.

Moravcsik, A. (1993). Preferences and power in the European Community: A liberal intergovernmentalist approach. *Journal of Common Market Studies*, *31*(4), 473–524.

Palonen, K. (2019). Politicisation: Disorder or chance? From literary to parliamentary debates. *Contemporary Poiltical Theory*, *18*(2), 249–254.

Quittkat, C., & Finke, B. (2008). The EU Commission consultation regime. In B. Kohler-Koch, D. de Bièvre & W. Maloney (Eds.), *Opening EU-governance to civil society: Gains and challanges* (pp. 183–222). Mannheim: MZES.

Radaelli, C.M. (1999). The public policy of the European Union: Whither politics of expertise? *Journal of European Public Policy*, *6*(5), 757–774.

Radaelli, C.M. (2002). Democratising expertise? In J. Grote & B. Gbikpi (Eds.), *Participatory governance: Political and societal implications* (pp. 197–212). Wiesbaden: Springer.

Reckwitz, A. (2020). *The society of singularities*. Cambridge: Polity Press.

Robert, C. (2012). Expert groups in the building of European public policy. *Globalisation, Societies and Education*, *10*(4), 425–438.

Sabido, P. (2013). *A year of broken promises: Big business still put in charge of EU expert groups, despite commitment to reform*. Brussels: The Alliance for Lobbying Transparency and Ethics Regulation in the European Union (ALTER-EU).

Sanchez-Cuenca, I. (2017). From a deficit of democracy to a technocratic order: The postcrisis debate on Europe. *Annual Review of Political Science*, *20*(20), 351–369.

Saurugger, S. (2010). The social construction of the participatory turn: The emergence of a norm in the European Union. *European Journal of Political Research*, *49*(4), 471–495.

Scharpf, F.W. (1997). Economic integration, democracy and the welfare state. *Journal of European Public Policy*, *4*(1), 18–36.

Schmidt-Wellenburg, C. (2017). Europeanization, stateness, and professions: What role do economic expertise and economic experts play in European political integration? *European Journal of Cultural and Political Sociology*, *4*(4), 430–456.

Schmidt-Wellenburg, C. (2019). For or against the European banking union: Position-takings and positions of 'German-speaking economists' in times of crisis? In J. Blasius, B. Le Roux, F. Lebaron & A. Schmitz (Eds.), *Empirical investigations of social space* (pp. 211–228) Cham: Springer.

Schmidt-Wellenburg, C., & Bernhard, S. (2020a). How to chart transnational fields: Introduction to a methodology for a political sociology of knowledge. In C. Schmidt-Wellenburg & S. Bernhard (Eds.), *Charting transnational fields: Methodology for a political sociology of knowledge* (pp. 1–33). Oxon and New York: Routledge.

Schmidt-Wellenburg, C. & Bernhard, S. (Eds.). (2020b). *Charting transnational fields: Methodology for a political sociology of knowledge*. Oxon and New York: Routledge.

Schmidt, V.A. (2012). Democracy and legitimacy in the European Union revisited: Input, output and 'throughput'. *Political Studies*, *61*(1), 2–22.

Schudson, M. (2006). The trouble with experts—and why democracies need them. *Theory and Society*, *35*(5/6), 491–506.

Scicluna, N. (2014). Politicization without democratization: How the Eurozone crisis is transforming EU law and politics. *International Journal of Constitutional Law*, *12*(3), 545–571.

Statham, P. & Trenz, H.-J. (2015). Understanding the mechanisms of EU politicization: Lessons from the Eurozone crisis. *Comparative European Politics*, *13*(3), 287–306.

Strassheim, H. (2015). Politics and policy expertise. In F. Fisher, D. Torgerson, M. Orsinin & A. Durnova (Eds.), *Handbook of critical policy studies* (pp. 319–340). Cheltenham: Edward Elgar.

Sunstein, C.R. (2016). The most knowledgeable branch. *University of Pennsylvania Law Review*, *164*(7), 1607–1648.

Tansey, R. (2014). The EU's revolving door problem: How big business gains privileged access. In D. Dialer & M. Richter (Eds.), *Lobbying in der Europäischen Union: Zwischen Professionalisierung und Regulierung* (pp. 257–268). Wiesbaden: Springer VS.

Turner, S.P. (2001). What is the problem with experts? *Social Studies of Science*, *31*(1), 123–149.

Turner, S.P. (2014). *The politics of expertise*. London: Routledge.

Vassalos, Y. (2008). *Secrecy and corporate dominance—a study on the composition and transparency of European Commission expert groups*. Brussels: The Alliance for Lobbying Transparency and Ethics Regulation in the European Union (ALTER-EU).

Weber, M. (1978). *Economy and society: An outline of interpretive sociology* (1921 ed.). Berkeley, Los Angeles and London: University of California Press.

Wiesner, C. (2019a). *Inventing the EU as a democratic polity: Concepts, actors and controversies*. Cham: Palgrave Macmillan.

Wiesner, C. (2019b). Rethinking politicization as a multi-stage and multilevel concept. *Contemporary Political Theory, 18*(2), 255–259.

Wille, A. (2013). *The normalization of the European Commission: Politics and bureaucracy in the EU Executive*. Oxford: Oxford University Press.

Part 2

Sociological perspectives on liberal democracy

6 The ideology of anti-populism and the administrative state

Stephen Turner

Introduction

The people, the state, and expertise form an unstable triad, and relating the three in a coherent way, either institutionally or theoretically, is ultimately not possible. Finding a way of dealing with these relations nevertheless is a problem that needs to be solved and re-solved. The theorization of the problem goes back to Plato's *Republic* and the 'solution' of making philosophers kings. The example of the *Republic* is revealing, but one might also take the long European tradition of the three orders, those who pray, those who work, and those who fight (Duby, [1978] 1980). Unstable triads are mythogenic: making sense of their relations requires fictions, or myths, which legitimate arrangements, and these may temporarily stabilize what is inherently unstable, as Plato used the myth of the metals, and as Aquinas used a hierarchical natural law. As one would expect, the particular need for constructing myths of this kind will vary according to the circumstances, including the inherited institutional structures. What needs to be justified will differ.

Harvey Mansfield defined populism, by which he meant populism as a political idea, as the belief in the virtue of the people. 'A populist let us say is a democrat who is satisfied with his own and with the people's virtue' (Mansfield, 1996, p. 7). Populism is thus based on a myth as well. But it is a myth whose role is primarily negative: it does not constitute an order, but rejects one in the name of the people. Actual rule requres more. But to deny the myth of the superior wisdom of the people is to threaten the democratic idea itself. And this poses a special problem for ostensibly 'democratic' regimes. The need for rulers requires its own 'democratic' myths, such as the theory of representation. But the myth of the people constrains these myths.

Mansfield follows his line on the populist with another: 'This distinguishes him from a reformer who is satisfied with his own virtue but not with other people's. Giving over government to the people is not the same as lecturing them' (Mansfield, 1996, p. 7). Progressivism took this tack. The progressives of the early twentieth century wanted the support and enthusiasm of 'the people', and envied populism for this. But they wanted to lead the people themselves. And they asserted themselves not in the name of people's interests and wishes, but in the name of expertise. Progressivism was to be the alliance of experts and an aroused 'people' (Turner, 1996). And this followed an emerging practice of social movements based on expertise, notably the prohibition movement, which employed the techniques presently associated with climate science under the heading alcohol science (Okrent, 2010; Turner, 2001, 2014), through this and other movements, became the third leg in the modern triad. And anti-populism came to take the form of a set of assertions about expertise and governance. My concern in this chapter will be the genealogy and significance of these assertions, and their function as governing myths.

The anti-populist, who is, unlike the populist, not satisfied with the people's virtue, faces a fundamental problem: to deny populism is to deny democracy, or a founding element of the democratic idea, that the people should be, and are the best, governors of themselves. Thus anti-populism, if it pretends to be democratic, cannot overtly deny the myth of the people. But the need for rulers and for the justification of their rule creates an opportunity to redefine the democratic idea, to create an appropriate counter-myth that enables the people to have a place, but not to rule. Anti-populism consists of myths and fictions of this kind, which can be identified in history.

Calling them myths is not to discount them. As W.I. Thomas and Dorothy Swaine Thomas said, '[if] men define situations as real, they are real in their consequences' (Thomas & Thomas, 1928, pp. 571–572). But it is to call attention to their role in discourse. My concern in what follows will be with the role they play, though it will be evident that many of the concepts at play in these discussions diverge from the thinking and experience of the people involved, and that these divergences are the source of the instability of the solutions to the triadic relation between people, state, and expertise. I will try to cut through some of these myths, by explaining the issues that gave rise to them.

The problematic idea of 'the people'

The place to begin, with populism, is with the pure democratic idea itself. Classically, it means rule by the people, the *demos*. But we are accustomed to adding disclaimers and qualifications, or specifications, to this idea: that expressions of the will of the people must take the form of laws and procedures, such as election laws and laws governing representation; or from a liberal perspective, that genuine democratic will-formation requires free individuals with freedom of speech and various individual rights; or from the Left, that substantive equality rather than mere formal equality is required for meaningful democratic participation. These additions function as temporary stabilizers to the relations between the three elements. But they each have their own difficulties, and are mythic on their own.

The critics of the concept of 'the people' are correct in one respect: the construction of the concept in different contexts has varied enormously, and there is no continuity between the various manifestations of the concept, which arise situationally and create unities in response to particular concrete issues. Where there is commonality between populisms is in the targets of their antagonism. Populism is intrinsically a denial of the special superiority of rulers and elites.

This conflict has taken multiple forms in the history of government, and in the history of political thought. Indeed, one can think of government as a scheme of reconciling the two: of adjusting the relation between the wishes of the ruled and the superior power of the ruler necessary to achieve political goods.

'Democratic' solutions require some sort of democratic backstop. Democratic accountability through the direct election of officials is one such means; discretionary power of administrators coupled with a general sense of the beneficial character and hence legitimacy of their actions is another. These correspond to the shoe-wearer and the shoe-maker, respectively. And the latter solution has long been intertwined with the problem of expertise, for the simple reason that the main claim for the need for discretionary power is that desirable governmental actions require expertise that the public lacks. But this is not an unproblematic solution to the problem of triadic balance: indeed, it depends on its own fragile myths.

We tend to think of the problem of democracy in terms of modern democratic theory, which pertains primarily to liberal democracy, and its conception of the people. But there is a long separate history of rule by the people, *il populo*, and people's parties in Europe, which is the subject of extensive discussion by Weber under the heading of 'non-legitimate domination' (Weber, [1921] 1966) reaching back to the Greek notion of democracy itself. These parties and these constitutional forms were separated by several centuries from the political alignments of Europe in the nineteenth century at the time of the rise of the People's Party in the United States, the source of the term populism itself.

The American People's Party – what I will call Populism with an upper-case P in what follows – differed from these earlier parties in an important respect. Expertise was not a major component of the earlier historical conflict between the people – who in the case of *il populo* were a fixed social class – and the governing elite, also a fixed social class. Expertise was even then part of the claim of the elite to rule. The conflict is as old as Aristotle, who compared the expertise of the shoemaker to the needs of the customers whose foot was pinched. But expertise as an independent source of authority, expertise other than expertise about ruling itself, was a new element. The Populists challenged not only the elites, but an economic dogma supported by expert opinion.

Expertise adds complexity to the relation between rulers and ruled, but also stabilizes this two-element relation by adding a third leg. To claim expertise is to add a legitimacy claim. To claim to be acting in accordance with expertise is even better: it displaces the authoritarian character of the relationship onto a neutral third source. To have the third source accepted as neutral and authoritative is better yet: it means that consensus between the three elements of the triad has been achieved, and that there is no room for conflict. The exercise of discretionary power no longer needs democratic accountability. The people accept the experts, and the administrators merely use their discretion in accordance with their expertise. Both those who exercise power and those it is exercised upon accept the legitimacy of the expert. And the expert never exercises power: the neutrality of the expert raises expertise above politics.

Populism, by asserting the superior wisdom of the people, rejects the identification of power and expertise. But in doing so it calls into question the notion of democracy itself. If governments are legitimated by experts, what, exactly, is the point of democratic accountability? What role do 'the people' have other than to obey, or perhaps to occasionally ratify the system of governance as a whole? This no longer seems to be democracy. It is, rather, paternalism.[1] But explicit arguments for paternalism, or elite rule, cannot be squared with the rhetoric of democracy: 'the people' still need to have an active role for a regime to be democratic. As a consequence, anti-populism takes an odd form: as an alternative account of democracy itself that developed in the course of the campaign against populism. My main concern will thus be with explaining anti-populism as an ideology, an ideology that gets concealed, in a Foucauldian way, in subsequent practice. As I will show, anti-populism is a product of a particular ideological need: to reconcile practices derived from absolutism with the claim to be a 'democracy'. As it happens, this is a need that is continually renewed, as new extensions of governmental practice rooted in the traditions of royal bureaucracies need to be justified, and new forms of 'populist' resistance to these practices need to be rejected. Claims about expertise play a large role in this reconciliation.

Populism is democratic in a specific sense: it is a reassertion of popular control as a remedy for the perceived failure or injustice of normal political and administrative practice, especially failures of representation and abuses by bureaucrats. In response to failures of representation, populists endorse referenda, plebiscites, constitutional amendments, or direct elections over mediated ones, depending on the system they are trying to circumvent. Populist movements happen when political parties, traditional leaders, elites, and politics as usual fail to deliver the expected goods, or fail to accord with the popular sense of reality, or are perceived as untrustworthy and corrupt.

What is typical in such cases is conflict with elites, and elite failure, as well as a rejection of the workings of the political system itself, particularly the parties. Populisms thus normally operate in conflict, with, or as an alternative to, parties, and commonly rely on charismatic leaders, or else create an alternative party, or attempt to take over an existing party. Populist tendencies are prone to co-optation, and typically do not outlast the situations that produced them, though they do represent a reserve of general sentiment against elites and particular ruling groups that can be activated in new situations. They differ from ideologies and ideological parties in that they are situational rather than analytic, in the sense that they have concrete targets and grievances rather than a developed analysis of political life that is extended to new situations and refined and elaborated. This accounts for many of the distinctive features of populist movements, especially the preference for leaders who promise to act decisively, in contrast to normal 'politicians', and their hostility to 'politics as usual'.[2]

Populisms are situation-driven rather than analysis-driven, or to put it differently, driven by specific crises or grievances, rather than by a permanent ideological viewpoint, though these movements of course have an analytic component. The situational character of populism also bears on another important contrast. It is necessary to distinguish two aspects of governance, sometimes known as input and output legitimacy, but normally treated as the distinction between representation or legislation and administration, or between democracy as government by the people or government for the people. Traditional parties and normal politics are concerned with representation and legislation. Populism typically arises in situations in which there are larger failures, failures which extend beyond normal political processes, and therefore beyond mere legislation within existing political practices. They typically seek reform of these practices, such as the role of lobbyists.

The antinomy of populism is elite rule. Elites rule through particular strategies, and fail through typical issues. Elite solidarity is essential to elite rule; division among the elite is a typical cause of elite failure (Shipman, Edmunds & Turner, 2018). Elites rule through alliances between the elite and a significant non-elite group. The most stable of these alliances have been with the middle classes, normally under an ideology of meritocracy, property rights, and support of business, an alliance which is played off against the demands of the excluded group, the poor. But an upstairs-downstairs alliance is always possible, and the upper hand the elite has in dealing with the non-elite segments of society depends on its ability to choose alternative groups to ally with. Thus pluralism favours the elite, because it provides more opportunities to change alliances. Populism, in contrast, must produce enough unity in the population to effectively counter the elite, and must therefore transcend differences between segments of society in the name of the people. Both Left and Right populisms are anti-pluralist, as a simple consequence of the dynamics of elite alliance-making: neither kind of populism could succeed if the elite used its alliance-making power to divide the movement. To the extent that elite rule depends on manipulating and shifting alliances with non-elite groups, as is the norm (Shipman, Edmunds & Turner, 2018), an attack on pluralism is a threat to elite rule as a political system itself.

The distinction between situation and analysis driven has other consequences. Žižek captures this distinction in thinking by contrasting Marxism to populism:

> [For] a populist, the cause of the troubles is ultimately never the system as such but the intruder who corrupted it (financial manipulators, not necessarily capitalists, and so on); not a fatal flaw inscribed into the structure as such but an element that doesn't play its role within the structure properly. For a Marxist, on the contrary (as for a Freudian), the pathological (deviating misbehavior of some elements) is the symptom of the normal, an indicator of what is wrong in the very structure that is threatened with 'pathological' outbursts.
>
> (Žižek, 2006, pp. 556–557; see also Laclau, 2005)

The Marxist, in short, needs an analysis, or a theory, about the system; the Populist needs only villains, such as 'the 1%'. Žižek goes on to, in effect, reject the populists' target, the elite, characterizing the 'pseudo concreteness of the figure that is selected as the enemy, the singular agent behind all threats to the people' (Žižek, 2006, p. 556). His is, therefore, a kind of Left-wing anti-populism. What makes Right-wing populism 'dangerous' is that the villains it identifies include not only the elite, but groups that are excluded from the populist's conception of the people, and therefore populism undermines 'pluralism'. The excluded groups are necessarily small, however, because the populist's strategy must be to break the alliances of the elite with subgroups and absorb them into 'the people'.

Populism is a response to the failure of ordinary political processes, and is therefore hostile to business as usual. Parties intervene between the 'people' and the state, in the course of electoral processes, so they are often understood as part of the obstacle to electoral control by 'the people' in the situation of the time. In the American case the solution was to form a new party. This failed, yet the issues raised by the populists were taken up by the extant parties.[3] Weber himself admired Gladstone for being able to go over the heads of the party leaders and speak directly to the people, and took this as a model for democratic control of the bureaucracy, which he saw as the preeminent danger to human freedom. This positive view of demagoguery points to something important: that the expression of non-elite opinion may be channelled in a variety of ways, dependent on the local political circumstances. Demonstrations, or manifestations, are a standard tactic in Europe, but less effective in the US. Charismatic leaders may represent popular opinion, either on the Left or the Right. These forms of expression are independent of the views being expressed. What is common to them is that they are responses to the imperviousness of the existing political order.

The common theme of populisms is accountability to the people, electoral accountability where possible, but through other means if necessary. Anti-populism is an attempt to restrict accountability. And here the claim of expertise becomes relevant. Experts are by definition not directly accountable to the public, but to their expertise, or their expert community, or collectively, as members of an expert class, or as part of an expert institution. Bureaucracies, notoriously, displace responsibility to rules that the bureaucracy interprets for itself, and conceal decision-making by distributing its contributory elements to multiple officials none of whom have complete responsibility, and by protecting officials from personal liability for actions. So there is a sense in which expertise and bureaucracy have an elective affinity, which is actualized as a means of avoiding accountability to 'the people'. One is an organizational, the other an epistemic means to the same end. Not surprisingly, they play a large role in the ideology of anti-populism.

Real populism

American Populism of the late nineteenth century is the source of the term and the model for the category. Some thinkers, eager to associate populism with fascism, either deny it was a genuine case of populism, or alternatively insinuate that it was a nascent form of fascism. My own reason for choosing the American late nineteenth and early twentieth centuries are simple. It illustrates issues that are submerged, for historical reasons, in cases of recent Right-wing European populism, which are nevertheless illuminated by the American case. My concern will be with the co-eval phenomenon of the American administrative state, and its justifying theory, which was explicitly anti-populist, and which becomes solidified in a vast subsequent theoretical literature in public administration. The parallel European literatures on this general topic, for historical reasons that will become apparent, lack the degree of explicit theorizing on the relation of democracy to administration that figures in the American discussion.

The major difference was this: the Continental administrative state did not need to be justified or explained in relation to democracy; it already existed prior to the many gradual steps toward 'democracy'. The American form had to be created, and was created through borrowing from, and reflecting on, Continental models. This meant that there was an explicit analysis of the administrative state and its relation to democracy, one which happens to have produced a specific intellectual tradition and body of practice, in which the issue of democracy is central. Much of the discussion focused on legal and constitutional issues, a topic I will not pursue here, but they may be briefly summarized. The People's Party in the United States invoked the original democratic impulses of the ordinary people as expressed in the American founding, and especially in the thinking of the anti-federalists, such as Sam Adams, that office holders should be voted on every year, thus maximizing electoral accountability. In comparative perspective, the fundamental constitutional feature of American government was rule by elected officials at all levels of administration, a practice that never emerged in Europe. It was this feature, and the complaints about such things as machine politics, that produced the negative view of American democracy that dominated European perspectives in the late nineteenth century, and is also central to the narrative of anti-populism.

The Populist movement arose in response to the world wheat price crisis of the 1880s, which coincided with the rapid expansion of cities, the world economy, and consequently the demand for capital, creating a crisis for credit that affected much of the capitalist world. Here the claim that the people had superior wisdom, an element not directly addressed in the UN definition, was important. There was an expert consensus on this, at least in the United States among economists and the elite, for strong currencies and the gold standard and against the radical expansion of money supplies. The platform of the People's Party of 1892 is the standard source for their views, though the movement, and the idea of reversing the turn to the gold standard, preceded it. This was the source of their key anti-elitist social analysis:

> Silver, which has been accepted as coin since the dawn of history, has been demonetized to add to the purchasing power of gold by decreasing the value of all forms of property as well as human labor, and the supply of currency is purposely abridged to fatten usurers, bankrupt enterprise, and enslave industry. A vast conspiracy against mankind has been organized on two continents, and it is rapidly taking possession of the world. If not met and overthrown at

> once it forebodes terrible social convulsions, the destruction of civilization, or the establishment of an absolute despotism.
>
> (National People's Party Platform, [1892] 1966, p. 91)

The platform, and the movement itself, went far beyond this, and in ways that are typical of populisms generally. The core of their position was an account of the situation:

> The conditions which surround us best justify our co-operation; we meet in the midst of a nation brought to the verge of moral, political, and material ruin. Corruption dominates the ballot-box, the Legislatures, the Congress, and touches even the ermine of the bench. The people are demoralized; most of the States have been compelled to isolate the voters at the polling places to prevent universal intimidation and bribery. The newspapers are largely subsidized or muzzled, public opinion silenced, business prostrated, homes covered with mortgages, labor impoverished, and the land concentrating in the hands of capitalists. The urban workmen are denied the right to organize for self-protection, imported pauperized labor beats down their wages, a hireling standing army, unrecognized by our laws, is established to shoot them down, and they are rapidly degenerating into European conditions. The fruits of the toil of millions are boldly stolen to build up colossal fortunes for a few, unprecedented in the history of mankind; and the possessors of those, in turn, despise the republic and endanger liberty. From the same prolific womb of governmental injustice we breed the two great classes – tramps and millionaires.
>
> (National People's Party Platform, [1892] 1966, p. 90)

The aim of the movement was 'to restore' popular rule, and in this respect it was a form of identity politics *avant la lettre*, but the identity was discussed not in the language of class, but in terms of 'the plain people', who were identified with the founders.

> [We] seek to restore the government of the Republic to the hands of 'the plain people,' with which class it originated. We assert our purposes to be identical with the purposes of the National Constitution; to form a more perfect union and establish justice, insure domestic tranquility, provide for the common defense, promote the general welfare, and secure the blessings of liberty for ourselves and our posterity.
>
> (National People's Party Platform, [1892] 1966, p. 92)

The populist movement allied itself with the Knights of Labor, the largest union of the time, and the Knights, whose 'identity' was so broad as only to exclude bankers, were ultimately supplanted by trade unions. There were, however, exclusions that followed from their account of the situation. The Knights and the trade unions generally were also opposed to unrestricted immigration, and for the same reasons. The party platform reflected this:

> That we condemn the fallacy of protecting American labor under the present system, which opens our ports to the pauper and criminal classes of the world and crowds out our wage-earners; and we denounce the present ineffective laws against contract labor, and demand the further restriction of undesirable emigration.
>
> (National People's Party Platform, [1892] 1966, p. 95)

Their attitude to the state was, however, paradoxical. On the one hand they wanted an increase in government power:

> We believe that the power of government – or in other words, of the people – should be expanded (as in the case of the postal service) as rapidly and as far as the good sense of an intelligent people and the teachings of experience shall justify, to the end that oppression, injustice, and poverty shall eventually cease in the land.
>
> (National People's Party Platform, [1892] 1966, p. 92)

But they did not want the creation of an unaccountable administration or massive bureaucracy.

Thus in a platform item calling for government control of the railroads, they qualified this demand by asking for an amendment to the Constitution by which

> all persons engaged in the government service shall be placed under a civil-service regulation of the most rigid character, so as to prevent the increase of the power of the national administration by the use of such additional government employes [sic].
>
> (National People's Party Platform, [1892] 1966, p. 93)

This may seem to be a contradictory demand: more government action without more power for the national administration and more bureaucrats, and less money in the hands of the state. But their suspicions of state power were foremost. They held that 'the money of the country should be kept as much as possible in the hands of the people', and thus demanded 'that all State and national revenues shall be limited to the necessary expenses of the government, economically and honestly administered' (National People's Party Platform, [1892] 1966, p. 94).

These demands were made in the larger context of a demand for greater electoral control, for example for the popular election of senators, and the imposition of one-term limits for the President and Vice-President, and for the secret ballot. The theme is clear: democracy requires the maximization of electoral control of the state, and a state that is responsive to the demands of the people as expressed in voting, with as little mediation as possible by professional politicians. But the situational aspects of the demands were epistemic: they were rejections of the guiding, and often 'expert', opinions of the elite.

The enemies of populism

Woodrow Wilson, writing in the nineteenth and early twentieth century as a professor, the only American president with this background, provides a complete intellectual articulation of anti-populist thinking. The basic elements are these: the people cannot be trusted to perform certain tasks, such as voting for administrators. But they can be led, by opinion leaders, which gives them the illusion of choice, to accept what they are given, and administrators can be given actual discretionary power, and a great deal of it, under the fiction that what they do is not 'politics' but pure administration, and that political choices determine the ends which administrators seek. The justification for this arrangement is that the people are rather stupid, and administrators possess knowledge, expertise, that the amateurs who get elected to the excessive multitude of democratically accountable office do not. Moreover, the electoral process needs to be radically curtailed: it is corrupted by political machines and the like. So the vast number of political offices needs to be reduced, by centralization, thus eliminating the need for local, independent, politically accountable office holders. The administrators who will replace them can be trusted and are accountable to the public because their responsibilities are well-defined, despite the lack of an electoral method, or indeed any method but trust, of holding them accountable. Pluralism means that there is no 'people' left for them to be democratically accountable to, as there once was, so the ideal of democratic accountability in the present leads instead to corruption and incompetence. Hallowed political ideas, such as the separation of powers and the rule of law, need to be discarded. Similarly for the rule of law, it is inefficient to have the courts and lawyers in a position to correct and supervise administrators. They need a wide zone of discretionary power, and this needs to include powers to regulate of the sort normally thought to be part of legislation. This arrangement 'saves' democracy, but saves it from itself: it not only produces better results, but it limits the domain of democracy to the range of things that opinion leaders of a kind resembling the British aristocracy, responsible but also benignly concerned with the general good, can exercise their influence over.

The temporal and logical order of this argument matters. It was not an argument of the form 'we have the relevant expertise, and are prevented from using it by an ignorant public, and therefore need positions of authority which are free from electoral supervision, which we can be trusted to use correctly'. Instead it took the form of 'the public is ignorant, officials need to be protected from them, they can be trusted if they are given a free hand, and then they can develop the expertise to act'. It is more an argument *against* the people than an argument for the alternative. Obviously, this was not, so to speak, an argument that could be made as part of an open political agenda. It needed to be disguised as something else. And the disguise came in the form of a variety of claims about the inadequacies of the electoral process. Wilson's solution was, invariably, to limit electoral accountability. And this directly clashed with Populism.

The novelty with Populism was that the case for the people no longer rested on the virtues of the Yeoman Farmer. Now it rested on the falsity of the beliefs of the elite, particularly with respect to the Gold Standard. The anti-populists seized on this. This was a matter on which the elite claimed overwhelming expert support. Wilson's own animus against Populism verged on the hysterical, despite his professorial language.

> There could be no better illustration of this than the constant re-argument, *de novo*, of the money question among us, and the easy currency to be obtained, at every juncture of financial crisis, for the most childish errors with regard to the well-known laws of value and exchange. No nation not isolated like ourselves in thought and experience could possibly think itself able to establish a value of its own for gold and silver, by legislation which paid no regard either to the commercial operations or to the laws of coinage and exchange which obtained outside its own borders. That a great political party should be able to win men of undoubted cultivation and practical sense to the support of a platform which embodied palpable and thrice-proven errors in such matters, and that, too, at a great election following close upon protracted, earnest, frank, and universal discussion, and should poll but little less than half the votes of the nation, is startling proof enough that we have learned to think, for the most part, only in terms of our own separate life and independent action, and have come to think ourselves a divided portion of mankind, masters and makers of our own laws of trade.
>
> (Wilson, 1901, p. 294)

This represents an early appearance of an appeal to expertise and a complaint about its lack of effect on the voting masses. Wilson concedes to at least some of his opponents the Jeffersonian virtues of cultivation and practical sense. But 'practical sense' now becomes an insult: this did not protect them from childish errors.[4]

The solution was to be found in reforming basic political institutions, under the pretext of 'efficiency', with the effect of eliminating electoral accountability, the basic aim of Populism. But the pretext was not based on an attack on the governance of big cities. As Woodrow Wilson expressed the complaints motivating him:

> Our later life has disclosed serious flaws, has even seemed ominous of pitiful failure, in some of the things we most prided ourselves upon having managed well: notably, in pure and efficient local government, in the successful organization of great cities, and in well-considered schemes of administration. The boss – a man elected by no votes, preferred by no open process of choice, occupying no office of responsibility – makes himself a veritable tyrant amongst us, and seems to cheat us of self-government; parties appear to hamper the movements of opinion rather than to give them form and means of expression;

> multitudinous voices of agitation, an infinite play of forces at cross-purpose, confuse us; and there seems to be no common counsel or definite union for action, after all.
>
> (Wilson, 1901, p. 291)

These were, so to speak, Populist complaints against the existing system, and paralleled the People's Party platform's strictures against rail lobbyists. But Wilson and the Populists had diametrically opposed solutions. Wilson believed that what was needed was elite rule, based on the model of the English aristocracy. Ever the Anglophile and secret Germanophile, Wilson used a German source to describe it.

> Until 1888, influential country gentlemen, appointed justices of the peace by the crown upon the nomination of the Lord Chancellor, were the governing officers of her counties. Practically every important matter of local administration was in their hands, and yet the people of the counties had absolutely no voice in their selection. Things had stood so for more than four hundred years. Professor Rudolph Gneist, the great German student of English institutions, in expounding English ideas of self-government as he found them exemplified in the actual organization of local administration, declared that the word *government* was quite as emphatic in the compound as the word *self*. The people of the counties were not self-directed in affairs: they were governed by crown officials. The policy of the crown was indeed moderated and guided in all things by the influence of a representative parliament; the justices received no salaries; were men resident in the counties for which they were commissioned, identified with them in life and interest, landlords and neighbors among the men whose public affairs they administered. They had nothing to gain by oppression, much to gain by the real advancement of prosperity and good feeling within their jurisdictions: they were in a very excellent and substantial sense representative men. But they were not elected representatives; their rule was not democratic either in form or in principle. Such was the local self-government of England during some of the most notable and honorable periods of her history.
>
> (Wilson, 1901, p. 295)

This was elite rule *on behalf* of the people, not self-government. And it provided Wilson with the model he developed for saving 'democracy'. The problem was to find a class of people who fit this model of representation, and to give them power. The new class was an invented one: administrators who would be granted vast discretionary power.

The case for the administrative state

The argument he developed was an attempt to discredit elections, and sanitize and justify administrative power and discretion. Expertise played a role in this argument, but not a simple one. Wilson's argumentative strategy was clear: to limit elections, and to limit electoral control of 'administration', which is conceived in such a way as to replace offices under electoral control and to centralize power so as to eliminate them. The present system, he thought, gives

> so many elective offices that even the most conscientious voters have neither the time nor the opportunity to inform themselves with regard to every candidate on their ballots, and must vote for a great many men of whom they know nothing. They give us, consequently, the local machine and the local boss; and where population crowds, interests compete, work moves strenuously and at haste, life is many-sided and without unity, and voters of every blood and environment and social derivation mix and stare at one another at the same voting places, government miscarries, is confused, irresponsible, unintelligent, wasteful. Methods of electoral choice and administrative organization, which served us admirably well while the nation was homogeneous and rural, serve us oftentimes ill enough now that the nation is heterogeneous and crowded into cities.
>
> (Wilson, 1901, p. 296)

This brings together two ideas: that democracy requires homogeneity, and that heterogeneity requires administrative power. What this power was supposed to be was extensive and discretionary, but apolitical. 'Administrative questions are not political questions. Although politics sets the tasks for administration, it should not be suffered to manipulate its offices' (Wilson, [1887] 1941, p. 494). It requires not electoral accountability, but trust, and organization that inspires trust:

> *Trust is strength* in all relations of life; and, as it is the office of the constitutional reformer to create conditions of trustfulness, so it is the office of the administrative organizer to fit administration with conditions of clear-cut responsibility which shall insure trustworthiness.
>
> (Wilson, [1887] 1941, p. 497; italics in original)

But this has a specific meaning: 'large powers and unhampered discretion seem to me the indispensable conditions of responsibility' (Wilson, [1887] 1941, p. 497). The two are supposed to go hand in hand:

> If to keep his office a man must achieve open and honest success, and if at the same time he feels himself intrusted with large freedom of discretion, the greater his power the less likely is he to abuse it, the more is he nerved and sobered and elevated by it. The less his power, the more safely obscure and unnoticed does he feel his position to be, and the more readily does he relapse into remissness.
>
> (Wilson, [1887] 1941, p. 498)

So to advance efficiency required a different political model, and to be 'democratic' required not just the pretence of political neutrality and subordination to the goals set in the political realm, but a claim about expertise.

This represented a fundamental change in the very idea of representative government, which Wilson candidly admitted, and it was a change that directly implicated the populist idea of the wisdom of the people, which Wilson demoted to 'the opinion of the street'. Only the right opinions should count, and they should arise in a particular setting, controlled by bureaucrats.

> Representative government has had its long life and excellent development, not in order that common opinion, the opinion of the street, might prevail, but in order that the best opinion, the opinion generated by the best possible methods of general counsel, might rule in affairs; in order that some sober and best opinion might be created, by thoughtful and responsible discussion conducted by men intimately informed concerning the public weal, and officially commissioned to look to its safeguarding and advancement, – by discussion in parliaments, discussion face to face between authoritative critics and responsible ministers of state.
>
> (Wilson, 1901, pp. 290–291)

The error of the past was clear to Wilson, and it was shown in the misinterpretation of the concept of self-governance. 'We printed the *SELF* large and the *government* small in almost every administrative arrangement we made; and that is still our attitude and preference' (Wilson, 1901, p. 296; emphasis in the original).

This simply did not work.

> We have found that even among ourselves such arrangements are not universally convenient or serviceable. They give us untrained officials, and an expert civil service is almost unknown amongst us. The aim of this response was to save democracy from itself, from electoral control, and from the opinion of the street, though the creation of an efficient and expert administrative state.
>
> (Wilson, 1901, p. 296)

What is distinctive about Wilson's writing, and that of such figures as John Burgess, who founded the Columbia University School of Economic and Political Science (Hoxie, 1955) precisely for the task of creating a class of professional bureaucrats, is this: it relied on European models, and the protagonists were Francophiles, Germanophiles, and Anglophiles, but provided a 'democratic' rationale for practices with a constitutional origin in either royal centralization or absolutism. The model was state bureaucracy, or what was openly called by Wilson, in the parlance of this pre-Bolshevik time, 'state socialism'. As Carl Schmitt pointed out, in Europe bureaucratic rule was a constitutional form that stood on its own, and European constitutions were mixed constitutions, with different elements that depended on different forms of legitimacy, of which this was one (Schmitt, [1932] 2004; Schmitt, [1928] 2008). In the American setting, bureaucratic powers of the sort that were normal on the Continent raised constitutional issues, particularly over the doctrine of separation of powers, which forbade administrators from legislating, and conflicted with the practice of judicial review, which empowered the courts to oversee regulation. What Wilson hankered after was the Continental model. So he had to overcome resistance to the idea that it was incompatible with democracy.

> We have supposed that there could be one way of efficiency for democratic governments, and another for monarchical. We have declined to provide ourselves with a professional civil service, because we deemed it undemocratic; we have made shift to do without a trained diplomatic and consular service, because we thought the training given by other governments to their foreign agents unnecessary in the case of affairs so simple and unsophisticated as the foreign relations of a democracy in politics and trade, transactions so frank, so open, so straightforward, interests so free from all touch of chicane or indirection; we have hesitated to put our presidents or governors or mayors into direct and responsible relations of leadership with our legislatures and councils in the making of laws and ordinances, because such a connection between lawmakers and executive officers seemed inconsistent with the theory of checks and balances whose realization in practice we understood Montesquieu to have proved essential to the maintenance of a free government. Our theory, in short, has paid as little heed to efficiency as our practice. It has been a theory of non-professionalism in public affairs; and in many great matters of public action non-professionalism is non-efficiency.
>
> (Wilson, 1901, p. 291)

For efficiency, the system – democratic self-government – needed to go, or to be limited drastically. An area needed to be carved out that was free of the system of checks and balances between the branches, within the executive, that allowed for discretionary power free from direct electoral or judicial supervision.

> Our success is made doubtful by that besetting error of ours, the error of trying to do too much by vote. Self-government does not consist in having a hand in everything, any more than housekeeping consists necessarily in cooking dinner with one's own hands. The cook must be trusted with a large discretion as to the management of the fires and the ovens.
>
> (Wilson, [1887] 1941, p. 498)

The people would be given some say in the new model, but only on the terms granted by administrators, terms based on expert knowledge of 'the best means'. 'Let administrative study find the best means for giving public criticism this control and for shutting it out from all other interference' (Wilson, [1887] 1941, p. 499). Shutting it out of interference, judicial or political, was the goal.

The myths here are multiple, and they make up a more or less coherent whole. The 'less' in the coherence is itself valuable: the various parts can be substituted for or need not even be mentioned in contexts where they are taken for granted, so this does not look like an ideology. The key idea is the incompetence of the people to govern themselves, and the consequent need for the delegation of authority to administrators, who possess expertise that is beyond the ken of the people. These administrators needed no supervision: merely by being given responsibility and discretionary power they would become paragons of apoliticality. Without democratic control, and free from the interference of lawyers and courts, government would become efficient. By giving up democratic control, and accepting the pale substitute of trust, 'democracy' would be saved. No one need believe these myths. They simply need to be embodied in practice: political parties need to ignore the discretionary actions of administrators, and thus give their tacit consent. Courts need to invent doctrines that enable them to deny relief to those who are injured by these acts. Politicians need to pass political problems off to 'experts'. Experts need to claim and thus take questions out of politics, with the tacit or explicit consent of politicians.

Populism and democratic theory

Wilson caught Populism in a basic practical contradiction: it wanted more government, but without bureaucrats, and without giving up electoral control. In a sense, this problem is a variant of the classic problem of the conflict between liberalism and democracy, in which a democratic vote can eliminate the freedoms that are a condition of a functioning democracy. The wishes of the people may lead them to what amounts to a practical contradiction. But these issues are intrinsic to democracy itself, in its original and core meaning. So is the problem of minorities: democracy as a majoritarian system of rule inevitably favours majorities over minorities, whether these are minorities of interest, opinion, or ethnicities with different opinions or interests than the majority. Much of the mythology of democracy involves the papering over of these hard facts.

Anti-populism is, like liberalism itself, anti-democratic. But liberal anti-populism relied on liberal means – on the rule of law and on constitutional restrictions on the state itself – to tie the hands of 'the people'. Liberalism is based on fear of the people. Left anti-populism or progressivism is also anti-democratic. It denigrates the people – the notions of false consciousness, misrecognition, and so forth are anti-democratic in the guise of anti-populism. But the guise is important: it allows anti-democratic ideas to be presented as 'saving democracy', or true democracy, when it is in fact a means of expanding the power of the state, and its discretionary power, which can then be used for 'progressive' ends.

Weber famously praised Gladstone for his ability to break out of the constraints of party and speak directly to the people, and promoted a constitutional design that was intended to maximize the possibility of this kind of leadership. He thought of this as the only means to control the bureaucracy, which parties would not do. Just as Weber viewed the fundamental form of democratic rule as plebiscitarian, and wished to amplify plebiscitary possibilities and forms, the American populists endorsed 'the legislative system known as the initiative and referendum' (National People's Party Platform, [1892] 1966, p. 95). The point of anti-populism was to prevent the use of these means, and restrict accountability even more – to the point that it was anti-democratic in the name of democracy.

Notes

1 This, in fact, is what writers like Philip Kitcher (2001) actually argue for.
2 Left populism makes the same gestures, but in academic circles at least there is a model of democratic transformational change in which structures and societal norms are dissolved in a moment of collective fusion, i.e. without leadership; see Wolin (1993, 1996).
3 But not completely. Some issues were ignored or restructured. And populist sentiment remained a distinctive feature of local politics in many places, a half-century after the movement itself expired; see Key (1949).
4 It is worth noting that in three decades the gold standard was dead, on a worldwide basis.

References

Duby, G. [1978] (1980). *The three orders: Feudal society imagined.* Chicago: The University of Chicago Press.
Hoxie, R.G. (1955). *A history of the faculty of political science, Columbia University.* New York: Columbia University Press.
Key, V.O. (1949). *Southern politics in state and nation.* Knoxville: University of Tennessee Press.
Kitcher, P. (2001). *Science, truth, and democracy.* New York: Oxford University Press.
Laclau, E. (2005). *On populist reason.* London & New York: Verso.
Mansfield, H. (1996). Was it really a myth? The persistence of individualism in America. *The Times Literary Supplement.* February 9. Retrieved from The Times Literary Supplement Historical Archive (www.the-tls.co.uk/archive/).
National People's Party Platform. [1892] (1966). The Omaha platform, July 1892: National People's Party Platform. In G.B. Tindall (Ed.), *A populist reader: Selections from the works of American populist leaders* (pp. 90–96). New York: Harper and Row.
Okrent, D. (2010). *Last call: The rise and fall of prohibition.* New York: Simon and Schuster.
Schmitt, C. [1932] (2004). *Legality and legitimacy.* Durham: Duke University Press.
Schmitt, C. [1928] (2008). *Constitutional theory.* Durham: Duke University Press.
Shipman, A., Edmunds, J., & Turner, B.S. (2018). *The new power elite: Inequality, politics and greed.* London & New York: Anthem Press.
Thomas, W.I., & Thomas, D.S. (1928). *The child in America: Behavior problems and programs.* New York: Knopf.
Turner, S. (1996). The Pittsburgh survey and the survey movement: An episode in the history of expertise. In M.W. Greenwald & M. Anderson (Eds.), *Pittsburgh surveyed: Social science and social reform in the early twentieth century* (pp. 35–49). Pittsburgh: University of Pittsburgh Press.
Turner, S. (2001). What is the problem with experts? *Social Studies of Science, 31*(1), 123–149.
Turner, S. (2014). *The politics of expertise.* New York: Routledge.
Weber, M. [1921] (1966). *The city.* New York: The Free Press.

Wilson, W. (1901). Democracy and efficiency. *Atlantic Monthly*. March. Retrieved from www.theatlantic.com/magazine/archive/1901/03/democracy-and-efficiency/520041/.
Wilson, W. [1887] (1941). The study of administration. *Political Science Quarterly*, *56*(4), 481–506.
Wolin, S. (1993). Democracy, difference, and recognition. *Political Theory*, *21*(3), 464–483.
Wolin, S. (1996). Fugitive democracy. In S. Benhabib (Ed.), *Democracy and difference: Contesting the boundaries of the political* (pp. 31–45). Princeton: Princeton University Press.
Žižek, S. (2006). Against the populist temptation. *Critical Inquiry*, *2*(3), 551–574.

7 Roman Catholicism and democracy

Internal conservatism and external liberalism?

Rosario Forlenza and Bryan S. Turner

Introduction

Existing debates about the Catholic Church and democracy tend to focus on the external relationship of Catholicism to societies or political institutions such as governments. Typically, that impact is seen in a negative light. We can however develop a more comprehensive view of the issues if we consider this debate in terms of an external and an internal dimension of the Church. In this chapter therefore we examine the question of Catholicism and democracy in terms of the Church's internal ecclesiastical structure(s) and secondly in terms of its external relationships with political institutions and society more broadly. In terms of both dimensions, we treat Vatican II as a critical turning point in the Church's relationship to modernity in general and to democracy in particular, but the question remains as to what extent its internal hierarchical structures are compatible with modern notions of democratic participation. Vatican II, commencing under Pope John XII in 1962 and concluding with Pope Paul VI in 1965, revised the relations between the Church and the modern world. In particular, the Catholic Church adopted a more positive assessment of secular modernity and the value of democratic institutions. While we give prominence to Vatican II in our analysis of the transformation of Catholicism in the twentieth century, we note that the development of the political attitudes and strategies of the Church have to be located in the second half of the nineteenth century with the growth of Christian Democracy and its influence on political parties in Europe and Latin America.

The Catholic Church, at least historically, is an authoritarian institution in which the laity is largely excluded from any influence over its governance and leadership.[1] We argue that despite a major revision of its beliefs towards the outside world, it remains a hierarchical, priestly organization in which knowledge and power are controlled by the priesthood. Ultimately authority descends downwards from the Pope through his cardinals and bishops to local parishes. In more technical terms, the Church and its priests control the means of grace, that is, the keys that open the doorways to personal salvation. In short, Vatican II democratized the Church's relationship with the outside world, while leaving its conservative and authoritarian internal or domestic culture largely intact. We believe that describing the Church in this manner is not necessarily a normative judgement, but a statement regarding what defines any priestly institution. We conclude that, while the post-Vatican II Church has democratic credentials, the sex scandals that have rocked the Church illustrate its internal secretive structure.

Part one: The internal hierarchic structure of authority

We start by referring to the classical texts of the sociology of religion, namely to the work of Max Weber and Ernst Troeltsch. Sociology has generally seen Protestantism as a reformed version of Christianity that contributed to the emergence of democratic politics by its emphasis on vernacular languages, giving access to biblical truths to the 'common man', and by its emphasis, if not on lay leadership, then on lay participation. While we defend this interpretation, we must start with a warning from a historical perspective on the Reformation. David Ogg, writing in the eighth revised edition of *Europe in the Seventeenth Century*, cautioned

> the truth is that such a vague term as democratic can be used of seventeenth-century organizations only with very careful reservations. The political heritage of the Renaissance was absolutism in the state, and the Calvinists were quite as much influenced by this conception as their opponents.
>
> (1961, pp. 88–89)

While taking these reservations on board, we are more interested in a later period in the eighteenth century when Protestant sects flourished in Britain and the United States.

Turning then to classical sociology, Troeltsch's model of church-sect-mysticism illustrated the dramatic differences for example between the Roman Catholic Church as a universal authoritarian organization and the Protestant sects (Troeltsch, 1992). Sects often emerged as a form of lay resistance to the hierarchical and closed character of the universal Church, but these sects often over time evolved towards conservative churches or more strictly towards denominations. Bryan Wilson (1959, 1961) developed an analysis of sects in terms of their responses to secular society. With Weber's ideal types in mind, he identified five sectarian types: conversionist, revolutionist, gnostic, reformist, and utopian. Sects that had an emphasis on conversion moved most radically towards middle-class denominations. In particular second-generation members are prone to accommodation into secular values, and hence over time such organizations are open to secular social influences and can quickly evolve into a denomination. Sociology of religion in the United States came to favour the idea of the denomination as a more accurate description of what was happening to conversionist sects in secular societies. In particular, with the separation of church and sect, the absence of an established church, the denomination was seen to be more characteristic of American conditions than sects.

We need briefly to give a definition of the denomination because we argue subsequently that the process of denominationalization has characterized aspects of the transformation of the Catholic Church, especially in its external relationship to secular society, after Vatican II. In this regard, H. Richard Niebuhr's *The Social Sources of Denominationalism* (1962) has been influential. Niebuhr argued that Protestant denominations had adjusted to the dominant pattern of individualism, which was particularly attractive for middle-class-followers with a gospel message that did not preach sin and damnation. While the majority of sects rejected the values and institutions of secular society, Protestant denominations were more likely to accommodate to rather than reject secularization. This accommodation has gone furthest in the United States with the rise of the mega-church.

The idea that Protestantism, as a system of denominations, is more compatible with secular modernity than Catholicism is often attributed to Troeltsch (1912). However, his attitude towards Protestantism was in fact more complicated and circumspect. He believed that there were important differences between *Altprotestantismus* and *Neuprotestantismus* – the latter being more consistent with modernity. We might follow Lori Pearson in arguing that for Troeltsch 'Protestantism was fertile ground for the working out of a theory of modernity' (2018, p. 38) rather than simply an analysis of religious organizations.

Yet another aspect of the Troeltsch legacy concerns the history of human rights. Thus, he explored the religious and secular influences on the historical rise of rights in his *Stoic-Christian Natural Law and Modern Secular Law* in 1911 (Troeltsch, 2005). In general, he argued that Protestantism contributed to ideas about individualism and freedom via the notion of 'personalism'. Similarly Georg Jellinek's objective in 1895 in *The Declaration of the Rights of Man and of Citizens* (2009) was to uncover the early religious roots of human rights ideas and thereby to counter the standard view that it was the French Enlightenment that had been the fertile ground of 'the rights of man and of citizens'. Jellinek treated the quest for freedom of religion as the original foundation of subsequent claims for freedom of conscience in Protestantism in all matters of belief, both religious and secular. Rejecting Rousseau's social contract theory and the secular underpinnings of the French and American revolutionary declarations as origins of the modern idea of rights, he argued that 'sovereign individualism in the religious sphere led to practical consequences of extraordinary importance' (Jellinek, 2009, p. 33).

Interpretations of Catholicism as a negative constraint on the rise of modernity have perhaps been most heavily influenced by the sociology of religion in the work of Max Weber (Turner, 2016; Turner & Forlenza, 2019). In the two essays on the *Protestant Ethic and the Spirit of Capitalism* (Weber, 2002), he famously saw the Protestant ethic as having an elective affinity with capitalism in particular and modernity in general. By contrast Weber did not develop a systematic analysis of Catholicism, but he regarded its rituals (such as the Eucharist) as magical. Talking about the way in which rituals were assumed to have a coercive effect on the gods, he noted 'such coercive religion is universally diffused, and even the Catholic priest continues to practice something of this magical power in executing the miracle of the mass and in exercising the power of the keys' (Weber, 1966, p. 25). He goes on in his definition of priest to notice

> the term 'priest' may be applied to the functionaries of a regularly organized and permanent enterprise concerned with influencing the gods, in contrast with the individual and occasional efforts of magicians … as a pure type the priesthood is unequivocal and can be said to be characterized by the presence of certain fixed cultic centres associated with some cultic apparatus.
>
> (Weber, 1966, p. 28)

In short priests are functionaries in organizations whereas, by contrast, magicians are self-employed.

Weber's critical views on Catholicism were probably influenced by developments in German politics in the late nineteenth century. In particular, one critical development in German politics was the doctrine of papal infallibility in 1870 which pushed Bismarck into a struggle against Catholicism. Distrusting the Church's loyalty and fearful of its influence he developed the *Kulturkampf* (1871–1887) to limit its social and political influence.

We reflect here on the history of the Methodist Church to develop a contrast case to the Roman Catholic Church in terms of their different relationships to democratic values and structures. The idea that Protestantism (especially the Wesleyan movement – later the Methodist Church) contributed to the rise of democracy has been widely rehearsed – partly because its internal structures are seen to have created opportunities for lay education, participation, and leadership. E.P. Thompson's *The Making of the English Working Class* (1966), looking at Methodism as popular culture, claimed that Methodist 'quietism' had contributed to the failure of revolution in England in the creation of industrial capitalism. His argument was challenged by David Hempton (1984) in *Methodism and Politics in British Society 1730–1850* where he claimed that Methodist ideas complemented political radicalism, and similarly Bernard Semmel (1973) in *The Methodist Revolution* talks of Methodist 'democratic faith'. What is clear is that Methodist lay organization contributed to the rise of a literate working class with experience of leadership in their local chapels. In that sense, it was a training ground for democratic participation as active citizens. This argument has been continued in contemporary sociology of religion by David Martin (1990) who, for example in *Tongues of Fire: The Explosion of Protestantism in Latin America*, has looked at the transformation of religion in Latin America and interprets evangelical Protestantism as a democratic force in the mobilization of the working class – indeed the underclass.

Catholicism itself has not 'escaped' its influence leading to a 'pentecostalization' of Latin America. These developments have largely taken place after Vatican II opened up Catholicism to an internal process of modernization, albeit a partial modernization. One index of the changing culture of Catholicism is its relationship to human rights, not so much as a legal framework, but as a social movement. Contemporary work in the history of human rights has taken notice of the relationship between Catholic teaching and human rights. For example Samuel Moyn has argued that in the 1930s some Catholic dissidents 'argued against the alliance of Catholicism and reaction, advocating instead for a moralistic conservatism compatible with, or even dependent upon, a liberal democracy whose viability had long been doubted in mainstream Catholic circles' (Moyn, 2014, p. 27). It was Pope Pius XII in 1930 who promoted the idea of human dignity and his wartime addresses announced basic universal human rights.

How far has the internal hierarchy within Catholicism undergone a process of (partial) democratization through a process of what we might call 'protestantization' or 'denominationalization'? The contemporary crises around sex scandals inside the Catholic Church raise profound questions as to how far internal reform and democratization have gone. In a recent report in *Religion Watch* (2019) – an online publication of the Baylor Institute of Religion – examined evidence from 8,645 victims of abuse. Margaret Smith and Karen Terry found that almost 60 per cent of the victims were aged between 10 and 14 years. Data on abused children were the same in Germany and Australia. Similar results have emerged from state commission reports such as the report from Pennsylvania. The sexual abuses are not confined to any one country. A further example can be taken from the *Royal Commission into Institutional Responses to Child Sexual Abuse* which reported to the Australian Government in December 2017. It identified 4,444 claimants where 30 per cent of abusers were priests and 37 were non-ordained religious. The Commission spoke of 'catastrophic failures of leadership'. Abuse extended through the entire range of Church authority including the conviction of Cardinal George Pell in 2019 for child sexual abuse. The cardinal was eventually released in 2020 by a decision of the Supreme Court on the legal grounds that there was insufficient compelling evidence.

These legal proceedings and inquiries are interesting because in them we see the secular state intervening to regulate hierarchical ecclesiastical institutions that protect its own authorities from external scrutiny. The extent to which a democratically elected government may intervene in a hierarchical undemocratic church is further illustrated by the contemporary debate in Australia over the seal of the confession. Two states in Australia (South Australia and ACT) have moved through legislation to break the 'seal of confession'. In Catholic canon law the seal of the confessional is inviolable. Some priests have argued that the traditional confessional is in decline, but if this challenge by secular law is successful, then the power of the priesthood is diminished. We consider these developments as examples of a democratically elected secular state intervening into the authority structure of a hierarchical and undemocratic religious organization. We argue in conclusion to this chapter that the prevalence of child sexual abuse and its cover-up in the Catholic Church and its various adjacent institutions is an example of an institution in which priests enjoy extensive authority and where the laity is still excluded from leadership. It remains a top-down and somewhat secretive institution. Several inquiries have referred to the secrecy within the Church that was the basis of systematic cover-ups. Thus, the *Report of the Commission to Inquire into Child Abuse in Ireland* (2009), also known as the Ryan Report, commented that the pre-occupation of the Dublin Archdiocese with 'the maintenance of secrecy' amounted to an abuse of power (Berry & Renner, 2004). We take this systemic presence of secrecy as an empirical measure of what we might call internal 'organizational authoritarianism'.

Part two: Vatican II, Catholic politics, and Christian Democracy

It would be tempting and not entirely incorrect to place Catholicism as an adversary to democracy and to modern nation-state politics, siding with 'tradition' and an outspoken critique of the modern democratic project as a work of the devil. Ever since the Enlightenment, the Church had officially condemned modernity for its godlessness. The French Revolution pitted the Church against modern politics in ways that at the time seemed irreconcilable (Hellemans, 2001, pp. 117–119). In 1832, Gregory XVI's encyclical letter *Mirari Vos: On Liberalism and Religious Indifferentism* condemned Félicité Lamennais's proposal to welcome the new society and its civil liberties as an opportunity for Catholicism – to 'baptize', in Lamennais's term, the Revolution. The text reads: 'At the present moment a brutal malevolence and imprudent science, an unrestrained arbitrariness prevail' (*Alacris exultat improbitas, scientia impudens, dissolute licentia*).[2] In 1864 Pius IX concluded his *Syllabus Errorum*, attached to the encyclical *Quanta Cura*, by condemning the idea that 'the Pope would have to learn to accept progress, liberalism and modern civilization' (*Romanus Pontifex potest ac debet cum progressu, cum liberalismo et cum recenti civilitate sese reconciliari et componere*). As the Pope stated in the opening lines of the encyclical, modernity must be seen as the result of 'criminal plans by malevolent people' (*nefariis iniquorum hominum molitionibus*). This general outlook did not change until the Second Vatican Council, and certainly explains the Vatican's weak position towards right-wing dictatorships emerging in the twentieth century and its general distrust of national-democratic politics.

It was obvious, therefore, that for decades secular liberal thinkers and politicians considered Catholicism as an insurmountable obstacle to liberal democracy. Leading French Republican Léon Gambetta famously exclaimed to the Chamber of Deputies 'Le cléricalisme, voilà l'ennemi!' in May 1877. Far into the twentieth century prominent politicians and social scientists asserted that Catholicism explained the persistence of dictatorship in Latin America and on the Iberian Peninsula. Catholicism, in the words of the influential social scientist Seymour Martin Lipset, appeared 'antithetical to democracy in pre-World War II Europe and in Latin America' (Lipset, 1960, pp. 72–73). In a widely read, cited, and influential article, Lipset observed that 'the linkage between democratic instability and Catholicism may also be accounted for by elements inherent in Catholicism as a religious system' (1959, p. 92, n. 40). In seeking to explain in 1958 why 'French Canadians have not really believed in democracy for themselves', and did not have a functioning competitive party, political scientist Pierre Trudeau, who would later serve as Prime Minister of Canada for 16 years, claimed that

> French Canadians are Catholics; and Catholic nations have not always been ardent supporters of democracy. They are authoritarian in spiritual matters;

> and since the dividing line between the spiritual and the temporal may be very fine or even confused, they are often disinclined to seek solutions in temporal affairs through the mere counting of heads.
>
> (Trudeau, 1968, p. 108)

Catholic citizens were suspected of maintaining transnational ties and ultimate loyalties to spiritual institutions elsewhere. The same suspicion played a role in the election campaign of John F. Kennedy in 1960, but he successfully became the first Catholic president of the United States.

The Second Vatican Council served to shape a new self-image of the Church as an interpreter of the 'sign of the times', as a companion traveller, partner, or 'guide' of modernity. It was, seen in hindsight, a quite remarkable discontinuity. The Church now recognized freedom of religion and human rights as central to the Church's doctrines. Instead of rejecting modernity as a dark and godless force, the Church now expressed hopes, in particular in the final pastoral document *Gaudium et Spes*, that the Church and the good forces of the modern world united would be able to build a common house for all people. Vatican II was, thus, a critical turning point in the attitude of the Church towards the realm of secular politics and democracy. The Council addressed and updated Catholic doctrine in the modern world, recognizing the moral superiority of democratic government against rival alternatives and promoting the value of human rights. No longer did the Church claim to possess a monopoly over truth, and Catholics were encouraged to engage in dialogue with their fellow non-Catholic citizens, entering the stage of pluralism and democracy. The Vatican, with the Council, eventually endorsed democracy and pluralism in an unequivocal manner.

Soon after the Second Vatican Council, there was a major expansion of democracy across the globe, which in the early 1990s Samuel Huntington defined as 'the third wave of democratization' (Huntington, 1991a, b). As noted by Huntington, roughly three-quarters of the countries that transited to democracy between 1974 and 1989 were predominantly Catholic countries in Europe. The fundamental changes in the Church brought about the Vatican Council (*aggiornamento*, or update, reform) which allowed *official* Catholicism for the first time in history to openly support democracy and human rights in opposition to authoritarian rule were thus crucial for the Catholic countries of the Mediterranean (Portugal and Spain in the mid-to-late 1970s) and Latin America (from the 1970s to the 1980s), as well as in Asia (the Philippines in the 1980s), and eventually in Eastern Europe (Poland and Hungary in the late 1980s). The 'third wave' of democratization was, therefore, a proper 'Catholic wave' (Casanova, 1996, 2001; Huntington, 1991a, b; Philpott, 2004; Troy, 2009). Huntington noted the 'strong correlation' that existed between Catholicism and democracy, and underscored the historical record that

> before the mid-1960s, the Catholic Church usually accommodated itself to authoritarian regimes and frequently legitimated them. After the mid-1960s, the Church almost invariably opposed authoritarian regimes … This repositioning of the Catholic Church from a bulwark of the status quo, usually

> authoritarian, to a force for change, usually democratic, was a major political phenomenon.
>
> (Huntington, 1991b, p. 77)

Crucially, Huntington continued,

> the changes flowed from the Second Vatican Council … Vatican II stressed the legitimacy and need for social change, the importance of collegial action by bishops, priests, and laity, dedication to helping the poor, the contingent character of social and political structures, and the rights of individuals.
>
> (Huntington, 1991b, p. 78)

There were other changes that occurred 'simultaneously in popular involvement and priestly activity at the base of the Church' (Huntington, 1991b, p. 78), which were crucial for these democratic developments. As Juan Linz writes with reference to Spain in the 1960s,

New generations of priest, some of them late vocations, perhaps a less rural recruitment of the clergy, a greater awareness of social injustice and contact with the de-Christianized working class, sociological studies of religious practice, the identification of the clergy with the cultural, linguistic minorities in the Basque country and Catalonia, and above all, the impact of the Second Vatican Council, produced a ferment of criticism and unrest among younger Catholic intellectuals, laymen, and clergy and conflicts with authority. (Linz, 1980, p. 258; see Huntington, 1991b, pp. 78–79)

Catholic writers and intellectuals in particular have seen the Council, implicitly or explicitly, as the moment when the Catholic Church finally accepted a changing world, shook off its reactionary past, and adapted to secular reality (Schloesser, 2006; Wicks, 2006). Sociologist José Casanova specifically credits the Vatican II *aggiornamento* for allowing Catholicism, for the first time in its history, to openly support democracy and human rights struggles which contributed significantly to this wave of democratization (Casanova, 2001). And yet, it would be very wrong to locate the Catholic encounter and complex relationship with democracy solely within the third wave of democratization and as a consequence of the change brought about the Second Vatican Council. The picture is incomplete, and effectively misleading, without considering the development of political Catholicism since the end of the nineteenth century and, more importantly, the emergence and consolidation of Christian Democracy after World War II.

From the middle of the nineteenth century, an alternative model for Catholicism started be emerge. While always serving as a critique of political modernity and democracy, Catholic thought on the modern also started to undergo profound transformations. This happened very much in the context of the process of nation-state formation which took place in Italy (a traumatic event for the Church as the pontiffs lost their territorial domains and Rome became the capital of a new secular state in 1870), in Europe, and in Latin America. Everywhere liberal political elites attempted to reduce the influence of the Church in society and abolish its ancient rights, at the time increasing the authority and power of the state. As a reaction, Catholics entered into the secular political scene increasingly engaging with public matters and the defence of their own interests, and those of the Church, through a vast array of organizations such as politics clubs, peasants' leagues, youth and recreational associations, and, eventually, proper political parties.

The direct consequence of this development was the emergence of an effective Catholic political civilization *milieu*, which turned Catholicism into a political identity. This process was reinforced and further promoted by Pope Leo XII and his 'social encyclical' *Rerum Novarum* (1891). Catholics were now urged to actively unite and to engage themselves in all kinds of social domains, and to respond to the threat of liberal and anti-clerical governments as well as to the challenge of socialism. By then it had become clear that modern society was more than a revolutionary chaos soon to collapse. A full-fledged and well-organized Catholic subculture, a Catholic 'pillar' or compartment within society, was established in anticipation of a Catholic modernity proper. The movement in many ways resembled what the socialist labour movement was achieving around the same time in Europe and beyond.

Nevertheless, the Vatican continued to condemn modernity and democratic politics. Between the end of nineteenth century and the beginning of the twentieth century the Vatican was forced to face a new challenge from *within* its own ranks, incidentally called 'modernism'. Modernism was an intellectual amorphous movement which developed among Catholics in the late nineteenth century and early twentieth century, first in France and England, with the proclaimed aim of bringing the Church into harmony with modernity and with the post-Enlightenment world. Interestingly, the term 'modernist' was first employed as a condemnation of social change by the Church authorities. The official condemnation of modernism in 1907, with Pius X's encyclical *Pascendi Dominici Gregis*, signalled a victory for Catholic anti-modernists, and an anti-modern position that would last in most of Europe throughout the first half of the century.

After World War I, political Catholicism and Catholic-inspired parties flourished everywhere in Europe and Latin America and soon were to compete with socialists, communists, and then with fascists and with new emerging authoritarian regimes. The Vatican itself maintained a highly ambiguous relationship with these Catholic political organizations, as in the past, remaining sceptical of Catholic political activity. After all, pluralism as such was bound to remain a problem for an institution with universalistic aspirations. The Vatican continued to deal with secular governments, even when they were authoritarian or fascist regimes. Rather than put its affairs in the hand of groups and parties which could become independent, the Vatican realized that the more prudent approach was to sign concordats to solve issues concerning the place and roles of the Church in the modern state, and to above all else guarantee the fundamental prerogatives and rights of the Church, especially in the realm of religious education. Thus, the Vatican entered into agreement with fascist regimes to protect ecclesiastic influence. Crucially, on 11 February 1929 an historic treaty was signed between the fascist Italian government and the Vatican, re-establishing the political power and diplomatic standing of the Catholic Church, which had been lost when Italy seized Rome. The Lateran Pacts established the Vatican City as an independent State, restored the civil sovereignty of the Pope as a monarch, and regulated the position of the Church and the Catholic religion in the Italian state. Furthermore, a financial convention compensated the Holy See for the loss of the Papal States (Forlenza & Thomassen, 2016, p. 74).

These interwar years were crucial for the development of a Catholic modernity. As James Chappel has written recently, it was in the 1930s that Catholics abandoned anti-modernism and the dream of restoring a quasi-medieval form of Christendom and reconsidered their relationship with modern political ideologies. Vis-à-vis the threat of totalitarianism, either of the left or the right, Catholics began to elaborate new ways to engage with the body politic. Instead of trying to overturn modernity and supplant secular modern state and economy, they began asking themselves 'How can we shape secular modernity to our specifications?' (Chappel, 2018, p. 13). To answer the question, two rival strategies – or two Catholic forms of modernity – emerged among Catholic intellectuals and leaders. Both were legitimate ways of updating the long Catholic tradition. Both involved the creation of a private sphere where Catholic beliefs, values, and institutions would be protected from the intrusiveness and dubious impartiality of the secular state. The first strategy, which Chappel calls 'paternal Catholic modernism', congealed around the defence of the sanctity of the patriarchal reproductive family as the protected sphere of private religious values. Catholics could accept the legitimacy and authority of the secular welfare state, provided its benefits were felt by the family, and so long as Catholic teaching about the family (on abortion, homosexuality, and divorce) was translated into law. Paternal Catholic modernism was linked with the increasing importance of anti-communism in Catholic circles, serving, thus, as the main rationale for Catholic collaboration with fascist or authoritarian regimes that promised to defend the family against communism. The second strategy, or 'fraternal Catholic modernism' (Chappell, 2018), was a different story. For a minority of Catholics, the threat of fascism was greater than any danger from the left. Much more suspicious of the state and capitalism than their 'paternal' fellows, these Catholics believed in workers' solidarity, free trade unions, and a free press to limit the power of state and market. Chappel's distinction between 'fraternal' and 'paternal' modernism is at times overly simplistic and minimizes nuances and ambiguities, creating boxes in which leading Catholic intellectuals did not necessarily fit neatly (Forlenza, 2019a). His work, however, captures and explains well how Catholic intellectuals and politicians – at first not necessarily opposed to fascist and authoritarian regimes, but then more and more disappointed and distraught by fascist racial politics, by the acceleration of the totalitarian dynamics, and by the war and the political-existential uncertainty that it entailed – began to search for a Catholic response to the problem of mass politics. The French intellectual Jacques Maritain (1971) became the compass of this political and intellectual search.

Maritain had been close to the quasi-fascist *Action Française* in the 1920s, but had abandoned the movement when it was condemned by the Vatican in 1926.

Working within a neo-Thomist philosophical framework, in the 1930s he started to embrace human rights and modern democracy. In particular, his 1936 study *Humanisme Intégrale* (Maritain, 1996) and his 1942 pamphlet *Christianisme et démocratie* (2012) (which was dropped by Allied planes over Europe in 1943) had constituted a cautious, but nevertheless decisive endorsement of the ultimately Christian nature of democracy. Central to Maritain's theory and definition of democracy was the concept of the 'person' and its opposition to the 'individual'. However, critics have argued that the Catholic notion of the dignity of the person retained a notion of hierarchy that was not entirely compatible with the idea of equal citizenship (Moyn, 2014, 2015). The 'person' has a spiritual and transcendent quality, not reducible to material and biological nature; it flourishes only within a community, when open to God. It is via the transcendent principle that the good of all can be articulated in the first place. Many Catholics, who had been sympathetic to fascism, found in Maritain an antidote to fascism, authoritarian politics, and totalitarianism. Maritain made the conceptual incompatibility between Catholicism and totalitarianism clear to Catholic intellectuals, serving as a powerful antidote to clerico-fascism. His thought freed Catholics (or a large sector of Catholicism) from the medievalist, anti-modern utopia that drove many of them to adhere to fascist or authoritarian regimes, seen as a sort of allies in the fight against modernity and for the Catholic regeneration of the world.

Maritain had a direct influence on Christian Democracy, the new 'political animal' (Judt, 2005) that in the post-World War II era dominated the political scene in Western Europe but also in Latin America. Via Christian Democracy central principles of political Catholicism and Catholic social teaching, as well as the personalist and communitarian language of Maritain, were introduced into the constitutions of Italy, West Germany, France, and other European countries: the centrality of the person, a social view on economy, the defence of non-state entities from the family to the Church, and the validation of forms of organization which were both political (parties) and corporatist (trade unions). Via Christian Democracy, the Catholic philosophical-political luggage and some of its important federalist principles (such as subsidiarity)[3] were also translated into the nascent process of European supranational integration (Conway, 2012; Forlenza, 2010, 2017, 2019b; Thomassen & Forlenza, 2016). Even the second wave of democratization after World War II was influenced by Catholic views – a fact that it is typically overlooked by scholars.

Christian Democracy was also at the forefront of the struggle against authoritarian regimes in Latin America for the entire post–World War II period. In short, resting on the tradition of Catholic social teaching, as re-elaborated by Maritain, Christian Democracy became a central actor in the process of building a modern mass and post-totalitarian democracy and a welfare state. With Christian Democracy in the post–World War II era the purpose of Catholic action changed dramatically. Christian Democrats were in the political realm not to protect the Church from anti-clerical assault, but to articulate and develop (in competition or also in cooperation with non-Catholic forces) political and socio-economic platforms and plans implementing a Christian Democratic and Catholic response to the challenge of modernity and democracy. Thus, Christian Democracy achieved what traditional political Catholicism had until then only dreamt about: to gain a leading role within the modern world.

To what extent did the development of Christian Democracy influence the Church and its attitude towards modernity? And to what extent were Christian Democrats 'controlled' by the Vatican? Matters were complex. The changes in the attitude of the Church toward democracy were not simply caused by external pressures. Catholic philosophers and political thinkers were actively seeking out a position on the crucial social issues of the day from within a Christian-inspired worldview. Their argument was that the Church should take moral leadership with respect to questions of social justice, the welfare of citizens, the dignity of the person, peace, and democracy. Put briefly, Christian Democracy became agenda-setting. And this happened in a continuous dialogue between the Vatican and Catholic politicians – a dialogue that took place across an institutional divide which crystallized within the same historical process. Christian Democracy developed outside the control of the Vatican; but the mutual influence that took place in formulating a stance toward the modern is at the same time clear.

The redefinition of Catholicism as a modern intellectual-cultural project advanced by Christian Democracy as a basis for new politics and practices, reinforced by the wider social, economic, and cultural transformation of the 1950s, certainly impinged upon the Church's attitude to democracy and modernity. The Council, in particular with the *Gaudium et Spes*, encouraged Catholics to enter the stage of pluralism and democracy, but in fact European and Latin American Christian Democrats had engaged the political realm and embraced the cause of democracy at least from World War II.

Conclusion: The long protestantization of the church

The Protestant Reformation of the sixteenth century was in many respects neither the first nor the last reformation of Christianity. At the beginning of his monumental *Christianity: The First Three Thousand Years* Diarmid MacCulloch wisely observed that 'all the world faiths which have known long-term success have shown a remarkable capacity to mutate, and Christianity is no exception, which is why one underlying message of this history is its sheer variety' (MacCulloch, 2009, p. 9). This message obviously applies to Catholicism, and hence the idea that the Protestant Reformation was the last definitive and singular transformation of Christianity is misleading. Catholicism was both before and after the Reformation undergoing change, and recent historical interpretations have emphasized the importance of the Counter-Reformation and the emergence of Tridentine Catholicism which was a coherent framework of ecclesiastical change involving a uniform catechism, a standard liturgy, Latin over any vernacular tongue, obligatory celibacy, and recognition at least of the emerging exclusivity of papal authority. The Catholic Church was furthermore not responding simply to the challenge of Protestant dissent. It was transforming itself in response to the rise of the nation state and to imperial powers (O'Malley, 2002).

In this chapter we have treated Vatican II and its aftermath as a further profound reformation of the Catholic Church, but we have interpreted those changes as making the Church more Protestant by nudging it in the direction of a denomination now more comfortable, at least officially, with the claims of other religions, with the existence of political democracy, and with secularism. These steps towards denominationalism have occurred only haltingly. One significant challenge to the Church is from issues ultimately related to the human body, especially the female body – procreation, abortion, euthanasia, sexual liberation, and same-sex marriage (Turner, 2011, 2017). On the one hand, the sexual scandals in the Church will require huge resources to manage the damaged reputation of the Church. On the other hand, there are more specific challenges from feminism.

Women are constructed as separate but equal in their roles and responsibilities in the Church by its complementary understanding of gender, displayed in the theological 'economy of salvation'. The declaration explains this economy, in which the priest must be male because Jesus Christ was male (Alliaume, 2006, p. 96).

Radical feminism represents a deeply problematic challenge, not only to the Church's authority structure, but to its doctrine of divinity. While the Church has embraced Mariology without significant difficulties, the doctrine of the Blessed Mary as *coredemptrix* or *mediatrix* raises major theological issues. This recognition of Mary clearly separates Catholicism from Protestant churches, and the idea of Mary as 'remotely' co-operating in human redemption alongside Jesus was not supported by Vatican II. However, while this view of Mary goes back to at least Irenaeus in 200, it has not received the full blessing of the Church. In 2017 the Congregation of the Mother *Coredemptrix* was renamed the Congregation of the Mother Redeemer. Sexuality, the status of women, and ultimately the role of the family in Catholic teaching will constitute a significant challenge to Church authority and in all likelihood nudge the Church further along the path to a denomination reluctantly accepting this particular dimension of secularization (Turner & Forlenza, 2016).

We also believe that Catholic popular religion represents a challenge to official Catholicism. The struggle over Padre Pio whose acceptance was resisted by the Church for many decades is an illustration of these problems for a Church attempting to rid itself of attachments that threaten its credibility (Luzzatto, 2010). Throughout southern Italy, popular rituals survive outside the authority structure of the official ecclesiastical institutions (Forlenza, 2018). In the case of Mary as *Coredemptrix*, the popularity of this notion of the role of Mary was kept alive by the so-called Amsterdam Visions which appeared to Ida Peerdeman between 1945 and 1959 in the city of Alkmaar.

In conclusion we have argued that the question of religious authoritarianism has to be addressed in terms of two dimensions. While the Roman Catholic Church has embraced the political democratization of modern societies and accepted certain features of secularism, its internal structures have remained (more or less) authoritarian. However, we also recognize that institutions are constantly changing and various issues around sexuality represent a major challenge to the internal structures of the Church. Without some radical revisions of its Tridentine legacy, this transformation may be historically the most problematic.

Notes

1 We here use 'authoritarianism' to describe the internal operations of the Roman Catholic Church without the intention of making a value judgement. We claim that 'authoritarian' is used factually to describe the authority structure of the Catholic Church which is hierarchical and priestly and in which the laity is not a core component of its authority structure. Furthermore, while women play an important role in the life of the church – for example as nuns – the rule of celibacy tends to preclude female involvement, despite involving the Church in ideological battles with feminism over gender. The doctrine of papal infallibility is a critical component of its authoritarian structure. These features contrast sharply with the somewhat flatter and inclusive authority structures of Protestant denominations.

2 The text in English of all encyclicals and papal documents quoted in this article can be found at the official websites http://www.paplencyclicals.net and http://www.vatican.va.

3 In Catholic social teaching, the principle of subsidiarity designated the idea that powers which individuals can exercise adequately themselves should not be arrogated to a central authority. In the context of Europeanism, it refers to the principle that the supranational community should only make law in situations where individual nations are incapable of acting.

References

Alliaume, K.T. (2006). Disturbingly catholic: Thinking the inordinate body. In E.T. Armour & S.M. St. Ville (Eds.), *Bodily citations: Religion and Judith Butler* (pp. 93–119). New York: Columbia University Press.

Berry, J., & Renner, G. (2004). *Vows of silence: The abuse of power in the papacy of John Paul II*. New York: Free Press.

Casanova, J. (1996). Global Catholicism and the politics of civil society. *Sociological Inquiry*, *66*(3), 356–363.

Casanova, J. (2001). Civil society and religion: Retrospective reflection on Catholicism and perspective reflection on Islam. *Social Research*, *68*(4), 1041–1080.

Chappel, J. (2018) *Catholic Modern: The challenge of totalitarianism and the remaking of the Church*. Cambridge, MA: Harvard University Press.

Conway, M. (2012). *The sorrow of Belgium: Liberation and political reconstruction, 1944–1947*. Oxford: Oxford University Press.

Forlenza, R. (2010). A party of the Mezzogiorno: The Christian Democratic Party, agrarian reform and the government of Italy. *Contemporary European History*, *19*(4), 331–349.

Forlenza, R. (2017). The politics of the Abendland: Christian democracy and the idea of Europe after the Second World War. *Contemporary European History*, *26*(2), 261–286.

Forlenza, R. (2018). Magic, religion, and the south: Notes on Ernesto De Martino. *Journal of Religious and Political Practice*, *4*(2), 137–155.

Forlenza, R. (2019a). New perspectives on twentieth-century Catholicism. *Contemporary European History*, *28*(4), 581–595.

Forlenza, R. (2019b). *On the edge of democracy: Italy, 1943–1948*. Oxford: Oxford University Press.

Forlenza, R., & Thomassen, B. (2016). *Italian modernities: Competing narratives of nationhood*. New York: Palgrave Macmillan.

Hellemans, S. (2001). From 'Catholicism against modernity' to the problematic 'modernity of Catholicism. *Ethical Perspectives: Journal of the European Ethics Network*, *8*(2), 117–127.

Hempton, D. (1984). *Methodism and politics in British society 1730–1850*. London: Hutchinson.

Huntington, S.P. (1991a). Democracy's third wave. *Journal of Democracy*, *2*(2), 12–34.

Huntington, S.P. (1991b). *The third wave: Democratization in late twentieth century*. Norman: University of Oklahoma Press.

Jellinek, G. (2009). *The declaration of the rights of man and of citizens*. Lexington: World Library Classics.

Judt, T. (2005). *Postwar: A history of Europe since 1945*. New York: Penguin.

Linz, J. (1980). Religion and politics in Spain: From conflict to consensus above cleavage. *Social Compass*, *27*(2/3), 255–277.

Lipset, S.M. (1959). Some social requisites of democracy: Economic development and political legitimacy. *American Political Science Review*, *53*(1), 69–105.

Lipset, S.M. (1960). *Political man: The social bases of politics*. New York: Doubleday.

Luzzatto, S. (2010). *Padre Pio: Miracles and politics in a secular age*. New York: Henry Holt & Company.

MacCulloch, D. (2009). *Christianity: The first three thousand years*. New York: Penguin Books.

Maritain, J. (1971). *The rights of man and natural law*. New York: Gordian Press.

Maritain, J. (1996) *Integral humanism*. Notre Dame: Notre Dame University Press.

Maritain, J. (2012) *Christianity and democracy*. San Francisco: Ignatius Press.

Martin, D. (1990). *Tongues of fire: The explosion of Protestantism in Latin America*. Oxford: Blackwell.

Moyn, S. (2014). *Human rights and the uses of history*. London: Verso.

Moyn, S. (2015). *Christian human rights*. Philadelphia: University of Philadelphia Press.

Niebuhr, R.H. (1962). *The social sources of denominationalism*. New York: Meridian.

Ogg, D. (1961). *Europe in the seventeenth century*. (8th edition, revised). London: Adam & Charles Black.

O'Malley, J.W. (2002). *Trent and all that. Renaming Catholicism in the early modern era*. Boston: Harvard University Press.

Pearson, L. (2018). Troeltsch on Protestantism and modernity. In C. Adair-Toteff (Ed.), *The anthem companion to Ernst Troeltsch* (pp. 37–54). London: Anthem Press.

Philpott, D. (2004). Christianity and democracy: The catholic wave. *Journal of Democracy*, *15*(2), 32–46.

Religion Watch (2019). Researchers find Catholic Church's patterns of sexual abuse consistent across time and place. *Religion Watch*, *34*(6–7). Retrieved from http://www.religionwatch.com/wp-content/uploads/2019/05/2019_04-05_ReligionWatch.pdf.

Report of the Commission into Child Abuse in Ireland (2009). Retrieved from https://www.gov.ie/en/publication/3c76d0-the-report-of-the-commission-to-inquire-into-child-abuse-the-ryan-re/.

Royal Commission into Institutional Responses to Child Sexual Abuse Australia (2017). Retrieved from https://www.childabuseroyalcommission.gov.au/.

Schloesser, S. (2006). Against forgetting: Memory, history, Vatican II. *Theological Studies*, *67*(2), 275–319.

Semmel, B. (1973). *The methodist revolution*. New York: Basic Books.

Thomassen, B., & Forlenza, R. (2016). Catholic modernity and the Italian constitution. *History Workshop Journal*, *81*(1), 231–251.

Thompson, E.P. (1966). *The making of the English working class*. New York: Vintage Books/Random House.

Troeltsch, E. (1912). *Protestantism and progress: A historical study of the relation of Protestantism to the modern word*. New York: G. P. Putnam's Sons.

Troeltsch, E. (1992). *The social teachings of the Christian churches*. London: George Allen & Unwin.

Troeltsch, E. (2005). Stoic-Christian natural law and modern secular law. In C. Adair-Toteff (Ed.), *Sociological beginnings* (pp. 110–131). Liverpool: Liverpool University Press.

Troy, J. (2009). Catholic waves of democratization? Roman Catholicism and its potential for democratization. *Democratization*, *16*(6), 1093–1114.

Trudeau, P.E. (1968). *Federalism and the French Canadians*. Toronto: Macmillan of Canada.

Turner, B.S. (2011). *Religion and modern society: Citizenship, secularization and the state*. Cambridge: Cambridge University Press.

Turner, B.S. (2016). Max Weber and the sociology of religion. *Revue Internationale de Philosophie*, *276*(2), 141–150.

Turner, B.S. (2017). Ritual, belief and habituation: Religion and religions from the axial age to the Anthropocene. *European Journal of Social Theory*, *20*(1), 132–145.

Turner, B.S., & Forlenza, R. (2016). The last frontier: The struggle over sex and marriage under Pope Francis. *Rassegna Italiana di Sociologia*, *57*(4), 689–710.

Turner, B.S., & Forlenza, R. (2019). Max Weber and the late modernization of Catholicism. In E. Hanke, L. Scaff, & S. Whimster (Eds.), *The Oxford Handbook of Max Weber*. Oxford: Oxford University Press.

Weber, M. (1966). *The sociology of religion*. London: Methuen & Co.

Weber, M. (2002). *The protestant ethic and the spirit of capitalism*. Los Angeles: Roxbury Publishing Company.

Wicks, J. (2006). New light on Vatican Council II. *The Catholic Historical Review*, *92*(4), 609–628.

Wilson, B. (1959). An analysis of sect development. *The American Sociological Review*, *24*(1), 3–15.

Wilson, B. (1961) *Sects and society: A sociological study of three religious groups in Britain*. London: Heinemann.

8 Breaking bad

The crisis of democracy in the age of digital culture

Tibor Dessewffy

Introduction

We are living in the Age of Uncertainties. To understand this situation, it is important to step outside the established intellectual frameworks or to be at least open to new lines of thinking. That is what I will try to do in this paper. I seek to capture a general phenomenon, the crisis of liberal democracy, by drawing on a theoretical assessment of the joint impact of three approaches – popular culture, digital media, and emotionally driven decisions – the literature of which is already humongous and still growing. And even though I am keenly aware that to do even one of these topics justice would stretch far beyond the limits of the current paper, I still undertake this mission impossible because my goal is to illuminate how these three issues are interdependent and inextricably linked. Although these three components are rarely grouped together in the context of such an analysis, the present study does not merely wish to assert that the posited relationship obtains between them.

It is important to emphasize that I do not juxtapose these three areas because of some desire to make exotic comparisons. The line of argument proposed here is motivated by more mundane concerns: I wish to explain the phenomenon discussed at the beginning of this essay by drawing on a deductive logic.

Taking the underlying ideas a step further, the research is also fuelled by the idea that in order to answer the question which inspired this study, the crisis of democracy, giving these approaches their due importance in academic scholarship and published discourse is essential, even if this is not meant to imply that these are the only relevant areas with regard to the question at hand. Hence, in the following, after expounding on the crisis of democracy, I will sketch the relevant elements of these three lines of thought and then proceed to conclude the paper by discussing the respective roles of two communities, which are – even though they are very different in other dimensions – both rooted in popular culture and based on emotive foundations. Furthermore, they both play a role in the political realm, too.

Is there a crisis of democracy?

We are living in the *Age of Uncertainties* (Bauman, 2013). These uncertainties manifest themselves in all areas of life, but they are probably nowhere near as striking and obvious as in politics. The traditional structures are creaking under the weight of various pressures, and the mostly nineteenth-century institutions, such as for example political parties, are confronted with radically new challenges and the inexorable pressure to renew themselves. As Manuel Castells put it very aptly with respect to the Brexit debate:

> Perhaps the most interesting piece of information in examining the sheer extent of the anti-EU movement is this: the Conservatives, Labour and Liberal Democrats all took a pro-remain stance, and yet 40 per cent of Labour voters and 60 per cent of Conservative voters went against the leaders of the three parties to vote for Brexit.
>
> (Castells, 2018, p. 64)

The literature on the crisis of the democratic institutional structure has become enormously large by now. We cannot review it in any detail here. To capture and illustrate the depth of the crisis, however, it is worth harking back to one of the intellectual founders of liberal democracy, John Stuart Mill. While his thinking was geared towards trying to delineate all the possibilities for expanding the liberties of individuals who live in human communities, Mill was also keenly aware of the populist threat that was deeply embedded in majoritarian democratic decision making. He, after all, discussed the concept of the tyranny of the majority extensively. Mill nevertheless sided clearly with the institutional structure provided by representative democracy and the decision-making process that this implies (Mill, 1873).

He argued that a democratic method of drafting and enacting legislation is better than non-democratic methods in three vital ways: strategically, epistemically, and by bettering the character of democratic citizens.

> *Strategically*, democracy has an advantage because it forces decision-makers to take into account the interests, rights and opinions of most people in society … Democracy is thought to be the best decision-making method on the grounds that it is generally more reliable in helping participants discover *the right decisions* … Democracy tends to get *people to think carefully and rationally* more than other forms of rule because it makes a difference whether they do or not.
>
> (Christiano, 2018, pp. 2–3)

It is also important to draw on these types of democratic benefits (strategic, epistemological, and moral development) because it helps us put the problems of our world today into sharp relief. As opposed to Mill's idealized image of democracy, the reality is that toxic leaders across the world fail to take into account the will of the governed. They use sophisticated techniques of manipulation to attain the mass support that they misuse to assert their own interests – which are often opposed to those of their voters. As a result, this digital façade of democracy does not result in decisions that actually serve the public good; in effect they benefit a narrow elite instead. And, finally, while owing to digital technology and social media the participation of the public in political processes may actually increase, on account of algorithmic-driven polarization and the filter bubble phenomenon, this does not lead to a proliferation of rational and considered discourse but rather leads to a profusion of harsh rancour in society.

Democracy as a way of governing societies and as a decision-making mechanism is obviously in crisis when juxtaposed against the ideals set out by Mill. There are several reasons for us having strayed so far from the Millian ideals. In the following, I wish to concentrate on the cultural impact of digital technology in particular. I think that the digital element, to wit platform capitalism, and the cultural and value changes engendered by the latter, are what give the crisis of democracy – the history of which actually goes a long way back – an entirely new quality.

However, the issue is not simply one of a structural crisis, in which the effectiveness of democratic norms and operations is in decline, and all we are seeing is that a different kind of political practice tends to be on the rise. No, the collapse, the rupture we are seeing is definitely headed in a certain direction: populist forces all over the world – Bolsonaro, Trump, Orbán, and Duterte, to name but a few of the most prominent figures globally – have achieved their political success within the democratic framework, drawing on new dynamics and techniques. What these leaders have in common is that they have risen to power by way of democratic elections. Although the illiberal exercise of power displays some very particular procedural, institutional, and civil rights policy-related features, I will argue in this article that the defining characteristics of the populist breakthrough are not the aforementioned but the broader cultural and technological transformations currently underway. At the same time, this cultural context and the concomitant social fabric it generates also include numerous elements which potentially offer opportunities for successfully confronting the prevailing trend of populism.

Battle for hegemony

If one wishes to better understand the interrelationship between the cultural context and political power, consulting Gramsci is unavoidable. Hegemony refers to the idea that the transformation of cultural values, narratives, belief systems, and practices (the War of Position in Gramsci) is a pre-requisite for political power, as it lays the groundwork for the successful struggle to attain the latter (i.e., the War of Manoeuvre).

It is worth noting that already back then Gramsci realized that popular culture was a pre-eminent domain in the battle over meanings and understandings of reality (Jones, 2007). Given how deeply Gramsci was entrenched in politics, it is hardly surprising that starting in the 1960s he became one of the leading thinkers of the New Left. However, in a curious twist on his original theories, over the past decades the representatives of the New Right have also discovered Gramsci as a popular point of reference in their struggle against the presumed hegemony of the left-liberal side. Alain de Benoist, the top and globally probably most prominent representative of this school, refers in this context to 'cultural hegemony' in civil society, by which he means the control over dominant values, attitudes, and ways of seeing and being. This control holds out the promise of long-term and enduring power. 'Capture the hearts and minds of the masses, as well as of key elites, and liberal democracy would fall, reasoned Benoist' (Bar-On, 2011, p. 204). Gramsci's rediscovery by the New Right is palpable in the Eastern Europe context, too. Recently, for example, the Hungarian political thinker Márton Békés declared 'Gramsci is ours – read him, interpret him, use him!' (Békés, 2018).

Békés is not some marginalized left-wing intellectual, quite the contrary in fact. He is the Director of Research at the House of Terror, a Disneyland kind of history museum in Budapest that seeks to present to the public the crimes of totalitarian regimes in the twentieth century.

Thus Békés, who holds several other positions besides his integral role in the management of the House of Terror, is a key right-wing ideologue of the present governing majority. His fascination with Gramsci highlights a strange feature observed all across Europe: while the left is almost completely devoid of a desire to attain cultural hegemony, virulent right-wing demagogic populism is consciously and successfully striving to make headway in creating its own cultural hegemony.

This is not that surprising when one considers two facts. First, the fight for cultural hegemony (the War of Position) is very much a central component in the efforts of illiberal regimes. Rather than going into detail about the endless list of battles over cultural hegemony in Hungary that substantiate the accuracy of this claim (driving CEU out of Hungary, abolishing the autonomy of independent public research institutions, media acquisitions and closures, the removal of academics from their positions because of public statements they have made, etc.), let me cut to the chase with a recent quote by László Kövér:

> László Kövér argues that despite certain opinions to that effect, history has not ended today. In fact, certain historical problems threaten to rear their head once again. – Instead of territorial wars of conquest, there is a conquest of the public mind – he said, adding: Europe is the target of such efforts at occupying the mind, and those behind these efforts are supranational organizations. All the developments in the realm of the European economy, culture, migration, demography, family, and youth policy are geared towards the realization of this objective. But Hungary recognized these efforts early on and has learned how they operate. The speaker [of the Hungarian parliament] argues that one of the goals and ambitions of this new type of warfare is to estrange youths from their families, their nation, their homeland, and, ultimately, from themselves, in order to – László Kövér added – confuse them so much that 'in the end they literally don't even know anymore if they are boys or girls. The other objective – according to the speaker – is to make the general human values wither because in the absence of these values, humans are incapable of recognizing or standing up for their interests'
>
> (Baranyai, 2019).

Although László Kövér is not an internationally known figure, he is by no means irrelevant, either: he has been the speaker of the Hungarian parliament, the National Assembly, since 2010, and his informal role is more important still. He is practically the only Fidesz politician who has been at Viktor Orbán's side ever since the inception of the party, and although he has never turned against the prime minister, he is also the only one within the Fidesz organization who may be considered an autonomous Orbán ally; his authority as the 'party's conscience' is beyond dispute on the right. His opinion is not marginal, it sets the course for Fidesz.

At the same time, however, there is also another relevant dimension here. The diverse universe of popular culture in the globalized age of information includes a marked presence of highly successful texts that could be used to boost a liberal progressive worldview in society. These cultural texts could serve as a foundation for the resistance against the hegemonic efforts of those in power. Given the aspirations of the illiberal regimes to assert a new cultural hegemony, it is hardly surprising that this battle is fought with increasingly harsh instruments. In the countries where illiberal leaders have already ascended to power, they deploy a vast arsenal of administrative and financial instruments to consolidate a hegemony.

Digital hermeneutics

In the new millennium, popular culture unfolds against the backdrop of the new digital age of information, within the framework of platform capitalism. This does not mean that we have merely added another frontline in the war for cultural hegemony. To understand the significance of this process, we need to take a short theoretical excursion. As our starting point, the first concept we have to get to know is digital hermeneutics. As I have explained in another study in detail, one of the distinctive features of the digital age is that it simultaneously transforms the sociological reality in which we live while it also holds out new opportunities for understanding said reality and opens up new interpretations thereof (Dessewffy, 2019).

There is no room here for a detailed and itemized description of how the 'objective' sociological world is being transformed, nor is such a description necessary for our purposes. It is enough for now to recall the term *onlife* introduced by Luciano Floridi. Floridi argues that the separation between online and offline has now become outdated; these previously distinct worlds have become organically intertwined these days. And while they are always in flux – due to mobile and wearable technologies as well as the internet of things – these spheres are increasingly inseparably enmeshed with one another.

In terms of understanding this new reality, we distinguish – qua Bruno Latour – between two programmes, which we refer to as Latour's soft and hard programmes. In the soft approach, the availability of digital data makes it possible to approach relevant questions by drawing on new methods to home in on the relations between them: 'At the very least, the digitally available profiles open new questions for social theory that don't have to be framed through the individual/collective standpoint' (Latour et al., 2012, p. 595). And in the harder approach, the methodological apparatus that has emerged based on the observation of individual behaviour as it manifests itself in the form of digital footprints gives rise to an entirely new social epistemological space: 'Change the instruments, and you will change the entire social theory that goes with them' (Latour, 2010, p. 155).

What does this imply for the argument advanced by this paper? In order to understand the crisis of democratic politics and the potential avenues out of this crisis, we need to pay emphatic attention to the processes that are going on in the digital/onlife world. And to properly comprehend these new organizational forms in our social life, we need to be open to understanding the uses of digital devices on the one hand, and the particular features of the onlife world on the other.

This is vital because as we saw in Gramsci there is nothing new per se in the desire to attain a hegemony, yet the modus operandi of these efforts in the current setting, their reliance on the digital toolkit, differs substantially from previous aspirations at achieving a cultural/political hegemony. While for the Bolsheviks in the early twentieth century the occupation of the telegraph office was vital, and during the late decades of the previous century the storming of radio stations and television channels emerged as the customary ritual of various revolutions, coups, and regime transitions, these days the relevant processes unfold in the network-based structures of social media and its polyphonic world, following the special rules that apply in the aforementioned realms. In line with this insight, the literature on filter bubbles, fake news, and digital neo-propaganda is continuously expanding (Barclay, 2018; Benkler, Faris & Roberts, 2018; Farkas & Neumayer, 2018; Farkas & Schou, 2019; Susser, Roessler & Nissenbaum, 2019). These studies focus on a supremely important area, namely the abuse of political power in the digital age. Still, theirs is not the argument I will build on below – partially because even though this is a genuinely exciting new area, I believe it has been studied rather extensively already. The more intriguing issue for me in the context of the present study is that when political power enters the scene with a desire to shape reality and its interpretations, it never does so in a vacuum. On the contrary, it always operates within the values, rules, and organizational structures that frame the existing context; sometimes it quietly complies with these rules, while on other occasions it relates to them much like the proverbial bull in the china shop. Whichever the case may be in any given context, there are two considerations that we must keep in mind when entering the realm of analysing political intentions and ambitions: that, on the one hand, the relationship between these is interactive – that it is of a kind where both sides mutually shape each other – while at the same time their interaction takes place in a fragmented environment, which reflects the structure of the digital world; this means that the various culturally constructed communities may react differently to various political initiatives.

It is interactive; in other words it is characterized by mutual feedback effects – the values and performances of the cultural context influence the political events and vice versa – and all this unfolds dynamically over time. These theoretical concepts and abstract claims are readily illustrated by the scandal surrounding the inauguration of the Puskás Aréna in Budapest. At the inauguration celebration of the stadium in 2019, four young kids from the Hungarian regions in Slovakia performed the song *Nélküled* (Without You). The correspondent of Hungary's largest online newspaper, Index.hu, was taken by surprise, and he reported that – unlike most other people in attendance – he remained seated during the performance of the song that he had previously not even heard of. In his article, he argued that the ritual requirement to stand up is reserved for national anthems. What he did not know, however, was that this sentimental ballad by the band Ismerős Arcok – which has been around for two decades – has in fact become a sacred song, an anthem of sorts among nationalist soccer fans. The 'you' in Nélküled's 'Without You', which is primarily disseminated through YouTube, refers to Hungarian co-ethnics in the ethnic Hungarian regions across the border, and the connection experienced by Hungarians in Hungary proper with this community. The song was first popular among Hungarian soccer fans in Dunaszerdahely (formerly a Hungarian town, today it is the Slovakian municipality of Dunajská Streda). After the article by Index.hu's correspondent was published, the government party media launched into a vehement and coordinated attack against the liberal journalist's allegedly profane and traitorous comments, which they viewed as defamatory to the Hungarian nation.[1] A few days after the article was published, anti-Semitic posters cropped up across Budapest depicting the journalist, Zoltán Miklósi, and one of his colleagues posing in front of an Israeli flag and an inscription saying 'we, too, are from outside the border' (a thinly veiled allusion to the target persons' presumed Jewish background, which would make them part of the 'cross-border' Diaspora community).[2] The story is at the same time also illustrative of the permeability between genres and of cross-genre intertextuality, as evidenced by the fact that it used a line from Kipling's *Jungle Book*, to wit 'we be of one blood, you and I'. To Hungarian audiences, this line is mostly known from the musical based on the book written by the prominent liberal artistic duo Geszti-Dés, which has been performed for 23 years without interruption to sold-out theatre audiences in Hungary. Nevertheless, looking at the audience of 60,000 at the stadium inauguration, who shed real tears at the event, we can state that by virtue of being profusely shared on social media platforms, Nélküled has emerged as a quasi-sacred text that elicits emotional identification while it conveys ideological contents which resonate profoundly with right-wing audiences. In terms of their intensity, the scandal and the social media storm it engendered, and the emotions and passions it gave rise to, were far more intense than the debates surrounding any public policy issue.

Digital culture and emotions

Emotions have always played a role in politics. Already Aristotle stressed in his *Rhetoric* how important it is for a speaker to take into consideration the sentiments (pathos) of the audience. And Martin Luther King, too, was not referring to sleeping issues when he gave his famous *I Have a Dream* speech.

The social psychologist Jonathan Haidt defines the dominance of sentiments as something specific to human nature. In *The Happiness Hypothesis* he describes our minds as being made up of two parts, pictured as a rider who sits atop an elephant. Our irrational, hard-to-control, and intuitive brain is the metaphorical elephant, while our more rational and thoughtful self is the rider. But most of the time, the elephant is very much in charge.

The social sciences, by contrast, tend to posit the existence of rational actors, which is why we are flabbergasted by phenomena such as Brexit or the election of Trump. In examining human behaviour, the turn towards the emotional does not suggest a simultaneous turn towards irrationality, however. What it means instead is the rejection of the abovementioned cold dichotomy.

It is no coincidence that the sociology of emotions has increasingly moved to the foreground during the past two decades (Duyvendak, 2011; Goodwin, Jasper & Polletta, 2009; Hochschild, 2016a; Hoggett & Thompson, 2012; Jasper, 2018).

Even if the medium is not the same as the message, the affordances of the dominant broadcasting tools of a given age do push certain communication styles into the foreground, while at the same time they relegate others to the background. It should not take long explanations to justify the claim that social media memes, few-second-long TikTok videos, or single-line posts are not the ideal realm for detailed rational arguments but instead a primary terrain for the expression of sentiments and massively fluctuating emotional reactions. The 'emotional design' of the online arsenal, of the new online instruments, is one of the prerequisites of political success in this day and age. And it appears that populist political forces enjoy a massive edge in this area. A good example of the latter is the success of the emotional messages which concluded the anxieties and chaos engendered by the 'Get Brexit Done' campaign. The underlying messages resonated enormously even though no one was – or in fact even could be – fully aware of the actual and rational substance of the Brexit issue. In her excellent book, Arlie Russel Hochschild reconstructs the deep stories and emotional dynamics of Tea Party supporters. She shows that even as the place where she did her fieldwork, the state of Louisiana, has been hit by an ecological disaster over the last decade, rather than ire at the polluting industrial corporations, the locals heaped blame on *excessive* state intervention. As a result, they emerged as the popular base in Louisiana of the radically anti-state Tea Party (Hochschild, 2016a). This – deeply troubling – example also illustrates how we need to start from the dynamics of emotions in coming up with the relevant emotional designs. Hochschild clearly identifies the secret behind the populist surge: charismatic leaders can credibly fill the need that arises from the emotionally based deep stories of the given communities. But, Hochschild asks, 'how does Trump, or any other charismatic leader, lay claim to being – and get received as – the messenger of a social group's deep story? By intuitively sensing and inhabiting a preexisting, recognizable cultural paradigm for conveying emotion' (Hochschild, 2016b, p. 687). For the political forces that stand opposed to populism, another major challenge – in addition to the lack of charismatic leaders – in coming up with competitive deep stories is that negative emotions (fear, hate, and anxiety) are stronger and more liable to motivate and mobilize people than positive sentiments (love, solidarity, and the pleasure of creating something).

Even as the everyday life of illiberal states and the ongoing cultural battle in these countries offer innumerable irrational and intriguing talking points, what matters for the purpose of the present analysis is that when we look at the relevant dynamics of politically and culturally organized online communities, then we need to take this emotional element into account. In the following, I will use two very different empirical examples to examine the vastly divergent strategies of two communities which are organized on an emotional basis – the strategies are *appropriation* and *organic cooperation*, respectively. These two types are positioned at the two extremes of a virtual axis: in one case, politics drew on an existing community and began to use it to its own ends, while in the other case a bottom-up organized, network-based community emerged, united along the lines of the members' common love for a popular culture product, their fandom.

(Re)appropriation

The year 2016 marked a sea change in the relations between democracy and digital populism, and it was the time of two seminal events with ramifications that we have yet to fully grasp – but we already know that they have fundamentally transformed our understanding of the aforementioned relationship. In both these instances, prior mistaken expectations played a major role. Specifically, what is at issue is the fact that these expectations had been arrived at based on the rules that had traditionally governed public discourse. That was part of the reason behind the victory of the new populist forces, since the movements in those segments of society that were hidden from the public gaze were for the most part obscured in the vision of the opposite side, which thus failed to either anticipate or properly react to the emerging situation. The two 2016 events in question were Brexit and the victory of Donald Trump in the US presidential election. For the traditional political forces, these demonstrated that the situation was worse than previously thought, and this insight gave rise to a legion of explanations. In the following, we want to highlight one aspect of the election of Donald Trump, which is vital for our own argument and has to some extent been relegated to the background in the dominant discourses thus far. This is not to imply that the filter bubble-generated reality fed by Russian interventions, the Cambridge Analytica scandal, the deep posts, fake news, and conspiracy theories all did not play a vital role and or lack strong explanatory power when it comes to these previously unexpected phenomena. Nevertheless, these explanations lack an important element – how was Trump capable of creating an extraordinarily active and aggressive troll army that multiplied and spread the power of his message in the online space, fighting the rhetorical battles for him and in his stead in the various forums of the public sphere? This online group was decisive for Trump's victory, and, in contrast to other explanations, the story of how they converged and how they operated could be reconstructed. At first glance, the most obvious layer of the story is a peculiar and nowhere near self-explanatory alliance between the real estate tycoon and media personality, Trump, who is connected to the old world by a thousand threads, and the alternative community of hackers, who are cocooned in a peculiar segment of the online world. After 2010, 4chan emerged as the primary channel of communication in the internal hacker universe, and it was followed in this role by 8chan. The structure of 4chan and 8chan, the lack of any regulatory forces, the full transparency of posts and comments, and of course their anonymity readily lent themselves to launching collective actions. These platforms, which initially adhered to an absolutist interpretation of libertarian principles and recognized no rules whatsoever, soon began to be dominated by practices that latter spread through the entire internet, such as schadenfreude-oriented pranks, flamings, and 'lulz'. But in earlier times, for example back in 2008 during an attack against Scientology, Fox News star host Bill O'Reilly labelled them as far left, and their support for the Occupy Movement seemed to confirm that charge. An anthropologist looking at the Anonymous troll movement for years during this period concluded that by using pranks, flamings, and DoS attacks, the hackers tested the outer limits of state power and ultimately used these operations as a vehicle to experience their own sense of autonomy (Coleman, 2015). The initially innocuous pranks, which were originally intended to be funny, increasingly turned into nasty and ruthless attacks, while the verbal gestures morphed into collective digital lynchings. The relatively rapid changes occurred due to two factors. For one, under the protective shield of freedom of speech openly Nazi voices entered the scene, such as for example the Daily Stormer, which seceded from 4chan. Yet, despite the fact that openly political contents had become more pronounced by 2014, the scene remained extraordinarily heterogeneous. As Milo Yiannopoulos, one of the key voices of the alt-right, noted at the time:

> The alt-right is a movement born out of the youthful, subversive, underground edges of the internet. 4chan and 8chan are hubs of alt-right activity. For years, members of these forums – political and non-political – have delighted in attention-grabbing, juvenile pranks. Long before the alt-right, 4channers turned trolling the national media into an in-house sport.
>
> (Bokhari & Yiannopoulos, 2016)

But then another development emerged, which was the #Gamergate scandal – when gamers felt that the journalists who covered and evaluated new products, such as Grand Auto Theft 5 and Day Z were biased with respect to the substance of the games and the sexist discourse around them. They launched savage attacks on journalists, specifically female journalists, and the feminist community, for its part, did not let these pass without a counter-reaction. 'Gamergate' has become shorthand for a particular kind of geek masculinity that feels victimized and disenfranchised by mainstream society, particularly popular feminism (Marwick & Lewis, 2017, p. 8).

That was the moment when Breitbart News, which had hitherto completely ignored the universe of online communities, suddenly turned to embrace the gamers' cause. In the opening article of Breitbart's swiftly created tech section, Yiannopoulos sent out the following invitation to gamers:

> Readers are sick of getting called trolls, harassers, misogynists, abusers, all because they don't agree with the opinions of journalists … Join me … as we take on the big tech companies, the government, VCs [venture capitalists], social justice warriors, and anybody else who wants to get between you, free speech and the truth.
>
> (Moore, 2018, p. 23)

This was obviously not a mere announcement about Breitbart adding a new section to its news division; it was a call to arms, a recruitment message sent out to Trump trolls. More specifically, it was a direct outreach to a heterogeneous community and the signalling of an effort to incorporate them into a pre-existing, Breitbart-centred alt-right subculture. It would be difficult to overstate the significance of this alliance. Despite all his personal idiosyncrasies, Trump was nevertheless the GOP candidate for president, and through the abovementioned gesture of his main media booster, Breitbart, he managed to align a multitude of very angry (and mostly white) young men with his cause. And these young men were technologically sophisticated, digitally highly literate, with a keen knowledge of meme production and collective attacks. They inserted themselves into the war of memes and opinions with the dynamism, resoluteness, and combativeness that tends to characterize neophytes. And this was not a traditional political campaign – neither for Trump nor for the hacker army backing him – but a war over life and death. As one of the veterans of the Great Patriotic Meme Wars put it in his recollections:

> The reason I fought in the meme war is that as Andrew Breitbart said we are at literal war with the left. There is an ideological Cold War going on right now and the victor will determine the fate of Western Civilization.
>
> (Moore, 2018, p. 25)

The hate-mongering and cruel tone that had been previously 'incubated' in 4chan and 8chan groups suddenly burst out into the political mainstream, putting those who were originally intent on following the rules of democratic discourse into a tight spot that seemed to offer no way out. This had a self-perpetuating impact: the more savage the tone adopted by the partisans of the meme war, the more likely those actors on the other political side who were used to the traditional public discourse were likely to be deterred – thereby fuelling the notion that the gamer army represents a majority of society.

To sum up, we talk about (re)appropriation when a political force recognizes and finds within the online space a relevant – and maybe even only casually organized – group, learns its concerns and grievances, and presents them with an offer that will end up binding the group to them.

Organic organizations

One of the side effects of the climate crisis is that the metaphors that draw on imagery associated with this crisis have moved to the fore in our social discourse.

In the analysis at hand, too, it would be useful to think of democracy as a continuously shrinking ice sheet, the boundaries of which are melting under the scorching heat of populism. Yet, in our view this would be a misleading metaphor which fails to take account of other processes that are ongoing at the same time and are aimed at building new forms of democratic organizations. Thus, in actuality, a more apt metaphor to capture what is happening in the world would be that of a shoreline, which is subject to both destructive and constructive processes at the same time, where the real dynamics are best captured not simply by destruction but by the twin notions of collapse and rebuilding. That is why in the following we are going to present organizations that match the constructive aspect of the metaphor. For the sake of symmetry, we are looking at groups that have been created to stand up for democratic values along new lines of logic. They enter the political arena organically, following their own values, based on the previously described logic of re-appropriation. From an analytical perspective, it is important to note that of course there may also be grassroots, organic groups that are working on destroying democracy.

One of the most intensely researched and most often cited culturally based groups that focus on political activism is the Harry Potter Alliance (HPA). The HPA is a non-profit organization operated by Harry Potter fans. It was founded by Andrew Slack in 2005 to draw attention to human rights violations in Sudan. The members of the group are brought together by the values conveyed in the Harry Potter novels, by their common beliefs. Their goal is to have an impact on political life as a civil organization, and they try to engage and mobilize people, involving them in the promotion and public dissemination of the values they stand for. In the words of the founder, Andrew Slack, 'we show them fun and accessible ways that they can take action and express their passion to make the world better by working with one of our partner NGO's' (Jenkins, 2015, p. 206).

Today, the Harry Potter Alliance boasts 112 chapters in 44 US states, and it is also present in a further 18 countries across 5 continents (HPA, n.d.a). Their operations span a wide range of activities, from helping earthquake victims in Haiti to campaigning for internet neutrality. J.K. Rowling herself has expressed support for the Harry Potter Alliance, while Jenkins identified it as a new type of civic organization.

HP Alliance has created a new form of civic engagement which allows participants to reconcile their activist identities with the pleasurable fantasies that brought the fan community together in the first place (Jenkins, 2015).

The 15-year operation of the HPA has resulted in a highly evolved and effective operation including education, a Wizard Activist School, and Hero Training, as well as toolkits that help raise awareness of social problems by analyzing certain pre-eminent texts in popular culture (e.g., *Star Wars*, *Doctor Who*, *Jessica Jones*, etc.), and use these to get people to take action. In the spirit of Gramsci, these educational materials are meant to highlight the political issues raised in the various contents at the core of popular culture fandom, trying to discern what parallels these texts offer to real life and what kinds of potential actions these parallels could give rise to. But the focus is on taking action because, as their slogan says, the goal is 'turn fans into heroes'.

More recently, HPA has begun to focus on the global immigration problem. It is worth quoting their call to action at length because it provides a good reflection of their organization's values, style, and operations:

> Summon your inner Hufflepuff to find immigrant-led and immigrant-serving organizations and fight for immigrant justice right in your own neighborhood! *The world is talking about immigration now, and what we hear isn't always kind.* In the U.S., our political leaders have turned hateful rhetoric into horrifying policy as immigrants are harassed and detained by I.C.E. in detention centers at the U.S. border and across the country. Around the world, countries debate who should take in refugees and how they should be treated – a problem that will only grow as climate change displaces more people in the years to come. *These national and global problems play out directly in our neighborhoods.* Knowing how to help – whether that means volunteering, donating, standing up to I.C.E., or more – requires being connected to your local immigrant community. *That's where the Hufflepuffs come in.* Hufflepuffs are kind, loyal, and unafraid of toil – that's why our #DAFightsBack Hufflepuff action is dedicated to working hard and being kind directly in your community! Using our new Ravenclaw-researched database, DA Fights Back Near You, *you can find immigrant-led and immigrant-serving organizations near you.* Making these local connections, strengthening the bonds between community members, and taking the lead from immigrant organizers is the only way communities can keep each other safe. *It's the only way we'll win.*
>
> (HPA, n.d.b)

The HPA went on to list 207 organizations that were looking for volunteers or financial or in-kind donations, and made the spreadsheet with this list available on its website. The HPA is also capable of uniting the previously mentioned topics in its activities: it combines the battle in the cultural realm with political action, and uses the emotional charge of fandom to organize through digital platforms.

With respect to the logic proposed above, it is also important to note that the HPA is a classic 'onlife' organization: its decentralized yet coordinated actions would be unimaginable without the concerted efforts of online and digital communication or the public engagement of local groups. The HPA is thus an example of a relatively formalized pro-democracy organization that operates based on a network structure and was created as a reflection on popular culture contents.

Although the HPA is a special formation, the operations of which are – despite the presence of a global network – centred around the US, its theoretical implications are broader nevertheless. My research in Hungary has shown that even in places where the HPA lacks a presence, the intertextual Potterverse may still exert a massive impact – and this popularity went hand in hand with a level of public engagement and willingness to demonstrate and attend political rallies and events at a far higher rate than was typical of the given age group (Dessewffy & Mezei, 2020).

Conclusion

The institutional structure and social acceptance of liberal democracy are in a closely interconnected crisis. One of the most important reasons behind this crisis is the complexity of possibilities opened up by the continuous growth in the expansion of digital culture.

It is precisely the spiralling growth of technological progress which makes it impossible to find a way out of the crisis of democracy by relying on the tools offered by Habermasian rational communication; it would be a mistake to tackle the crisis by trying to move just in that direction. On the contrary, beyond the undoubtedly necessary regulatory interventions, the way out of the crisis could lie in the deeper appreciation and knowledge of digital culture, the reinforcement of the positive values and practices therein, as well as the proper use of emotional design based on an understanding of the underlying emotional dynamics. The future trajectory of the present situation is by no means set in stone. Ultimately, the outcome will be decided based on the social and political struggles which are to come in the approaching epoch.

Notes

1 For a decent summary of the incident, see Balogh (2019).
2 The scope of the scandal is readily apparent in the fact that the Budapest embassies of the United States and Israel – two countries whose governments otherwise nurture close ties with Viktor Orbán – both protested against the posters, see Horváth (2019).

References

Balogh, E.S. (2019). Fidesz and ‘our homeland’ join forces in an anti-semitic campaign against ‘nation haters’. *Hungarian Spectrum*. November 24. Retrieved from https://hungarianspectrum.org/2019/11/24/fidesz-and-our-homeland-join-forces-in-an-anti-semitic-campaign-against-nation-haters/.

Baranyai, G. (2019). Kövér László: Területfoglaló háború helyett tudathódítás zajlik. Magyar Nemzet. November 29. Retrieved from https://magyarnemzet.hu/belfold/kover-laszlo-teruletfoglalo-haboru-helyett-tudathoditas-zajlikk-7542890/.

Barclay, D.A. (2018). *Fake news, propaganda, and plain old lies: How to find trustworthy information in the digital age*. London: Rowman & Littlefield.

Bar-On, T. (2011). Transnationalism and the French nouvelle droite. *Patterns of Prejudice*, *45*(3), 199–223.

Bauman, Z. (2013). *Liquid times: Living in an age of uncertainty*. New York: John Wiley & Sons.

Békés, M. (2018). Gramsci jobbról. *Mandiner*. July 31. Retrieved from https://mandiner.hu/cikk/20180731_bekes_marton_gramsci_jobbrol.

Benkler, Y., Faris, R., & Roberts, H. (2018). *Network propaganda: Manipulation, disinformation, and radicalization in American politics*. New York: Oxford University Press.

Bokhari, A., & Yiannopoulos, M. (2016). An establishment conservative's guide to the alt-right. *Breitbart*. March 29. Retrieved from http://www.breitbart.com/tech/2016/03/29/an-establishment-conservatives-guide-to-the-alt-right/.

Castells, M. (2018). *Rupture: The crisis of liberal democracy*. Cambridge and Medford: John Wiley & Sons.

Christiano, T. (2018). Democracy. In E.N. Zalta (Ed.), *The Stanford encyclopedia of philosophy*. Retrieved from https://plato.stanford.edu/archives/fall2018/entries/democracy/.

Coleman, G. (2015). *Hacker, hoaxer, whistleblower, spy: The many faces of Anonymous*. New York: Verso Books.

Dessewffy, T. (2019). *Digitális Szociológia*. Budapest: Typotex.

Dessewffy, T., & Mezei, M. (2020). Fans and politics in an illiberal democracy. In Ashley Hinck and Amber Davisson (Eds.), *Fandom and politics*. Special issue of Transformative Works and Cultures, no. 32. Retrieved from https://doi.org/10.3983/twc.2020.1757.

Duyvendak, J.W. (2011). *The politics of home: Belonging and nostalgia in Europe and the United States*. London: Palgrave Macmillan.

Farkas, J., & Neumayer, C. (2018). Disguised propaganda from digital to social media. In J. Hunsinger, M.M. Allen & L. Klastrup (Eds.), *Second international handbook of internet research* (pp. 1–17). Dordrecht: Springer.

Farkas, J., & Schou, J. (2019). *Post-truth, fake news and democracy: Mapping the politics of falsehood*. New York: Routledge.

Goodwin, J., Jasper, J.M., & Polletta, F. (Eds.) (2009). *Passionate politics: Emotions and social movements*. Chicago: University of Chicago Press.

Hochschild, A.R. (2016a). *Strangers in their own land: Anger and mourning on the American right*. New York: The New Press.

Hochschild, A.R. (2016b). The ecstatic edge of politics: Sociology and Donald Trump. *Contemporary Sociology*, *45*(6), 683–689.

Hoggett, P., & Thompson, S. (Eds.) (2012). *Politics and the emotions: The affective turn in contemporary political studies*. New York: Bloomsbury.

Horváth, B. (2019). Az amerikai nagykövetség is elítélte az Index újságíróit támadó antiszemita plakátokat. !!444*!!!*. November 25. Retrieved from https://444.hu/2019/11/25/az-amerikai-nagykovetseg-is-elitelte-az-index-ujsagiroit-tamado-antiszemita-plakatokat.

HPA—The Harry Potter Alliance. (n.d.a). Featured chapter. The Harry Potter Alliance. Retrieved from https://www.thehpalliance.org/chapters.

HPA—The Harry Potter Alliance. (n.d.b). Take action w/ #DAFIGHTSBACK. The Harry Potter Alliance. Retrieved from https://www.thehpalliance.org/dafightsback.

Jasper, J.M. (2018). *The emotions of protest*. Chicago: University of Chicago Press.

Jenkins, H. (2015). Cultural acupuncture: Fan activism and the Harry Potter Alliance. In L. Geraghty (Ed.), *Popular media cultures: Fans, audiences and paratexts* (pp. 206–229). Basingstoke: Palgrave Macmillan.

Jones, S. (2007). *Antonio Gramsci*. London: Routledge.

Latour, B. (2010). Tarde's idea of quantification. In M. Candea (Ed.), *The social after Gabriel Tarde: Debates and assessments* (pp. 145–163). London: Routledge.

Latour, B., Jensen, P., Venturini, T., Grauwin, S., & Boullier, D. (2012). 'The whole is always smaller than its parts'—A digital test of Gabriel Tardes' monads. *The British Journal of Sociology*, *63*(4), 590–615.

Marwick, A., & Lewis, R. (2017). *Media manipulation and disinformation online*. New York: Data & Society Research Institute.

Mill, J.S. (1873). *Considerations on representative government*. London: Longmans, Green.

Moore, M. (2018). *Democracy hacked: How technology is destabilising global politics*. London: Oneworld Publications.

Susser, D., Roessler, B., & Nissenbaum, H. (2019). Technology, autonomy, and manipulation. *Internet Policy Review*, *8*(2), 1–22.

Index

Note: Page numbers in italics denote figures while bold denotes tables.